IRISH WRITERS' GUIDE
1996-1997

The Lilliput Press
in association with
BOOKS IRELAND

Published by The Lilliput Press Ltd
4 Rosemount Terrace, Dublin 7, Ireland.

ISBN 1-874676-70-8

Cataloguing in Publication data available
from the British Library.

Typeset by Books Ireland
Printed by ColourBooks, Dublin.

Books Ireland is supported by
both Arts Councils in Ireland.

CORRECTIONS & ADDITIONS

New or updated information for the listings,
headed with the list for which they are intended,
should be posted or faxed to

Books Ireland,
11 Newgrove Avenue, Dublin 4
fax (01) 269 2185

They will be published in the next issue of
Books Ireland magazine
and incorporated in the next edition of
the *Irish Writers' Guide*.

Preface

WHEN WE STARTED work on the *Irish Writers' Guide* just over a year ago, we thought we knew a good deal about producing books, but we had a lot to learn.

For one thing directories never end. Enterprises start up and crash and people change their jobs and addresses faster than you can set type and read proofs, and always when you think "Surely we can go to press now" there are twenty good reasons for holding on a little longer. But if you wait until a directory is complete before you publish it you'll wait for ever. All you can do is fix a day, grit your teeth, publish and—in a phrase coined by an Irishman—be damned.

We know the guide will fill a long-felt gap and we can only hope that the people and bodies we've inadvertently omitted or got wrong will inform us as well as damning us, so that the next edition will be even more complete and useful. We are particularly grateful to the people who returned our questionnaires.

One of our problems was that we were also producing *Books Ireland* magazine, which celebrates its twentieth year of unbroken—and always punctual—publication in 1995, and nothing is ever allowed to delay it. *Books Ireland* lists and reviews the extraordinary output of Irish publishers, and henceforth it will also make space for additions and changes to the lists in this directory, so that you don't have to wait for the next edition of the book if you want to keep up to date.

Another thing we learned was that the market for writers by no means begins and ends with books and magazines. We knew Ireland was remarkable for its publishing industry, but we had no idea until we started compiling these lists how many theatre, film or video companies there are. The only thing that disappointed us was to find that local radio is not seen as a fruitful market for the professional or freelance writer. There's surely room for development—and, who knows, when local television comes on the scene it may take its cue and be accessible to local talent too?

In *Books Ireland* we often complain about books that should have indexes and don't. Before critics give us our own medicine, we ask them to consider that the *Irish Writers' Guide* is itself supposed to be an index. We hope you find what you want in it.

September 1995   JEREMY ADDIS AND SHIRLEY KELLY

So you want to be a writer?

HAVE YOU CONSIDERED what that means? If you think it means spending half the day beavering away at a typewriter and the other half waiting for the muse to call, then think again. Creative genius is a rare and wonderful thing, but there's much more to writing than putting pen to paper, and any aspiring writer who fails to appreciate this will never do more than aspire.

Skill and artistry

Writing is a craft or skill as well as an art form, and the latter is dependent on the former. There are many good craftsman writers plying their trade who are not artists, but no 'creative' writers who are not *also* craftsmen. Just because writing sentences is a more common skill than making pictures or music does not mean there is less to be learned than by a painter or a composer. On the contrary, it is probably harder to teach the techniques of effective writing than other skills, and all but impossible to teach real 'creative' writing. Skills really have to be learned by failing and failing again—by hard-won experience—and only when they are learned may your creative artistry (if you are blessed with any) be recognised.

Writing is also a business, and as with any other business, there are procedures to be followed, conventions to be observed and customers to be served. Even if you've got strong traces of James Joyce's DNA in your blood, it pays to play by the rules.

Market research

Every successful business is founded on sound market research, and the same should apply to every writing project. If, for instance, you're writing a non-fiction book, it makes sense to conduct a thorough search of bookshops and libraries to see how many other books, if any, have been published on that subject, and then decide whether or not yours is sufficiently different. If you're writing a novel, then it's not so simple; even publishers find it difficult to assess the market for new fiction.

But whatever you write—short stories, novels, poetry, non-fiction, feature articles, film scripts, stage plays—you must establish who might be interested in publishing or producing it. The listings in this directory and in similar directories of the British, US and other markets, should be your starting point. Thereafter, it's a question of examining the previous and current output of your target publisher, magazine editor, film producer or whatever, to see if your work roughly matches their requirements.

Re-read, revise, rewrite

You've just typed the last word of your magnum opus and you can't wait to get it in the post. But wait: have you scoured your work for basic errors of grammar, spelling and punctuation? Have you checked the accuracy of everything which purports to be factual? Have you surgically removed every redundant verb, adverb and adjective, and cast out every contemptible cliché? Has anyone else read it but you? Remember, you are your own worst critic and proof-reader. Make sure that your work gets the once-over from someone whose judgement you trust.

Professional presentation

You've narrowed the market for your work to three or four possible outlets, and you're ready to approach the first. Like any good business-man, you want to make an impression on your prospective client, so you do things the way he or she likes them done. As you will see in the subsequent listings, different editors, publishers and producers have their own preferences when it comes to dealing with unsolicited submissions, and procedures vary slightly from one form of writing to another, but in the first instance most prefer to see an introductory letter, with a succinct outline of the proposed project.

Hardly anybody will dignify a handwritten note with a reply, and most editors are highly sceptical of elaborate letterheads and glossy presenta-tion packs, but it's not difficult to strike a happy mean between the two extremes. Remember to enclose a stamped, self-addressed envelope with your submission—you're not inviting rejection, just showing that you appreciate your contact's busy schedule and limited resources. If, in accordance with your contact's expressed preference, you are submitting any part of your finished work, make sure it's typed, double-spaced, on A4 paper (one side only), with wide margins.

Selling yourself

You've submitted your proposal to each of your possible outlets and had nothing but rejections. What are you doing wrong? Probably one of two things. Either the proposal itself is a non-starter, or your sales pitch isn't sufficiently confident. Often, these amount to the same thing. The key to a successful sales pitch is self-belief, and if you don't have absolute faith in your project, then you can't expect anyone else to show any interest in it. On the other hand, if you know for a fact that there's a substantial market for your product, and you're sure that you're the best person to produce it, your enthusiasm and confidence will rub off on your target buyer. If, however, you've written something which you know in your heart of hearts is less than perfect, your lack of confidence in your work will be spotted a mile off. So it's back to the drawing board for a long hard look at your typescript.

Then again, of course, it could be your natural modesty which is coming between you and your first commission. If it's a magazine article, have you bothered to include your best cuttings from other newspapers and magazines? If it's a collection of short stories, have you mentioned the fact that you've just won a prize in a national short-story competition? But be careful not to go over the top: if your track record is genuine, there's no need for hype.

Down to business

Should you be fortunate enough to secure your first commission without recourse to addictive substances, be sure to make the most of the opportunity. Don't imagine for a minute that anyone is going to make allowances for your novice status; in fact, you may even have to do better than more established writers to make an impression. Remember, too, that you're trying to build a lasting, professional relationship with your editor or producer, and that requires a combination of diplomacy and honesty. A certain degree of deference is expected, but sycophancy impresses nobody.

And whatever you do, don't promise more than you can deliver, especially when it comes to deadlines. Editors and producers have been known to make unreasonable and unrealistic demands, and novice writers are easily intimidated, but if you're honest about what you can achieve within a certain time-frame then you're less likely to end up with egg on your face.

Publishing

Writers should understand the publishing processes and should collaborate actively in the production and marketing of their work, short of becoming a nuisance to the publisher or producer.

The notes and lists we provide on publishing in this guide should therefore not be of interest only to those who consider self-publishing or setting up in that difficult business. If they make you realise that the people who reject your work—or accept, produce and market it—are not malign enemies but potential or present partners in your enterprise who do a difficult job and take considerable financial risks on behalf of writers, your reading will not be in vain.

Writing for periodicals

David Rice

ONCE UPON A TIME I mailed a packet of five feature articles to the managing editor of one of America's biggest metropolitan newspapers, with the outrageous suggestion that he might like to use me as a regular columnist. I got a reply by return, saying yes, they'd run me every Saturday. The story is told in full in my new paperback, *Blood Guilt* (Blackstaff). Although it's a work of fiction, the sequence about the journalist becoming a syndicated columnist is based on my personal experience.

Yet I don't recommend the procedure, because you need a neck like mine, and you also need to have been a journalist for some years before you attempt the like. But why not work towards it? First of all, of course, you have break into journalism.

The most effective way is to go through one of Ireland's three schools of journalism—Rathmines (now on the DIT Aungier Street campus); Dublin City University; or University College Galway. These are the recognised gateways to the profession, but they are hard to get into.

So, if you do not manage to get into one of these schools, or returning to full-time education isn't an option, what can you do? You can start as a freelance, and here are some tips on how to begin.

Target a periodical

If you already have something to say, pick out the magazine or newspaper that is most likely to let you say it. If you have no topic in mind, pick the magazine you would like to be published in, and see what kinds of topics they run. Then develop a topic that would suit it.

This directory offers one of the most comprehensive listings of periodicals available in Ireland. Most British publications are listed in the *Writers' Handbook* (Macmillan) or the *Writers' and Artists' Yearbook* (A. & C. Black); and you'll find thousands of American publications in the annual *Writers' Guide* (Writers' Digest Books). Ask for these at your bookshop or library.

Study the periodical

Prepare a profile of your chosen magazine. You will gain a certain amount of information from this and other directories, but if you're serious about contributing to a publication you must also carefully examine several of its recent issues.

You'll need the following information:

- The publisher's address, telephone and fax number.

- The name of the commissioning editor for freelance work. It helps enormously to send your work to the correct person. It is most often the features editor, but not always.

- The target readership—age, sex, social class, education level, etc. You can hardly write a suitable article until you know what kind of readers you will have.

- The kind of articles published in the magazine, and the preferred topics. A study of several back issues will give you a good idea of this, and can trigger new ideas for suitable topics. But beware of suggesting topics that have already been exhaustively dealt with.

- The magazine's attitude. Right wing? Liberal? Feminist? Environmentalist? There's no point in offering, say, a piece on condoms to *Osservatore Romano*.

- The preferred length of articles. Count the words in several articles, and make sure your piece is about average length.

- The lead time—i. e. how far in advance of publication must you present your article? Most monthly magazines have a two or three month lead time; weekly publications two weeks to a month.

- The preferred method of approach. Do editors prefer to receive a complete manuscript in the first instance, or a query letter?

- The best time to contact the magazine—obviously not close to deadline.

Periodicals differ considerably in their requirements. For example, Smurfit publications (*Woman's Way, U, IT*) welcome a brief query letter, outlining your idea. You can attach clippings of previous work to show what you can do. They don't want unsolicited manuscripts and have a lead time of two months. *Image* magazine, on the other hand, prefers phone calls to query letters and has a lead time of three months.

The *Irish Independent* prefers you to send a brief list of your ideas for articles, and will contact you if any intrigues the features department. You can follow up with a phone call (Monday, Tuesday or Wednesday mornings), but don't overdo it. Lead time varies, but a couple of weeks is suggested.

The *Irish Press* group wanted beginners to cut out preliminary enquiries and just send the manuscript. Make sure they have been revived before you send them anything!

Choosing a topic

Suitable topics are all around you. The key is to remember the motto of feature writers: to make familiar things new, and new things familiar.

When you get down to writing, make sure the very first paragraph grabs the readers and makes them want to read what follows. Be sure the article is cleanly typed, double spaced, on one side of the page only. If you can handle a word processor, use it in preference to a typewriter: it makes for a better looking page. Leave plenty of room for the editor's pencil, especially on the first page (start the article halfway down the page).

At the top of the first page, put your name, the catchline (a single word to identify the article), and the page number. These three things should be at the top of every subsequent page. On a cover sheet put your name, address, telephone (and fax number if you have access to one); the general title of the article; and the number of words in the article.

Attach a brief covering letter. You can fax the lot, or post it. If sending by post, use paper clips, not staples, and put it in a large envelope so it arrives flat and fresh. And for heaven's sake keep a copy.

It is hard to break into freelancing, just as it is hard for young barristers to get a first brief, or for new surgeons to find anyone willing to submit to their virgin scalpels. But, as in all walks of life, perseverance pays off.

The good workman

And if you do persevere, remember that, like surgeon or plumber, you are going to need tools. The tools used to be pen, paper and typewriter—now they are word processor, fax, telephone, answering machine, tape recorder, and, ultimately, modem. Most publishers are still accepting hard copy (i.e. typewritten pages) from freelances, but more and more they are preferring computer discs, simply because they have fewer and fewer people to typeset your manuscript. So, if you plan to stick with journalism, start saving for the tools.

David Rice is the author of four books, including a number one bestseller *Shattered Vows* (Blackstaff Press). He lectures at Rathmines School of Journalism.

Periodicals

This list includes general-interest as well as most trade, professional and specialised periodicals. National and daily newspapers are listed separately, as are provincial, regional and local papers and magazines. After frequency, we give approximate circulation and then the International Standard Serials Number. In the italic notes the following information (where supplied to us) is given in this order: material considered, with *maximum* number of words and news deadline; whether photos (b/w and or colour) or other artwork is considered; preferred approach by contributors—whether an enquiry by letter, fax or post, or submission of typescript in the first instance. If copy is acceptable on disc, we state either MS-DOS (IBM-compatible) or Apple Mac, disc size and sometimes a note of the word-processing system used (when in doubt, use ASCII)—but note that it is normal to submit a print-out with the disc. Whether membership of NUJ is required or preferred follows, and finally the approximate payment for material.

Accountancy Ireland

87-89 Pembroke Road, Dublin 4. tel. 01-668-0400 fax 01-668-0842. 6 a year, 16,026 (ABC). 0001-4699. Editor: Charles O'Rourke.

Business related news and articles on business, accountancy and information technology. Photos inc. colour. Letter or fax enquiry. Apple Mac 3½ inch ASCII £50 per article.

Administration

Institute of Public Administration, Vergemount Hall, Clonskeagh, Dublin 6. tel. 01-269-7011 fax 01-269-8644. Quarterly, 1,500. Editor: Tony McNamara.

Professional-level material on public affairs. Submit typescript. MS-DOS WordPerfect 5.1. No payment.

Afloat

2 Lower Glenageary Road, Dun Laoghaire, Co Dublin. tel. 01-284-6161 fax 01-284-6192. Monthly, 9,000. 0332-4486. Editor: W. M. Nixon. News: David O'Brien. South: Claire Bateman. North: Elaine First. Inland: Tom O'Brien.

News (15th of month) and articles of boating interest. Apple Mac ASCII Standard NUJ rates.

Africa

St Patrick's Missionary Society, Kiltegan, Co Wicklow. tel. 0508-73233 fax 0508-73281. Editor: Revd Gary Howley.

Aisling Magazine, The

Eochaill, Inis Mór, Árainn, Co na Gaillimhe. tel. 099-61245 fax 099-61245. Quarterly, 1,500. Editors: Dara Molloy and Tess Harper.

Articles on Irish spirituality, justice issues, social analysis etc., short stories, 2,500 words. Poetry. Featured artist in each issue illustrates chosen articles; no photos. Letter with full typescript. Apple Mac. No payment for articles.

albedo one

2 Post Road, Lusk, Co Dublin.

Science fiction, fantasy, horror plus interviews with leading writers in these genres and book reviews. Stories of 2,000-6,000 words welcomed, plus articles on science fiction literature or media, artwork and cartoons.

Amnesty International

48 Fleet Street, Dublin 2. tel. 01-677-6361 fax 01-677-6392. Bi-monthly, 12,000. Editor: Morina O'Neill.

AMT Magazine

Computer Publications of Ireland, 66 Patrick Street, Dun Laoghaire, Co Dublin. tel. 01-280-0424 fax 01-280-8468. Monthly. 4,500. Editor: John McDonald.

Articles on advanced manufacturing technology.

Anois

27 Cearnóg Mhuirfean, Baile Átha Cliath 2. tel. 01-676-0268 fax 01-661-2438. Weekly, 4,500 (ABC). Managing Editor: Donall Ó Móráin.

Irish-language news (Thursday p.m.), articles (500 words), short stories (any length) and poetry (300 words). Photos inc. colour.

Apple Mac. *'Attractive payment for quality material'.*

Apple Report
Computerscope, 1 Prospect Road, Dublin 9. tel. 01-830-3455 fax 01-830-0888. Quarterly, 6,000. Editor: Frank Quinn.

Archaeology Ireland
PO Box 69, Bray, Co Wicklow. tel. 01-286-2649 fax 01-286-4215. Editor: Dr Gabriel Cooney.
News of archaeological interest 500 words. Any disc. No fees.

Astronomy & Space
Astronomy Ireland, PO Box 2888. Dublin 1. tel. 01-459-8883 fax 01-459-9933. Monthly.

AudIT
19 Rutland Street, Cork. tel. 021-313855 fax 021-313855. 6 a year, 750. 0961-124X. Editor: Ken Ebbage, tel. 0044-1438-840770.
Articles on audit automation, 4,000 words. B/w photos. MS-DOS Word for Windows 2.0 3½ inch. £250 per article.

Bakery World
53 Glasthule Road, Sandycove, Co Dublin. tel. 01-280-0000 fax 01-280-1818. 2 months, 2,500. Editor: Natasha Swords.
Industrial and product news 800 words. Profiles, current politics 3,000 words. Stories, nostalgic pieces 1,500 words. Photos inc. colour. Submit typescript. Apple Mac HD large. £60-£70 for 2,000-word feature.

Béaloideas
Department of Irish Folklore, University College Dublin, Dublin 4. Annual, 1,000. 0332-270X. Editor: Pádraig Ó Héalaí (UCG). Advisory editor: Professor Bo Almquist.
Journal of the Folklore of Ireland Society. Scholarly articles on Irish folklore. Apple Mac Word 4/5. No payment.

Big Issues, The
Ormond Multi-Media Centre, 16-18 Lower Ormond Quay, Dublin 1. tel. 01-873-3500.

Books Ireland
11 Newgrove Avenue, Dublin 4. tel. 01-269-2185 fax 01-269-2185. 9 a year, 3,300.
0376-6039. Publisher: Jeremy Addis. Features: Shirley Kelly. Eagarthóir Gaeilge: Alan Titley.
News (16th of month) and articles or interviews (1,500 words) on authors, book trade, publishing, librarianship. Could add to panel of reviewers (always commissioned), particularly specialists. No fiction, poetry, essays or unsolicited reviews. B/w photos. Letter or fax enquiry about features or reviewing. MS-DOS both disc sizes. £50 for features, £35 for reviews, negotiable for newsy photos. News not paid for except by arrangement.

Bord Altranais News
31-32 Fitzwilliam Square, Dublin 2. tel. 01-676-0226 fax 01-676-3348. 3 a year, 45,000. Editor: Eugene Donoghue. Features: Maria Neary.

Bride & Groom and First Home
28-32 Exchequer Street, Dublin 2. tel. 01-677-4186/4279 fax 01-677-4516. 6 a year. Editor: Leanne de Cerbo.
Features on bridal fashion and services. Photos inc. colour. Letter or fax enquiry.

Build
Belenos Publications, 32 Upper Fitzwilliam Street, Dublin 2. tel. 01-661-9236 fax 01-661-2417. Monthly, 4,000 ABC. Editor: John Low.

Bulletin
Society of St Vincent de Paul, 8 New Cabra Road, Dublin 1. tel. 01-838-4164/4167.

Business and Exporting
Jude Publications, Tara House, Tara Street, Dublin 2. tel. 01-671-3500 fax 01-671-3074. Monthly. Editor: Neil Whoriskey.

Business and Finance
Belenos Publications, 50 Fitzwilliam Square, Dublin 2. tel. 01-676-4587 fax 01-661-9781. Weekly, 11,000. Managing Editor: William Ambrose. Editor: Dan White.

Business Ulster
Ulster Journals, 39 Boucher Road, Belfast. tel. 08-01232-681371 fax 08-01232-381915. Editor: Patricia Rainey.

Cara

Mac Publishing, Taney Hall, Eglinton Terrace, Dundrum, Dublin 14. tel. 01-296-0000 fax 01-296-0383. Bi-monthly, 70,000. Editor: Mary Dowey.

The Aer Lingus in-flight magazine, which is currently changing publisher and staff. Check latest information.

Car Driver

7 Cranford Centre, Montrose, Dublin 4. tel. 01-260-0899 fax 01-260-0911. Monthly, 9,135 (ABC). Editor: Karl Tsigdinos.

News and features on anything automobile-related. Photos inc. colour. Letter or fax enquiry. Apple Mac. £100 per 1,000 words.

Catering & Licensing Review.

Greer Publications, 151 University Street, Belfast BT7 1HR. tel. 08-01232-231634 fax 08-01232-325736. Monthly. Editor: Kathy Jensen.

Catholic Standard

55 Lower Gardiner Street, Dublin 1. tel. 01-874-7538 fax 01-836-4805. Weekly, 8,000. Editor: Cristina Odone.

Certified Accountant

19 Rutland Street, Cork. tel. 021-313855 fax 021-313496. Monthly, 55,000. 0306-2406. Editor: Brian O'Kane. News: Monica Igoe. Features: Conor O'Boyle. Books, products, services: Mary-Rose O'Sullivan.

News (250 words, 20th of month) and articles (2,500 words) on accountancy, tax and business for professional readership. Photos inc. colour. Letter or fax enquiry. MS-DOS Word for Windows 2.0 3½ inch. £125 per 1,000 words.

Checkout Magazine

22 Crofton Road, Dun Laoghaire, Co Dublin. tel. 01-280-8415 fax 01-280-8415. Monthly, 6,500. Editor: Mary Brophy.

Church of Ireland Gazette

36 Bachelor's Walk, Lisburn, Co Antrim. tel/fax 08-01846-675743. Weekly, 6,500. Editor: Canon C. W. M. Cooper.

Circa Art Magazine

58 Fitzwilliam Square, Dublin 2. tel. 01-676-5035 fax 01-661-3881. Quarterly, 7,000. 0263-9475. Editor: Tanya Kiang.

News: Gemma Tipton. Northern Ireland: Terry Loane.

News on visual arts and artists, awards, conferences, 350 words; articles on contemporary and historical visual art and culture, 3,500 words; reviews of exhibitions, films, books, 800 words. Photos (prints) inc. colour (large format). Apple Mac 3½ inch. £25 per review.

Comhar

5 Rae Mhuirfean, Baile Átha Cliath 2. tel. 01-678-5443 fax 01-678-5443. Monthly, 2,500. Editor: Tomás Mac Síomóin.

Commercial Law Practitioner

Brehon Publishing, 4 Upper Ormond Quay, Dublin 7. tel. 01-873-0101. Monthly. Editor: Thomas B. Courtney. Exec. Editor: Bart D. Daly.

Communications Worker

575 North Circular Road, Dublin 1. tel. 01-836-6388 fax 01-836-5582. 6 a year, 16,000. Editor: David Begg. News and features: Christopher Hudson.

News of interest to Telecom and An Post employees. Cartoons, photos inc. colour. Letter or fax enquiry.

ComputerScope

1 Prospect Road, Glasnevin, Duiblin 9. tel. 01-830-3455 fax 01-830-0888. 10 a year, 7,800. Editor: Tom Golden. Associate Editor: Paul Healy.

Constabulary Gazette

Ulster Journals, 39 Boucher Road, Belfast. tel. 08-01232-681371 fax 08-01232-381915. Editor: Martin Williams.

Construction & Property News

175 North Strand Road, Dublin 1. tel. 01-874-2265 fax 01-874-1242. Fortnightly, 4,000.

Consumer Choice

45 Upper Mount Street, Dublin 2. tel. 01-661-2442 fax 01-661-2464. Monthly, 11,000. 0790-486X. Editor: Kieran Doherty.

Unsolicited material not considered.

Cosantóir, An

Department of Defence, Parkgate Street, Dublin 8. tel. 01-837-9911 fax 01-677-9018. 10 a year. Editor: Ray Slattery.

CPA Journal of Accountancy

Certified Public Accountants in Ireland, 9 Ely Place, Dublin 2. tel. 01-676-7353 fax 01-661-2367. Quarterly, 2,900. Editor: Denis Hevey.

Cyphers

3 Selskar Terrace, Dublin 6. tel. 01-497-8866. 2-3 a year, 800. Editors: Leland Bardwell, Pearse Hutchinson, Eiléan Ní Chuilleanáin, Macdara Woods.
Short stories and poetry all types, including translations. Submit typescript or 6 poems. Apple Mac 3½ inch. £10 per page.

Dairy Executive

33 Kildare Street, Dublin 2. tel. 01-676-1989. Quarterly, 1,650. Editor: Kyran Lynch.

Dance News Ireland

65 Fitzwilliam Square, Dublin 2. tel. 01-676-2677 fax 01-661-0392. Quarterly, 2,000.
News and features on dance: events, training and people. Photos inc. colour. Letter or fax enquiry.

Diaspora

Ireland Worldwide, PO Box 3884, Dublin 4.

Doctrine and Life

Dominican Publications, 42 Parnell Square, Dublin 1. tel. 01-872-1611 fax 01-873-1760. Monthly, 3,000. 0012-466X. Editor: Bernard Treacy OP.
Religion, theology and social comment 2,500 words. Apple Mac. Submit typescript. £10 per 400 words.

d'Side

The Factory, 35A Barrow Street, Dublin 4. tel. 01-668-4966 fax 01-668-4157. 2-monthly, 15,000. Editor: Melanie Morris. Features: Gavin Lyons. Arts: Suzie Coen.
Youth-orientated articles (2,000 words), fiction (3,000 words), poetry (500 words) and photo-journalism (inc. colour). Letter or fax with sample typescript. Apple Mac.

Dublin Event Guide

7 Eustace Street, Dublin 2. tel. 01-671-3377 fax 01-671-0502. Fornightly, 13,000. Editor: Michael Beirne.
Features on arts and entertainment 700 words; reviews 400 words. B/w photos. Apple Mac 3½ inch.

Dublin Historical Record

Old Dublin Society, 58 South William Street, Dublin 2. Half yearly, 850. Editor: Patrick Johnston.

Economic and Social Review

4 Burlington Road, Dublin 4. tel. 01-676-0115. Quarterly. Editors: J. Boyle and C. T. Whelan.

Education Magazine

Tara Publishing, 112 Poolbeg Street, Dublin 2. tel. 01-671-9244 fax 01-671-9263. 8 a year, 3,000. 0791-6161. Editor: Evelyn Lee.
News (600 words) and articles (1,600 words) on education national or international, teaching resources and technology, careers, college profiles. No fiction or poetry. Photos inc. colour. Letter or fax enquiry.

Education Today

35 Parnell Square, Dublin 1. tel. 01-872-2533 fax 01-872-2462. 3 a year, 25,000. Editor: Sinead Shannon.
Articles of interest to primary-school teachers with strong educational content. Photos inc. colour. Letter or fax enquiry. Apple Mac for Quark Xpress. News not paid for except by arrangement.

element

2 Upper Mount Street, Dublin 2. 1 a year. Editor: Mari-aymone Djeribi.
Essays on art, society and food; short stories, experimental new writing and translations. Poetry only in translation. B/w photos, line drawings. Submit typescript. Apple Mac 3½ inch. No payment.

Engineers Journal

Dyflin Publications, 58 North Great Charles Street, Dublin 1. tel. 01-855-0477 fax 01-855-0473. Monthly, 10,000. Editor: Hugh Kane

Entertainer, The

5 Lower Abbey Street, Dublin 1. tel. 01-878-7894. Editor: Martin Thomas.

Environmental Management Ireland

Nestron Ltd, 58 Middle Abbey Street, Dublin 1. tel. and fax 01-872-0734. Bi-monthly. Editor: Annette O'Riordan

Far East, The

St Columban's, Navan, Co Meath. tel. 046-21525. 9 a year, 185,000 inc. Britain. Editor: Revd Alo Connaughton.

Farm Week

14 Church Street, Portadown, Co Armagh BT62 3LQ. tel. 08-01762-339421 fax 08-01762-350203. Weekly, 12,500. Editor: Hal Crowe.
Farming-related features 750 words. B/w photos. Letter or fax enquiry. 'Payment on merit': approx. £50 per 1,000 words.

Feasta

(Eag.) 13 Paráid na Díge, Corcaigh. tel. 021-307579; (Fógr.) 6 Sráid Fhearchair, Baile Átha Cliath 2. tel. 01-475-7401. Monthly, 2,500. Editor: Séamus Ruiséal.

Finance Magazine

162 Pembroke Road, Ballsbridge, Dublin 4. tel. 01-660-6222 fax 01-660-6830. Monthly, 3,000. 0790-8628. Editor: Ken O'Brien. Asst editor: Lorna Daly.
News and articles on investment and finance. Photos inc. colour. Submit typescript. MS-DOS 3½ inch. £100 per 1,000 words.

Flaming Arrows

County Sligo VEC, Riverside, Sligo. tel. 071-45844 fax 071-43093. Annual, 500. 0791-0932. Editor: Leo Regan.
Fiction (3,000 words), poetry, essays (1,500 words). B/w photos and graphics. Letter enquiry or typescript. Payment by arrangement.

Fleet Management Magazine

13 Ranelagh Village, Dublin 6. tel. 01-497-6050 fax 01-496-7408. Monthly, 5,300. Editor: Phil O'Kelly. News: Ronnie Bellew.
News (300 words) and features (1,000 words) on road transport management and freighting, Irish and international. Offbeat or unusual transport stories or pictures. Photos inc. colour. Letter or fax enquiry. Apple Mac. £40 per 1,000 words.

Focus

Maxwell Publicity, 49 Wainsfort Park, Dublin 6W. tel. 01-492-4034 fax 01-492-4035. Bi-monthly, 500. Editor: Terry Gogan.

Food Ireland

Tara Publishing, 1-2 Poolbeg Street, Dublin 2. tel. 01-671-9244 fax 01-671-9263. Editor: Bernard Potter.

Fortnight

7 Lower Crescent, Belfast BT7 1NR. tel. 08-01232-232353 / 311337 fax 08-01232-232650. 11 a year, 3,000. 0141-7762. Editor: Robin Wilson. Deputy editor: Damian Smyth.
News, 400 words; analysis and perspectives, 1,300 words. B/w photos. Fax enquiry. Apple Mac.

Forum

Alma House, Alma Place, Carrickbrennan Road, Monkstown, Co Dublin. tel. 01-280-3967 fax 01-280-7076. Monthly, 2,500. Editor: Geraldine Meagan. News: Niamh McGarry.
Journal of the Irish College of General Practitioners. Material of interest to (and mostly by) GPs. Photos inc. colour. Apple Mac.

Furrow, The

St Patrick's College, Maynooth, Co Kildare. tel. 01-628-6215 fax 01-708-3908. Monthly, 8,000. 0016-3120. Editor: Ronan Drury.
Articles on religion, education, pastoral practice, social problems; book reviews and chronicles of events. B/w photos. Submit typescript.

Futura

Unit 9 Sandyford Office Park, Dublin 18. tel. 01-295-8119 fax 01-295-8065. Monthly, 3,500. Editor: Pat Lehane.

Gaelic Sport

139A Lower Drumcondra Road, Dublin 9. tel. 01-836-0366 fax 01-836-0624. 6 a year, 30,000. 0791-1521. Editor: Tommy McQuaid. Features: Paul Sibson.
Material on Gaelic games. Letter enquiry.

Gaelic World

10 Burgh Quay, Dublin 2. tel. 01-679-8655 fax 01-679-2016. Monthly. Editor: Mick Dunne.
Material on Gaelic games. News deadline 20th of month. Fax enquiry. Payment negotiable.

Gaelsport Magazine

6-7 Camden Place, Dublin 2. tel. 01-478-

4322 fax 01-478-1055. Monthly, 15,000. Editor: Owen McCann

Garage Trader

Tel. 08-01762-355060 fax 08-01762-336959. Quarterly, 10,000. Editor: Lorna Brown.

News and features on the garage trade and equipment, component distributors, motor factors, car care products, accident repair, petrol forecourt retailing. Photos inc. colour. Letter or fax enquiry. Apple Mac 3½ inch. £50 per 100 words.

Garda Journal

Jude Publications, Tara Street, Dublin 2. tel. 01-671-3500 fax 01-671-3074. Monthly. Editor: Brendan K. Colvert.

Garda News

6th floor, Phibsboro Tower, Dublin 7. tel. 01-830-3166 fax 01-830-6396. Monthly, 5,000. Editor: Austin Kelly.

News (2nd Monday) and features of Garda interest. Photos inc. colour. Submit typescript.

Garda Review

5th Floor, Phibsboro Tower, Dublin 7. tel. 01-830-3533. Monthly, 6,000. Editor: Catherine Fox.

News (by 17th of month) and features on law enforcement and of Garda interest. Photos inc. colour. Letter enquiry.

Gay Community News

10 Fownes Street Upper, Temple Bar, Dublin 2. tel. 01-671-0939. Monthly, 6,500. Editor: Richard Prendiville. News: Suzy Byrne. Features: Anita Thomas. Health and Lifestyles: Ciarán O'Keeffe. Arts: Brian Finnegan.

Lesbian or gay related news, features, stories, poetry, letters, book reviews. B/w photos. Submit typescript. Apple Mac or MS-DOC, HD 3½ inch. No payment.

Gazette of the Law Society of Ireland

Blackhall Place, Dublin 7. tel. 01-671-0711. 10 a year, 6,200. Editor: Barbara Cahalane.

Go Direct

Ryan Media, The Basement, 12 Hume Street, Dublin 2. tel. 01-676-9538 fax 01-676-9538. 5 a year, 4,411. Editor: Damian Ryan. News: Niamh O'Reilly.

Guideline

14 Cherry Drive, Castleknock, Dublin 15. tel. 01-820-4501 fax 01-820-4501. 5 a year, 700. Editor: Loretta Jennings. Asst editor: Mary Coolahan, tel. 01-820-7848.

News and features on careers and further education. B/w photos. Letter or fax enquiry. MS-DOS WordPerfect or ASCII 3½-inch.

Health and Safety

Jude Publications, Tara Street, Dublin 2. tel. 01-671-3500 fax 01-671-3074. Monthly. Publisher: Kate Tammemagi.

Health Services News

Vergemount Hall, Clonskeagh, Dublin 6. tel. 01-269-7011 fax 01-269-8644. Quarterly, 3,000. 0791-363X.

Material on the health services, including policy and organisation, 1,000 words. B/w photos. Letter or fax enquiry. MS-DOS 3½ inch.

History Ireland

PO Box 695, James's Street PO, Dublin 8. tel. 01-453-5730 fax 01-453-5730. 4 a year, 6,000. Editors: Hiram Morgan and Tommy Graham.

History material, 3,000 words. Photos inc. colour. MS-DOS or Apple Mac, both disc sizes. Year's subscription in lieu of payment for feature articles.

Hot Press

13 Trinity Street, Dublin 2. tel. 01-679-5077 / 679-5091 fax 01-679-5097. Fortnightly, 20,983. 0332-0847. Editor: Niall Stokes.

Hotel and Catering Review

52 Glasthule Road, Sandycove, Co Dublin. tel. 01-280-0000 fax 01-280-1818. Monthly, 4,123. 0332-440. Editor: Frank Corr.

Industry news, 500 words by 15th of month; features on hotels and personalities, 1,000 words. Photos inc. colour. Letter or fax enquiry. Apple Mac. £80 per 1,000 words.

Image

22 Crofton Road, Dun Laoghaire, Co Dublin. tel. 01-280-8415 fax 01-280-8309. 10 a year, 21,065. Editor: Jane McDonnell. Asst editor: Carolyn McGrath

Features 500 words, fiction 3,000 words. Letter or fax enquiry with idea or outline only. Apple Mac.

Impartial Reporter and Farmers' Journal

William Trimble Ltd, 8-10 East Bridge Street, Enniskillen, Co Fermanagh. tel. 08-01365-324422 fax 08-01365-325047. Weekly, 14,000. Editor: Denzil McDaniel.

In Dublin

6-7 Camden Place, Dublin 2. tel. 01-478-4322 fax 01-478-1055. Fortnightly, 20,000. Editor: Siobhán Cronin.

Features on entertainment, 1,000 words. Photos inc. colour. £80 per 1,000 words.

Industrial Relations News Report

121-3 Ranelagh, Dublin 6. tel. 01-497-2711 fax 01-497-2779. Weekly. Editor: Brian Sheehan. Asst. Editor: Martin Frawley.

Industry & Commerce

Tara House, Tara Street, Dublin 2. tel. 01-671-3500 fax 01-671-3074. Monthly, 8,500. Editor: Carol Power.

National and European news (20th of month), articles on business, finance and personalities, 1,200 words. Humorous comment for 'Time out' section. Photos inc. colour. Letter or fax enquiry. Apple Mac. NUJ membership required. £80 per 1,200 words.

Innti

32 Albany Road, Ranelagh, Dublin 6. tel. 01-497-2353. Yearly, 1,000. Editor: Michael Davitt.

New poems in Irish and essays or reviews on poetry. Artwork accepted.

Inside Business

Dyflin Publications, 58 North Great Charles Street, Dublin 1. tel. 01-855-0477 fax 01-855-0473. Monthly, 10,000. Editor: Claire Reilly.

Inside Ireland

PO Box 1886, Dublin 16. tel. 01-493-1906. Quarterly, 7,000. 0332-2483. Editor, news and features: Brenda Weir. Asst editor: Vivienne Flanagan.

Direct-mail circulation mainly in USA, with some in Australia, Canada and Europe. Articles are commissioned, but ideas submitted in writing, with sample of previous work, are considered. £100 per 1,000 words on publication.

Insight Magazine

Harmony Publications, Roslyn Park, Sandymount, Dublin 4. tel. 01-269-8422 fax 01-283-0163. Quarterly. Editor: John Cunningham.

Intercom

Veritas, 7-8 Lower Abbey Street, Dublin 1. tel. 01-878-8177 fax 01-878-6507. Monthly, 8,000.

IPU Review

Butterfield House, Butterfield Avenue, Dublin 14. tel. 01-493-1801 fax 01-493-1801. Monthly, 1,600. Editor: David Butler MPSI. News: Michael Ryan.

Journal of the Irish Pharmaceutical Union. News (10th of month) and features of interest to pharmacists. B/w photos. Letter enquiry. 'Fee dependent on length'.

Ireland of the Welcomes

Bord Failte, Baggot Street Bridge, Dublin 2. tel. 01-676-5871 fax 01-676-4765. 6 a year, 100,000. Editor: Dr Peter Harbison. Asst Editor: Letitia Pollard. We understand that changes may be imminent.

Articles on people, places and things Irish, 1,500 words. Very occasional short story (1,200 words); poetry usually only in conjunction with other material. Photos inc. colour. Submit typescript. £15 per 100 words.

Ireland's Eye

Lynn Industrial Estate, Mullingar, Co Westmeath. tel. 044-48868. Monthly.

Features of Irish interest 2,000 words; stories with Irish flavour 1,500 words. Photos inc. colour. Submit typescript.

Ireland's Own

North Main Street, Wexford. tel. 053-22155 fax 053-23801. Weekly, 52,000. Editor (weekly): Margaret Galvin.

Popular general-interest and historical articles, 1,000 words; short stories, 3,000 words. Photos inc. colour. Submit typescript. Payment varies.

Irish Architect

CP Group, 66 Patrick Street, Dun Laoghaire, Co Dublin. tel. 01-280-0424 fax 01-280-8468. 6 a year. Editor: J. Owen Lewis. Contact: Alan R. Phelan.

Irish Banking Review
Irish Bankers' Federation, Nassau House, Nassau Street, Dublin 2. tel. 01-671-5311 fax 01-679-6680. Quarterly. Editor: Stewart MacKinnon.

Irish Brides & Homes Magazine
Crannagh House, 198 Rathfarnham Road, Dublin 14. tel. 01-490-5504 / 490-0550 fax 01-4906763. Quarterly, 10,000. Editor: Ruth Kelly. News: Mary McCarthy.
News, features, fiction. Photos inc. colour.

Irish Building Services News
Pressline, 5-7 Main Street, Blackrock, Co Dublin. tel. 01-288-5001 fax 01-288-6966. 10 a year, 2,500. Editor: Pat Lehane.

Irish Catholic, The
55 Lower Gardiner Street, Dublin 1. tel. 01-874-7538 / 874-2795 fax 01-836-4805. Weekly, 37,000. Editor: Bridget Anne Ryan. Features: Stephen Harris.
News 400 words by 4 p.m. Monday; features and stories 800 words, photos inc. colour. Letter or fax enquiry. Apple Mac.

Irish Chemical and Processing Journal
CP Group, 66 Patrick Street, Dun Laoghaire, Co Dublin. tel. 01-280-0424 fax 01-280-8468. 10 a year, 2,800. Editor: John McDonald.

Irish Computer
CP Group, 66 Patrick Street, Dun Laoghaire, Co Dublin. tel. 01-280-0424 fax 01-280-8468. Monthly, 7,000. Managing Editor: Donald McDonald.

Irish Criminal Law Journal
Round Hall Press, Kill Lane, Blackrock, Co Dublin. tel. 01-289-2922 fax 01-289-3072. 6 months, 450. 0791-539X. Editor: Shane Murphy BL.
Articles on criminal law. Letter enquiry or typescript. Any disc. No fee.

Irish Doctor
Jude Publications, Tara House, Tara Street, Dublin 2. tel. 01-671-3500 fax 01-671-3074. Monthly. Editor: Bridget Maher.

Irish Electrical Review
Unit 9 Sandyford Office Park, Dublin 18. tel. 01-295-8069 fax 01-295-8065. Monthly, 3,000.

Irish Farmers Journal
Irish Farm Centre, Bluebell, Dublin 12. tel. 01-450-1166 fax 01-452-0876. Weekly, 71,218. Editor: Matthew Dempsey. News: Des Maguire. Features: M. Moroney, Mairead McGuinness.
News, 500 words; technical, foreign articles, 1,000 words, country-based fiction for magazine section 400 words. Photos inc. colour. Any disc. Letter or fax enquiry. £200 per 1,000 words.

Irish Farmers Monthly
31 Dean's Grange Road, Blackrock, Co Dublin. tel. 01-289-3305 fax 01-289-6406. Monthly, 22,000. Editor: Brian Gilsenan. News: Willie Ryan.
News (24th of month) and features on farmers and their families 1,500 words. Photos inc. colour. Fax enquiry. Apple Mac. £50 per 500 words.

Irish Field
Irish Times, 11-15 D'Olier Street, Dublin 2. tel. 01-679-2022 fax 01-679-3029. Managing Editor: V. Lamb. Weekly, 10,000.

Irish Food
31 Dean's Grange Road, Blackrock, Co Dublin. tel. 01-289-3305 fax 01-289-6406. 7 a year. Editor: Brian Gilsenan. Asst editor: Róisín O'Hea.
News and features of interest to food buyers in other countries, company profiles. Photos inc. colour. Apple Mac. £50 per 500 words.

Irish Forestry
Mount Alto, Ashford, Co Wicklow. tel/fax 0404-40435. 2 a year, 600. Editor: Donal Magner.

Irish Geography
Dept of Geography, Trinity College, Dublin 2. tel. 01-702-1143 fax 01-671-3397. 2 a year. Secretary: Joe Brady, UCD.

Irish Hardware
52 Glasthule Road, Sandycove, Co Dublin. tel. 01-280-0000 fax 01-280-1818. Monthly 1,850. Editor: Pat Nolan.

Irish Health Professional
Maxwell Publicity, 49 Wainsfort Park, Dublin 6W. tel. 01-492-4034 fax 01-492-4035. Bi-monthly, 5,000. Editor: Terry

Gogan.

Irish Homes
48 North Great Georges Street, Dublin 1. tel. 01-872-1414 / 872-1636 fax 01-878-7749. 4 a year. Editor: Bernice Brindley. News and features: Geraldine Herbert. *Material on homes, interiors, gardening, cookery, travel. Photos inc. colour. Letter or fax enquiry.*

Irish Historical Studies
Dept of Modern History, Trinity College, Dublin 2. tel. 01-702-1578. 2 a year, 1,000. Editors: Ciaran Brady and Keith Jeffery.

Irish Journal of Education
Educational Research Centre, St Patrick's College, Dublin 9. tel. 01-837-3789 fax 01-837-8997. Annual, 1,000. 002-1257. Editor: Thomas Kellaghan. *Material on education for teachers at all levels.* MS-DOS 3½ inch.

Irish Journal of European Law
Round Hall Press, Kill Lane, Blackrock, Co Dublin. tel. 01-289-2922 fax 01-289-3072. 2 a year, 450. 0791-5403. Editors: James O'Reilly and Anthony Collins. *Legal articles and law reports. Any disc. No payment.*

Irish Journal of Medical Science
6 Kildare Street, Dublin 2. tel. 01-676-7650 fax 01-661-1684. Quarterly, 1,500. Editor: Thomas F. Gorey MCh,FRCSI. *Material on medical and allied subjects. B/w photos. No discs. £40 per page.*

Irish Journal of Psychology
13 Adelaide Road, Dublin 2. 4 a year. Editors: Ken Brown and Carol McGuinness (Belfast) tel. 08-01232-245133 fax 08-01232-664144.

Irish Law Times
Round Hall Press, Kill Lane, Blackrock, Co Dublin. tel. 01-289-2922 fax 01-289-3072. Monthly, 750. 0021-1281. Editor: Raymond Byrne. *Legal articles, 4,000 words. B/w photos. Letter or fax enquiry or typescript. £100 per article.*

Irish Library see Leabharlann

Irish Literary Review
15 St Stephen's Green, Dublin 2. Editor:

Richard Pyne.

Irish Marketing Journal
7 Leopardstown Office Park, Dublin 18. tel. 01-295-0088 fax 01-295-0089. Monthly, 5,000. Editor: Norman Barry.

Irish Medical Journal
10 Fitzwilliam Place, Dublin 2. tel. 01-676-7273 fax 01-661-2758. Bi-monthly, 5,500. Editor: John Murphy.

Irish Medical News
Mac Publishing, Taney Hall, Eglinton Terrace, Dublin 14. tel. 01-296-0000 fax 01-296-0383. Weekly, 6,250. Editor: Niall Hunter.

Irish Medical Times
15 Harcourt Street, Dublin 2. tel. 01-475-7461 fax 01-475-7467. Weekly, 6,909. Editor: Maureen Browne. *News (200 words, deadline Tuesday) and articles (500 words) of interest to practitioners. Photos inc. colour.*

Irish Motor Industry
Jude Publications, Tara House, Tara Street, Dublin 2. tel. 01-671-3500 fax 01-671-3074. Monthly. Editor: Maura Henderson.

Irish Pharmacy Journal
Kenlis Publications, 37 Northumberland Road, Dublin 4. tel. 01-660-0551 fax 01-668-1461. Monthly, 2,100. Editor: Val Harte.

Irish Political Studies
PSAI Press, College of Humanities, University of Limerick. tel. 061-333644 fax 061-338170. Annual, 600. 0790-7184. Editor: Vincent Geoghegan. *Academic articles, 10,000 words. No payment.*

Irish Printer
52 Glasthule Road, Sandycove, Co Dublin. tel. 01-280-0000 fax 01-280-1818. Monthly, 1,940. 0790-2026. Editor: Frank Corr. *News (by 4th of month) of the printing industry, 500 words; articles on technical or business matters, 1,000 words. Photos inc. colour. Letter or fax enquiry. Apple Mac. £80 per 1,000 words.*

Irish Psychologist, The

Seagrove, 9 Claremont Road, Howth, Dublin 13. tel. 01-832-6656 fax 01-832-3962. Monthly, 1,000. Editor: Chris Morris.

News (last Friday of month) and features on professional research, history and technical, 2,500 words. Cartoons, b/w photos. Letter or fax enquiry. Apple Mac. No payment at present.

Irish Reporter, The

PO Box 3195, Dublin 6. tel. 01-874-5158. Editor: Anthony O'Keefe.

Irish Review, The

Insitute of Irish Studies, Queen's University, Belfast. tel/fax 08-01232-439238. 2 a year. Editors: Kevin Barry et al.

Irish Roots

Belgrave Publications, Belgrave Avenue, Cork. tel. 021-500067 fax 021-500067. Quarterly. 0791-6329. Editor: Tony McCarthy.

Genealogy and the Irish diaspora: news 300 words, features 2,000 words. B/w photos. Apple Mac. Submit typescript. £30 per article.

Irish Scientist, The

Samton Ltd, 17 Pine Lawn, Blackrock, Co Dublin. tel. 01-289-6186 fax 01-289-7970. Annual, 16,000. Editor: Dr Charles Mollan.

News and features on science and technology supplied by institutions who contribute to the cost (but may themselves pay their writers). Photos inc. colour. Phone, fax or letter enquiry. MS-DOS MS Word 3½ inch.

Irish Skipper, The

Mac Publishing, Taney Hall, Eglinton Terrace, Dundrum, Dublin 14. tel. 01-296-0000 fax 01-296-0383. Monthly. Editor: Niall Fallon.

Irish Social Worker

114-116 Pearse Street, Dublin 2. tel. 01-677-4838 fax 01-671-5734. Quarterly, 700. Editor: Kieran McGrath. International issues: Charles Delap.

Articles on social work, 2,000 words; book reviews, 1,200 words. No fiction or poetry. B/w photos. Apple Mac. No payment.

Irish Stamp News

27 Upper Mount Street, Dublin 2. tel. 01-676-7228 fax 01-676-7229. Quarterly, 5,000. 0332-317X. Editor: Ian Whyte.

News and features on philately or postal history. Photos inc. colour. MS-DOS WordPerfect 1.44 mb. Letter or fax enquiry. Fee by arrangement.

Irish Sword, The

Newman House, 86 St Stephen's Green, Dublin 2. 2 a year, 1,000. 0021-1389. Editor: Dr H. Murtagh.

Learned articles on military history, 10,000 words. Photos inc. colour. Apple Mac. No payment.

Irish Tatler

Smurfit Publications, 126 Lower Baggot Street, Dublin 2. tel. 01-662-3158 fax 01-661-9757. Monthly, 156,000 (JNMR). Editor: Sarah Foot. Asst editor: Bernice Harrison.

Features of social interest, female politics, emotional politics 1,500 words. Fiction minimum 1,500 words. Phone enquiry. Payment negotiable.

Irish Travel Trade News

9 Western Parkway Business Centre, Dublin 12. tel. 01-450-2422 fax 01-450-2954. Monthly, 2,000. Editor: Michael Flood.

Irish Theological Quarterly

St Patrick's College, Maynooth, Co Kildare. tel. 01-628-5222. Quarterly, 1,000. Editors: Patrick McGoldrick, Patrick Hannon.

Irish University Review

Room K 203, UCD, Belfield, Dublin 4. 2 a year. Editor: Christopher Murray.

Irish Veterinary Journal

Jude Publications, Tara House, Tara Street, Dublin 2. tel. 01-671-3500 fax 01-671-3074. Monthly. Editor: Pat O'Mahony.

Irish Woman

An Grianán, Termonfeckin, Co Louth. tel. 041-22119 fax 041-22690. Quarterly, 5,000. Editor: James Creed.

News (mid-month) and features on women's issues and healthcare. B/w photos. Letter or fax enquiry.

Irish Youthwork Scene

National Youth Federation, 20 Lower Dominick Street, Dublin 1. tel. 01-872-9933 fax 01-872-4183. 5 a year, 1,000. 0791-6302. Editor: Avril Soper.

News and articles on youth issues, youth workers and youth-work practice: 1,500 words. Photos inc. colour.

Journal, The

5 Whitefriars, Aungier Street, Dublin 2. tel. 01-478-4141 fax 01-475-0131. Bi-monthly. Editor: James Wims.

Krino

PO Box 65, Dun Laoghaire, Co Dublin. 2 a year. Editors: Gerald Dawe, Aodan Mac Poilin, Eve Patten, Jonathan Williams.

Fiction and essays (3,000 words), poetry (6 poems), B/w photos and artwork. Letter or fax enquiry. Copies of the magazine in lieu of payment.

Leabharlann, An : The Irish Library

(Ronayne:) Donegal County Library, Rosemount, Letterkenny. tel. 074-21968 fax 074-26402, or (Quinn:) South-Eastern Education and Library Service, Ballyna-hinch, BT248DH. tel. 08-01238-562639 fax 08-01238-565072. Quarterly, 1,100. 0023-9542. Editors: Liam Ronayne and Kevin Quinn. News: Fionnuala Hanrahan. Reviews: Agnes Neligan, St Patrick's College, Maynooth.

Journal of the Library Association of Ireland and the Library Association, NI branch. News (100 words) and articles (6,000 words) on librarianship and information topics. B/w photos. Submit typescript. Apple Mac. No payment.

Licensing World

52 Glasthule Road, Sandycove, Co Dublin. tel. 01-280-0000 fax 01-280-1818. Monthly, 4,000. Editor: Pat Nolan.

Lifeboats Ireland

15 Windsor Terrace, Dun Laoghaire, Co Dublin. tel. 01-284-5050 fax 01-284-5052. Editor: Dermot Desmond.

Feature articles of maritime interest, 1,000 words. Photos inc. colour. Submit typescript. MS-DOS ASCII

Linen Hall Review

17 Donegall Square North, Belfast BT1 5GD. tel. 08-01232-321707 fax 08-01232-438586. 3 a year, 6,000. Editor: John Gray.

Local Authority Times

Institute of Public Administration, Lansdowne Road, Dublin 4. tel. 01-668-6233 fax 01-668-9135. Quarterly, 3,000. 0791-8267. Editor: E. MacCafferty.

News and features of interest to local authorities, 1,500 words. Letter enquiry.

Management

52 Glasthule Road, Sandycove, Co Dublin. tel. 01-280-0000 fax 01-280-1818. Monthly, 7,250. Editor: Frank Dillon.

Medical Missionaries of Mary

MMM Communications, Rosemount, Booterstown, Co Dublin. tel. 01-288-7180 fax 01-283-4626. Quarterly, 15,000. Editor: Sister Isabelle Smyth.

Messenger see Sacred Heart

Micléinn le Chéile

16 North Great George's Street, Dublin 1. tel. 01-878-6366 fax 01-878-6020. 6 a year. Editor: Colm Keaveney.

Milltown Studies

Milltown Institute of Theology and Philosophy, Milltown Park, Dublin 6. tel. 01-269-8802 fax 01-269-2528. 2 a year, 1,000. Editor: Gervase Corcoran OSA.

Modern Woman

Meath Chronicle Group, Market Square, Navan, Co Meath. tel. 046-21442 fax 046-23565. Monthly. Editor: Margot Davis.

Motoring Life

Cyndale Enterprises, 48 North Great George's Street, Dublin 1. tel. 01-872-1636. Monthly, 9,500. Editor: Fergal K. Herbert.

New Music News

Contemporary Music Centre, 95 Lower Baggot Street, Dublin 2. tel. 01-661-2105 fax 01-676-2639. 3 a year, 3,000. 0791-5268. Editor: Eve O'Kelly.

Material on contemporary classical music, 3,000 words. B/w photos. Letter or fax enquiry. Apple Mac. No payment.

Newmarket Business Report

9 Mellifont Avenue, Dun Laoghaire, Co

Dublin. tel. 01-280-9476 fax 01-280-9465. Fortnightly. Editor: Karl Glynn-Finnegan.

Northern Ireland Legal Quarterly

SLS Legal Publications, Faculty of Law, Queen's University, Belfast BT7 1NN. tel. 08-01232-245133 ext. 3597 fax 08-01232-325590. 4 a year, 700. 0029-3105. Editor: Dr Peter Ingram.

Legal notes and articles, 10,000 words. MS-DOS 3½ inch. No payment.

Oblate Missionary Record

Oblate Fathers, Inchicore, Dublin 8. tel. 01-454-2417. 5 a year, 8,000. Editor: Father J. Archbold.

Oghma

38 Faiche Steach Póilín, Baile Dúill, Baile Átha Cliath 13. Guthán 01-832-5672. Go bliantúil/Annual. Eagarthóirí: Seosamh Ó Murchú, Mícheál Ó Cearúil, Antain Mag Shamhráin.

Anailís agus taighde ar chúrsaí reatha, staire, eacnamaíochta, socheolaíochta, eolaíochta agus cúrsaí an tsaoil trí chéile. Prós: gearrscéalta, aistriúcháin ó theangacha eile seachas ón mBéarla, sleachta as obair idir lámha, etc.; critic liteartha d'ardchaighdeán. Litir nó glaoch gutháin. Córas MS-DOS-bhunaithe.

Outlook

169 Booterstown Avenue, Co Dublin. tel. 01-288-1789 fax 01-283-4307. Bi-monthly, 45,000. Editor: Revd Brian Gogan CSSp.

PC Live!

Computerscope, 1 Prospect Road, Dublin 9. tel. 01-830-3455 fax 01-830-0888. Publisher: Frank Quinn.

Phoblacht, An / Republican News

58 Cearnóg Pharnell, Baile Átha Cliath 1. 01-873-3611 / 873-3839 fax 01-873-3074. Weekly, 30,000. Editor: Mícheál Mac Donnacha.

Material in Irish is welcome. News on national question (by 1 p.m. Wednesday) 1,000 words. Political, social, economic, cultural features 3,000 words. Stories 3,000 words. No poetry. B/w photos. Letter or fax enquiry. Apple Mac. NUJ membership not required but preferred.

Phoenix, The

44 Lower Baggot Street, Dublin 2. tel. 01-661-1062 fax 01-668-2697. Fortnightly, 20,077. Editor: Paddy Prendiville. Deputy editor: Paul Farrell.

Investigative news and gossip, satire and humorous verse. No fiction. B\w photos. Enquire by phone. NUJ membership. Apple Mac 3½ inch.

Pioneer

27 Upper Sherrard Street, Dublin 1. tel. 01-874-9464 fax 01-874-8485. Contact Maureen Manning.

Plan Magazine

8/9 Sandyford Office Park, Dublin 18. tel. 01-295-8115/6 fax 01-295-9350. Monthly. Editor: Emer Hughes.

News on property, environment and building 250 words. Features on architecture, building and technology 1,200 words. Photos inc. colour. Letter or fax enquiry. Apple Mac. £100 per 1,000 words.

Plantman

1 The Green, Kingsway Heights, Dublin 24. tel. 01-452-0898. Monthly, 3,960. Editor: Patrick Murphy. News Editor: Derek Gibson.

News on plant machinery, first week of month. Photos inc. colour. Letter or fax enquiry.

Poetry Ireland News

Bermingham Tower, Upper Yard, Dublin Castle, Dublin 2. tel. 01-671-4632 fax 01-671-4634. 6 a year, 750. Editor: Niamh Morris.

Poetry news; no further data supplied.

Poetry Ireland Review

Bermingham Tower, Upper Yard, Dublin Castle, Dublin 2. tel. 01-671-4632 fax 01-671-4634. Quarterly, 1,000. 0332-2998. Editor: Moya Cannon.

Poetry; features by arrangement. Letter enquiry. Apple Mac. £10 per poem; articles by arrangement.

Presbyterian Herald.

Church House, Fisherwick Place, Belfast BT1 6DW. tel. 08-01232-322284 fax 08-01232-248377. Monthly, 17,500. Editor: Arthur Clarke.

Public Sector Times
1 Eglinton Road, Bray, Co Wicklow. tel. 01-286-9111 fax 01-286-9074. Monthly, 20,000. Managing Editor: James D. Fitzmaurice.

Public Service Review
PS Executive Union, 30 Merrion Square, Dublin 2. tel. 01-676-7271 fax 01-661-5777. 6 a year, 6,000. Editor: Tom McKevitt

Reality
75 Orwell Road, Rathgar, Dublin 6. tel. 01-492-2488 fax 01-492-2654. 11 a year, 20,000. Editor: Father Gerard Moloney.
News (by end of month), features and fiction, 1,500 words. Photos inc. colour. Submit typescript.

Recover
St Camillus, South Hill Avenue, Blackrock, Co Dublin. tel. 01-288-2873 fax 01-288-3380. Quarterly. Editor: Father G. Price.

Religious Life Review
42 Parnell Square, Dublin 1. tel. 01-873-1355 fax 01-873-1760. 2 months, 3,000. Editor: Austin Flannery OP.
Material of interest to members of religious communities, 2,500 words. Apple Mac. Submit letter or fax. £10 per 400 words.

Republican News see Phoblacht

Retail News
Tara Publishing, 112 Poolbeg Street, Dublin 2. tel. 01-671-9244 fax 01-671-9263. Editor: Jane Mulhall.

Riverine
Laurel Cottage, Dowlin, Piltown, Co Kilkenny. Annual. 0790-8423. Editor: Edward Power.
Fiction, 3,000; poetry, 100 lines; reviews and critical essays. B/w photos of contributors only. Submit typescript. Payment in copies.

RTÉ Guide
Commercial Enterprises, RTÉ, Donnybrook, Dublin 4. tel. 01-208-3111 fax 01-208-3085. Weekly, 182,000. Editor: Heather Parsons.

Sacred Heart Messenger, The
Messenger Publications, 37 Lower Leeson Street, Dublin 2. tel. 01-676-7491/2 fax 01-661-1606. Monthly, 180,000.

Editor: Brendan Murray SJ. Asst. editor: Anne Duff.
Articles on spiritual, family and social issues, short stories and serials; no poetry. 1,200 words. Photos inc. colour. Submit letter. Apple Mac.

Salesian Bulletin
Salesian House, St Teresa's Road, Dublin 12. tel. 01-455-5605 fax 01-455-8781. Quarterly, 20,000. Editor: Eddie Fitzgerald SDB.

Search
RE Resource Centre, Holy Trinity Church, Rathmines, Dublin 6. tel. 01-497-2821. 2 a year, 700. 0332-0618. Editor: Revd Michael Burrows; Reviews: Revd R. L. Clarke.
A Church of Ireland journal; theological articles and reviews of interest to Irish Anglicanism, 3,000 words. Letter or fax enquiry.

ShelfLife Magazine
CPG, 66 Patrick Street, Dun Laoghaire, Co Dublin. tel. 01-280-0424 fax 01-28-8468. Monthly, 7,500. Editor: Colette O'Connor. Off-trade: Jacinta Delahaye.
The new title of TSN News. News (15th) and features for grocers, off-licences, TSN, forecourt, H&B trade and relevant legislation: 2,000 words. Photos inc. colour. Letter or fax enquiry. Apple Mac. £100 per 1,000 words.

SMA Magazine: the African Missionary
Society of African Missions, Blackrock Road, Cork. tel. 021-292871. 5 a year, 39,000. Editor: Father Peter McCawille.

Social and Personal
27 Lower Baggot Street, Dublin 2. tel. 01-66200500 fax 01-661-6153. Monthly, 18,000. Editor: Nell Stewart-Liberty.
Interviews and articles on interiors, 1,500 words; short stories, 2,500 words. Also party stories, the arts, actors, at homes. Letter or fax enquiry. Apple Mac. £100 per 1,000 words.

Socialist Voice
43 East Essex Street, Dublin 2. tel/fax 01-671-1943. Fortnightly.

Specify
Greer Publications, 151 University Street, Belfast BT7 1HR. tel. 08-01232-231634 fax

08-01232-325736. Monthly, 4,700. Editor: Brian Russell.

Sporting Press
Davis Road, Clonmel, Co Tipperary. tel. 052-21422. Weekly 8,000. Editor: Jerry Desmond.
Anything to do with greyhounds. Photos inc. colour. News deadline Tuesday.

Sportsworld
48 North Great Georges Street, Dublin 1. tel. 01-872-1414 / 872-1636 fax 01-878-7749. Monthly, 23,000. Editor: John Martin.

Studia Hibernica
St Patrick's College, Drumcondra, Dublin 9.

Studies
35 Lower Leeson Street, Dublin 2. tel. 01-676-6785 fax 01-676-2984. Quarterly. Editor: Noel Barber SJ.
Theology, philosophy, politics, social sciences, letters, history.

Studies in Accounting & Finance
19 Rutland Street, Cork. tel. 021-313855 fax 021-313496. 3 a year, 1,000. 0791-864X. Editor: Brian O'Kane.
Articles on accountancy and business, 4,000. B/w photos. Letter or fax enquiry. MS-DOS Word for Windows 2.00 3½ inch. £200 per article.

Technology Ireland
Glasnevin, Dublin 9/ tel. 01-837-0101 fax 01-837-7122. 10 a year. Editors: Tom Kennedy and Mary Mulvihill.

Trade-Links Journal
4 St Kevin's Terrace, Dublin 8. tel. 01-454-2717. 6 a year, 3,750. Editor: Cathal Tyrell.

Tuarascáil
INTO, 35 Parnell Square, Dublin 1. tel. 01-872-2533 fax 01-872-2462. 10 a year, 20,000. Editor: Billy Sheehan.

U Magazine
126 Lower Baggot Street, Dublin 2. tel. 01-660-8264 fax 01-661-9757. Monthly. Editor: Maura O'Kiely. Asst Editor: Annette O'Meara. Fashion: Cathy O'Connor. Health: Áine McCarthy. Arts: Tony Clayton-Lea.
Reports and interviews, humour, curent af-fairs, relationships, sex, analysis, arts, fashion, travel, health, sport: 2,000 words. No fiction or poetry. Letter enquiry. Apple Mac.

Ulster Business
Greer Publications, 151 University Street, Belfast BT7 1HR. tel. 08-01232-231634 fax 08-01232-325736. Monthly, 6,000. Editor: Richard Buckley.

Ulster Countrywoman
209/211 Upper Lisburn Road, Belfast BT10 0LL. tel. 08-01232-301506 fax 08-01232-431127. Monthly, 6,500. Editor: Mrs Mildred Brown.
Sells only to members.

Ulster Farmer
Irish Street, Dungannon, Co Tyrone. tel. 08-018687-22557 fax 08-018687-27334. Editor: D. Mallon.

Ulster Grocer
Greer Publications, 151 University Street, Belfast BT7 1HR. tel. 08-01232-231634 fax 08-01232-325736. Monthly. Editor: Brian McCalden.

Ulster Tatler
39 Boucher Road, Belfast BT12 6UT. tel. 08-01232-681371. Monthly, 11,000. Editor: R. M. Sherry

Unity
Community Party of Ireland, 43 East Essex Street, Dublin 2. tel/fax 01-671-1943. Weekly. Editor: James Stewart.

Walking World Ireland
109 Old County Road, Dublin 12. tel. 01-454-5135/6 fax 01-454-5141. Quarterly, 12,000. 0791-8801. Editor: Frank Greally. Art editor: Conor O'Hagan.
News 250 words, features 1,500 words, poetry. Photos inc. colour. Fax enquiry. £70 per 1,000 words.

Woman's Way
126 Lower Baggot Street, Dublin 2. tel. 01-662-31588264 fax 01-661-9757. Weekly 66,260. Editor: Celine Naughton. Asst editor: Marianne Hartigan. Cookery: Honor Moore. Home: Carita McCullagh. Fashion: Valerie Shanley.
Features and fiction 1,500 words. Photos inc. colour. Letter or fax enquiry. Apple Mac with hard copy.

Women's Clubs Magazine

49 Wainsfort Park, Terenure, Dublin 6W. 01-492-4034 fax 01-492-4035. Quarterly, 10,000. 0532-446X. Editor: June Cook. News: Terry Gogan. Features: Mel White. *Journal of the Irish Federation of Women's Clubs; copy contributed by members.*

Word, The

Divine Word Missionaries, Moyglare Road, Maynooth, Co Kildare. tel. 01-628-9564 fax 01-628-9184. Monthly, 55,500. Editor: Revd Thomas Cahill SVD.

Writings

PO Box 3707, Dublin 6. 5 a year, 5,000. Editor: Edward Browne.
Short stories, 2,000 words; poetry, 500 words. Letter enquiry with copy prefereably on disc. MS-DOS or Apple Mac 3½ inch.

Xchange

Telecom Éireann, St Stephen's Green West, Dublin 2. tel. 01-701-5057 fax 01-478-1211. 10 a year, 17,000. Editor: Seán Creedon.
News and features (1,500 words) of interest to Telecom or RTE staff. Photos inc. colour. Letter or fax enquiry. Apple Mac. Rates negotiable.

Youth in Print

National Youth Council of Ireland, 3 Montague Street, Dublin 2. tel. 01-478-4122 fax 01-478-3974. 4 a year, 5,000.
Articles on youth work and youth sociology. Fax enquiry: no unsolicited manuscripts. NUJ membership required. Payment negotiable.

Newspapers, national

It is a sign of how busy national papers are—and how little concerned with freelance contributions—that only one of the following replied to our questionnaire. Don't waste their time! We mean no disrespect to any newspaper that enjoys national circulation by listing some such under Provincial and Local Periodicals. We have followed the *IPA Yearbook and Diary* in this, whose editor kindly permitted us to use information provided in the invaluable 1995 edition.

Anois
27 Cearnóg Mhuirfean, Baile Átha Cliath 2. tel. 01-676-0268 fax 01-661-2438. Eagarthóir: Bernard Harris. Eagarthóir Comhairleach: Micheál Mac Aonghusa.

Belfast Telegraph
124-144 Royal Avenue, Belfast BT1 1EB. tel. 08-01232-321242 fax 08-01232-242287. Daily, evening, 134,000. Editor: Edmund Curran.

Cork Examiner, The
PO Box 21, Academy Street, Cork. tel. 021-272722 fax 021-275477. Dublin office 96 Lower Baggot Street, Dublin 2. tel. 01-661-2733 fax 01-661-2737 telex 76014. Daily, 52,000. Editor: Brian Looney. Deputy Editor: Brendan O'Neill. Features Editor: Dan Buckley. Business Editor: Kevin Mills. Arts & Entertainment Editor: Declan Hassett. Agricultural Editor (Farm Exam Supplement): Steven Cadogan. Women's Editor: Irene Feighan. Sports Editor: Tom Ahern.

Evening Echo
Address as for *Cork Examiner*. Daily, 25,000. Editor: Nigel O'Mahony. Deputy Editor: Brian Feeney.

Evening Herald
Independent Newspapers (I) Ltd, Middle Abbey Street, Dublin 1. tel. 01-873-1666 fax 01-873-1787 telex 33473. Daily, 92,000. Editor: M. Denieffe.

Evening Press *
Irish Press Newspapers Ltd, 13-15 Parnell Square East, Dublin 1. tel. 01-671-3333 fax 01-671-3097. Daily, 59,000. Editor: Dick O'Riordan.

Irish Family, The
PO Box 7, Mullingar, Co Westmeath. tel. 044-42987 fax 044-42987. Editor: Dick Hogan.

Irish Independent
Independent Newspapers (I)Ltd, Middle Abbey Street, Dublin 1. tel. 01-873-1333 fax 01-873-1787 telex 33472. Daily, 144,000. Editor: Vincent Doyle. Deputy Editor: Michael Woolsey. Business Editor: Matt Cooper. Features Editor: Gerry Mulligan. Arts Editor: Tom Brady. Literary Editor: Bruce Arnold. Sports Editor: Karl McGinty.

Irish News
113-117 Donegall Street, Belfast BT1 2GE. tel. 08-01232-322226 fax 08-01232-231282 telex 08-01232-747170. Daily, 43,000. Editor: Tom Collins. Deputy Editor: Noel Doran. News Editor: Pauline Reynolds. Political Editor: Billy Graham. Business & Agriculture Editor: Seamus Boyd. Arts Editor: Colm McAlpin. Women's Editor: Anne Molloy.

Irish Press *
13-15 Parnell Square East, Dublin 1. tel. 01-671-3333 fax 01-671-3097. Daily, 44,000. Editor: Hugh Lambert.

Irish Times, The
10-16 D'Olier Street, Dublin 2. tel. 01-679-2022 fax 01-679-3910 telex 93639. Daily, 93,000. Editor: Conor Brady. News Editor: Niall Kiely. Features Editor: Caroline Walsh. Political Editor: Dick Walsh. Arts Editor: Paddy Woodworth. Literary Editor: John Banville. Education Editor: Christine Murphy. Sports Editor: Malachy Logan.

News Letter
Century Newspapers Ltd, 45-56 Boucher Crescent, Belfast BT126QY. tel. 08-01232-

680000 fax 08-01232-664412. Daily, 100,000. Editor: Geoff Martin. News: H. Robinson. Features: G. Hill. Sport: Brian Millar. Business: David Kirk. Arts: Charles Fitzgerald.

Publishes editions under the titles Belfast News Letter *and* Ulster News Letter. *News by 8 p.m., Features 1,000 words. No fiction, occasional poetry. Photos inc. colour. Letter or fax enquiry. Apple Mac. Fee negotiable.*

Star, The

Independent Star Ltd, Star House, Terenure Road North, Dublin 6W. tel. 01-490-1228 fax 01-4902193. Daily. Editor: Gerry O'Regan. Deputy Editor: Paddy Murray. News Editor: John Donlon. Assistant Editor: Dave O'Connell. Features Editor: Bernie O'Toole.

Sunday Business Post

27-30 Merchants Quay, Dublin 8. tel. 01-679-9777 fax 01-679-6496. Weekly, 29,000. Editor: Damien Kiberd. News Editor: Nick Mulcahy.
Deputy/Features Editor: Aileen O'Toole. Political Editors: Emily O'Reilly, Mark O'Connell.

Sunday Independent

Independent Newspapers (I) Ltd, Middle Abbey Street, Dublin 1. tel. 01-873-1333 fax 01-873-1787. Weekly, 253,000. Editor: Aengus Fanning. Deputy/News Editor: Willie Keeley. Deputy/Features Editor: Anne Harris. Business Editor: Shane Ross. Arts Editor: Ronan Farren. Sports Editor: Adhamháin O'Sullivan.

Sunday Press *

Irish Press Newspapers Ltd, 13-15 Parnell Square East, Dublin 1. tel. 01-671-3333 fax 01-679-7452. Weekly, 170,000. Editor: Michael Keane.

Sunday Times

30 Upper Merrion Street, Dublin 2. tel. 01-676-5166. fax. 01-676-5254. Weekly. Irish Editor: Alan Ruddock.

Sunday Tribune

15 Lower Baggot Street, Dublin 2. tel. 01-661-5555 fax 01-661-5302 telex 90995. Weekly. Editor: Peter Murtagh. News Editor: Diarmuid Doyle. Political Editors: Joe Joyce, Cathal McCoille, Olivia O'Leary. Features Editors: Deirdre McQuillan, Rosalind Dee. Sports Editor: Johnny Waterson.

Sunday World

Sunday Newspapers Ltd, Newspaper House, Rathfarnham Road, Dublin 6. tel. 01-490-1980 fax 01-490-1838 telex 93586. Weekly, 268,000. Editor: Colm MacGinty. News Editor: Seán Boyne.

* The three papers of the Irish Press group were not being published as we went to press, but there are plans to resuscitate some if not all. The last correct details are given here.

Periodicals, provincial and local

This list includes newspapers and magazines of both general and special interest that mainly target a readership in one part of the country. Only the *Belfast Telegraph* and *Cork Examiner*, of papers with a place name in the title, are generally acknowledged to have national-news-paper status, though many listed below sell nationally and even internationally. Unlike the national newspaper publishers, these ones mostly returned our questionnaire, and often showed a genuine interest in encouraging and helping freelance writers.

Anglo-Celt, The
Cavan. tel. 049-31100 fax 049-32280. Weekly, 16,000. Editor: Johnny O'Hanlon.

Antrim Guardian
1A Railway Street, Antrim. tel. 08-01849-462624. Wednesday, 23,000. Editor: Liam Hefron.
Localised edition of Ballymena Guardian.

Argus, The
Jocelyn Street, Dundalk, Co Louth. tel. 042-34632 fax 042-31643. Weekly, 9,000. Editor: Kevin Mulligan.

Armagh-Down Observer.
Irish Street, Dungannon, Co Tyrone. tel. 08-018687-22557 fax 08-018687-27334. Weekly. Editor: M. O'Neill.

Armagh Observer.
26 English Street, Armagh. tel. 08-018687-22557 fax 08-018687-27334. Weekly. Editor: D. Mallon.

Artsfocus
Down Recorder, 2-4 Church Street, Downpatrick, Co Down. tel. 08-01396-613711 fax 08-01396-614624. 2 a year, 3,000. Editor: Gary Law.
Local-interest news, features or fiction. B/w photos. Submit typescript. No payment.

Ballymena/Antrim Times and Ballymena Observer
see Morton Newspapers

Ballymena Chronicle and Antrim Observer
Irish Street, Dungannon, Co Tyrone. tel. 08-018687-22557 fax 08-018687-27334. Weekly. Editor: M. O'Neill.

Ballymena Guardian
Northern Newspaper Group, Railway Road, Coleraine. tel. 08-01266-41221 fax 08-01266-653920. Weekly, 24,000. Editor: M. O'Neill.

Banbridge Chronicle
14 Bridge Street, Banbridge, Co Down. 08-018206-62322 fax 08-018206-24397. Weekly, 7,500. Editor: Bryan Hooks.

Banbridge Leader
see Morton Newspapers

Bray People
Main Street, Bray. tel. 01-286-7393. See People Newspapers.

Business Contact
58 North Great Charles Street, Dublin 1. tel. 01-855-0477 fax 01-855-0473. 10 a year, 4,500. 0791-9182. Editor: Karen Hesse.
News and articles about business in Dublin, 1,200 words. Photos inc. colour. Fax enquiry. NUJ membership required; payment at NUJ rates.

Carrickfergus Advertiser
31A High Street, Carrickfergus, Co Antrim. tel 08-019603-63651 fax 08-019603-63092. Weekly (Wed.), 14,000. Editor: Ian Greer.

Causeway
6 Murray Street, Belfast BT1 6DN. tel. 08-01232-236030 fax 08-01232-236081. 4 a year, 2,500. 1350-6013. Editor: Tony Canavan.
News and articles on all aspects of Northern culture and heritage, 3,000 words. B/w phots. MS-DOS MS Word 3.5 inch. Payment negotiable.

Clare Champion
Barrack Street, Ennis, Co Clare. tel. 065-28105 fax 065-20374. Weekly, 20,000. Editor: J. F. O'Dea.

Coleraine/Ballymoney Times
see Morton Newspapers

Coleraine Chronicle
Northern Newspaper Group, Railway Road, Coleraine, Co Derry. tel. 08-01265-43344. Weekly, 23,000. Editor: Hugh McGratten.

Connacht Sentinel, The
The Connacht Tribune, 15 Market Street, Galway. tel. 091-67251 fax 091-67970. Weekly, 6,000. Editor: John Cunningham.

Connacht Tribune, The
15 Market Street, Galway. tel. 091-67251 fax 091-67970. Weekly, 27,500. Editor: John Cunningham. Assistant Editor: Michael Glynn.

Connaught Telegraph
Castlebar, Co Mayo. tel. 094-21711 fax 094-24007. Weekly, 16,000. Editor: Tom Courell.

Corkman, The
see Kerryman

County Down Spectator
D. E. Alexander & Sons, 109 Main Street, Bangor, Co Down. tel. 08-01247-270270 fax 08-01247171544. Weekly, 16,000.

Craigavon Echo.
14A Church Street, Portadown, Co Armagh. tel. 08-01762-350041 fax 08-01762-350203. Free weekly, 23,000. Editor: David Armstrong.

Democrat, The
Irish Street, Dungannon, Co Tyrone. tel. 08-018687-22557 fax 08-018687-27334. Managing Editor: D. J. Mallon.

Derry Journal
Buncrana Road, Derry. tel. 08-01504-265442 fax 08-01504-262048. Or at Church Street, Letterkenny, Co Donegal. tel. 074-26240 fax 074-26329. Tuesday and Friday 25,000. Editor: P. McArt.

Derry People and Donegal News
Ulster Herald Series, Crossview House, Letterkenny, Co Donegal. tel. 074-21024 fax 074-22881. Thursday, 10,400. Editor: E. J. Quigley. New Editor: J. McCrory.

Donegal Democrat
Donegal Road, Ballyshannon, Co Donegal. tel. 072-51201 fax 072-51945. Weekly, 17,500. Editor: John Bromley.

Donegal People's Press
Champion Publications, Wine Street, Sligo. tel. 071-69222 fax 071-69040 or at Letterkenny tel. 074-21842 fax 074-24787. Weekly, 9,000. Editor: Seamus McKinney

Down Recorder
Church Street, Downpatrick, Co Down. tel. 08-01396-613711 fax 08-01396-614624. Weekly, 13,000. Editor: Paul Symington.

Drogheda Independent
9 Shop Street, Drogheda, Co Louth. tel. 041-38658 fax 041-34271. Weekly, 13,000. Editor: Paul Murphy. Deputy Editor: Jim McCullen.

Dromore Star
see Morton Newspapers

Dundalk Democrat
Thomas Roe Ltd, 3 Earl Street, Dundalk. tel. 042-34058 fax 042-31399. Weekly, 16,000. Editor: T. P. Roe.

Dungannon News and Tyrone Courier
58 Scotch Street, Dungannon, Co Tyrone. tel. 08-018687-22271 fax 08-018687-26171. Weekly, 13,000. Editor: R. G. Montgomery.

Dungannon Observer
Irish Street, Dungannon, Co Tyrone. tel. 08-018687-22557 fax 08-018687-27334. Weekly. Editor: D. Mallon

Dungarvan Leader and Southern Democrat
Colm J. Nagle, 78 O'Connell Street, Dungarvan, Co Waterford. tel. 058-41203 fax 058-41203. Weekly, 13,000. Editor: Colm J. Nagle.
Local interest. Fax enquiry. B/w photos

Dungarvan Observer and Munster Industrial Advocate
Shandon, Dungarvan, Co Waterford. tel. 41205 fax 058-41559. Weekly, 10,500. Editor: P. Lynch.

East Belfast Herald and Post
see Herald and Post

Echo, The
Mill Park Road, Enniscorthy, Co Wexford. tel. 054-33231 fax 054-33506. With *Wexford*

Echo, Gorey Echo, New Ross Echo, weekly, 21,800. Editor in Chief: James Gahan.

Farming Echo
see Echo

Fermanagh Herald
Ulster Herald Series, John Street, Omagh, Co Tyrone. tel. 08-01662-243444 fax 08-01662-242206; or Belmor Street, Enniskillen, Co Fermanagh. tel. 08-01365-322066 fax 08-01365-325521. Weekly (Wed.), 10,500. Editor: E. J. Quigley (Omagh). News Editor: M. Breslin (Enniskillen).

Fermanagh News
Irish Street, Dungannon, Co Tyrone. tel. 08-018687-22557 fax 08-018687-27334. Editor: D. Mallon.

Five County News
see Longford News

Fold, The
St Maries of the Isle, Cork. tel. 021-312330 fax 021-965209. Monthly, 9,000. 0790-6838. Editor: Revd Bernard Cotter. Features: Tom Hayes.
The diocesan magazine of Cork and Ross. News of religious and local interest (400 words), features on religion, people, communities and self-help (1,000 words); occasional fiction on seasonal themes; no poetry. Photos inc. colour. Letter or fax enquiry. £20 per 1,000 words. MS-DOS or Apple Mac.

Galway Advertiser
2-3 Church Lane, Galway. tel. 091-67077 fax 091-67079. Weekly (Thurs.), 32,000. Managing Editor: Ronnie O'Gorman.

Gorey Echo
see Echo

Guardian, The
Court Street, Enniscorthy, Co Wexford. tel. 054-33833 or Thomas Street, Gorey. tel. 055-21423. See People Newspapers

Herald and Post Newspapers
124 Royal Avenue, Belfast BT1 1EB. tel. 08-01232-239049 fax 08-01232-239050. Weeklies, combined circ. 159,000. Editor: Nigel Tilson.

In Cork
Hatfield House, 14 Tobin Street (off South Main Street), Cork. tel. 021-278544/5 fax 021-278546.
Editor: Gerry McCarthy.
Listings and events guide, plus news and features on local issues and personalities.

Kerryman, The
Clash Industrial Estate, Tralee, Co Kerry. tel. 066-21666 fax 066-21608. Weekly, with *The Corkman*, 33,500. Editor: Gerard Colleran. Assistant Editor: Gerard Colleran. Sports Editor: John Barry.

Kerry's Eye
Kenno Ltd, 22 Ashe Street, Tralee, Co Kerry. tel. 066-23199 fax 066-23163. Weekly 17,500. Editor: Padraig Kennelly.

Kilkenny People
34 High Street, Kilkenny. tel. 056-21025 fax 056-21414. Weekly, 20,000. Editor: John Kerry Keane.

Larne/Carrickfergus/Newtownabbey Times
see Morton Newspapers

Leader, The
The Square, Dromore, Co Down. tel. 08-01846-692217 fax 08-01846-699260. Weekly, 10,500. Editor: Carlton Baxtor.

Leinster Express
Dublin Road, Portlaoise, Co Lais. tel. 0502-21666 fax 0502-20491. Weekly inc. *Offaly Express*, 17,000. Editor: Teddy Fennelly.

Leinster Leader
19 South Main Street, Naas, Co Kildare. tel. 045-97302 fax 045-71168. Weekly, 15,000.

Leitrim Observer
St George's Terrace, Carrick-on-Shannon, Co Leitrim. tel. 078-20025 fax 078-20112. Weekly, 11,000. Editor: Anthony Hickey.

Liffey Champion
51 Main Street, Leixlip, Co Kildare. tel. 01-624-5533. Fortnightly. Editor: V. Sutton.

Limavady Sentinel
see Londonderry Sentinel

Limerick Chronicle
Limerick Leader Ltd, O'Connell Street, Limerick. tel. 061-315233 fax 061-314804. Weekly (Tues.), 7,000. Editor: Brendan

Halligan.

Limerick Leader
O'Connell Street, Limerick. tel. 061-315233 fax 061-314804. 4 per week, 7,500-28,000. Editor: Brendan Halligan.

Lisburn Echo
12A Bow Street, Lisburn, Co Antrim. tel. 08-01846-679111 fax 08-01846-602904. Weekly, 22,614. Editor: Joseph Fitzpatrick. *News (noon Friday), features, poetry of local interest inc. churches, cultural, sporting, entertainment. B/w photos. Letter or fax enquiry. NUJ membership preferred. Payment negotiable.*

Local News Publications
(Southside edition:) 9 Lower Kevin Street, Dublin 8. tel. 01-475-7132 fax 01-834-2079. Editor: Frank Bambrick. Features & News Editor: Derek Kenny.
News, 50-800 words (20th of the month), features, 1,000 words, poetry, humour and cartoons. B/w photos or quality colour. Letter or fax enquiry. Apple Mac. Payment £15-£35.
(Northside edition:) Rosehill House, Main Street, Finglas, Dublin 11. tel. 01-836-1666 fax 01-834-2079.

Londonderry/Roe Valley Sentinel
see Morton Newspapers

Londonderry Sentinel
33 Strand Road, Derry. tel. 08-01504-267571 fax 08-01504-269646. Weekly with *Limavady Sentinel*, 11,000. Editor: James Cadden.

Longford Leader, The
Market Square, Longford. tel. 043-45241 fax 043-41489. Weekly (Wed.), 25,000. Editor: Eugene McGee.

Longford News
Dublin Street, Longford. tel. 043-46342 fax 043-41549. Weekly (Wed.), 24,000. Group Editor: Paul Healy. Deputy Editor: Siobhán Cronin. Features: Audrey Moorehead. Sports: Eamonn Sweeney.

Lurgan and Portadown Examiner
Irish Street, Dungannon, Co Tyrone. tel. 08-018687-22557 fax 08-018687-27334. Weekly. Editor: D. Mallon.

Lurgan Mail
4A High Street, Lurgan, Co Armagh. tel. 08-01762-327777 fax 08-01762-325271. Weekly, 10,000. Editor: Richard Elliott.

Mayo News
The Fairgreen, Westport, Co Mayo. tel. 098-25311 fax 098-26108. Weekly, 12,000. Editor: Seán Staunton.

Meath Chronicle and Cavan and Westmeath Herald
Market Square, Navan, Co Meath. tel. 046-21442 fax 046-23565. Weekly, 20,000. Editor: Kevin Davis. Fashion: Margot Davis. Sports: Paul Clarke.

Meath Topic
Topic Newspapers, Lynn Industrial Estate, Mullingar. tel. 044-48868 fax 044-43777. Weekly. Editor: Dick Hogan.

Midland Tribune, The
Emmet Street, Birr, Co Offaly. tel. 0509-20003 fax 0509-20588. Weekly, 16,000. Editor: John O'Callaghan.

Mid-Ulster Echo
see Morton Newspapers

Mid-Ulster Mail
Magherafelt. see Morton Newspapers

Mid-Ulster Observer
Irish Street, Dungannon, Co Tyrone. tel. 08-018687-22557 fax 08-018687-27334. Weekly. Editor: M. O'Neill.

Morton Newspapers Ltd
21-35 Windsor Avenue, Lurgan, Craigavon, Co Armagh BT67 9BG. tel. 08-01762-326161 fax 08-01762-343618.

Mourne Observer
Castlewellan Road, Newcastle, Co Down BT33 0QZ. tel. 08-013967-22666 fax 08-013967-24566. Weekly, 13,200. Editor: Terence Bowman. Sports: Raymond Stewart *News (noon Tuesday) and features of local interest. Fiction and poetry by local authors. B/w photos. Letter or fax enquiry. Payment (not for fiction or poetry) negotiable.*

Munster Express, The
37 The Quay, Waterford. tel. 051-72141 fax 051-73452. Twice weekly, 18,500. Editor: K. J. Walsh.

Nationalist and Leinster Times
42 tullow Street, Carlow. tel. 0503-31731. Weekly, 17,000. Editor: Thomas Mooney.

Assistant Editor: Eddie Coffey. Sports: Paul Donaghy.

Nationalist Newspaper

Queen Street, Clonmel, Co Tipperary. tel. 052-22211 fax 052-25248. Weekly, 15,500. Editor: Tom Corr.

Nenagh Guardian

13 Summerhill, Nenagh, Co Tipperary. tel. 067-31214 fax 067-33401. Weekly, 7,750. Editor: Gerry Slevin.

New Ross Standard

South Street, New Ross, Co Wexford. tel. 051-21184. See People Newspapers.

Newry Reporter, The

Ed Hodgett Ltd, 4 Margaret Street, Newry, Co Down. tel. 08-01693-67633 fax 08-01693-63157. Weekly, 16,000. Editor: D. O'Donnell.

Newtownabbey Guardian

as for Northern Constitution.

Newtownards Spectator

109 Main Street, Bangor, Co Down. tel. 08-01247-270270 fax 08-01247-271544. Weekly, 4,000. Editor: Paul Flowers.

North and Newtownabbey Herald and Post

see Herald and Post

North Down Herald and Post

see Herald and Post

North-West Echo

33 Strand Road, Derry. tel. 08-01504-268459 fax 08-01504-269646. Weekly free, 30,000. Editor: James Cadden.

Northern Constitution

Northern Newspaper Group, Railway Road, Coleraine, Co Derry. tel. 08-01265-43344. Weekly, 8,750. Editor: Grant Cameron.

Northern Standard

The Diamond, Monaghan. tel. 047-81867 fax 047-84070. Weekly, 14,500. Editor: Martin Smyth.

Offaly Express

Bridge Street, Tullamore. tel. 0506-21744 fax 0506-51930. Weekly, edition of *Leinster Express*.

Offaly Topic

see Meath Topic

Outlook, The

Castle Street, Rathfriland, Co Down. tel. 08-018206-30202 fax 08-018206-31022. Weekly, 7,500. Editor: Ken Purdy.

People, The

1A North Main Street, Wexford. tel. 053-22155 fax 053-23801. See People Newspapers

People Newspapers Ltd

1 North Main Street, Wexford. tel. 053-22155 fax 053-23801. Five regional titles together 36,000. Editor: Gerard Walsh.

Portadown Times

see Morton Newspapers

Property Echo

see Echo

New Ross Echo

see Echo

Portadown Times

14 Church Street, Portadown. tel. 08-01762-336111 fax 08-01762-350203. Weekly, 13,000. Editor: David Armstrong
News 500 words. B/w photos.

Roscommon Champion

Abbey Street, Roscommon. tel. 0903-25051 fax 0903-25053. Weekly, 10,500. Editor: Paul Healy.

Roscommon Herald

Boyle, Co Roscommon. tel. 079-62622 fax 079-62926. Weekly, 16,500. Editor: Christina McHugh.

Sligo Champion

Champion Publications Ltd, Wine Street, Sligo. tel. 071-69222 fax 071-69040. Weekly, 16,500. Editor: S. Finn.

Sligo Weekender

Castle Street, Sligo. tel. 071-42140 fax 071-42255. Weekly, 11,000. Editor: Brian McHugh.
News by Tuesday, or Thursday if important. Features. B/w photos. Letter or fax enquiry. Apple Mac.

South Belfast Herald and Post

see Herald and Post

South News

Unit 5 Wood Park, Glenageary, Co Dublin. tel. 01-284-0266 fax 01-284-0860. Irregular, free, 51,000. Editor: Ken Finlay.

Southern Star

Skibbereen, Co Cork. tel. 028-21200 fax 028-21071. Weekly, 16,000. Editor: L. O'Regan.

Strabane Chronicle

John Street, Omagh, Co Tyrone. tel. 08-01662-243444 fax 08-01662-242206. Weekly (Thurs.) 4,000. Editor: E. J. Quigley.

Strabane Weekly News

25-27 High Street, Omagh, Co Tyrone. tel. 08-01662-242721 fax 08-01662-243549. Editor: N. F. Armstrong.

Tipperary Star

Nationalist Newspaper Co Ltd, Friar Street, Thurles, Co Tipperary. tel. 0504-21122 fax 0504-21110. Weekly, 10,500. Editor: Michael Dundon.

Trinity News

DU Publications, House 612:3 Trinity College, Dublin 2. tel. 01-702-2335. Monthly in term time, 10,000. Editor: Barbara Collins. Arts: Aengus Collins, Siobhán Doyle, Eoin Brannigan.
Student news, 800 words; features, reviews, author interviews, 2,000 words. B/w photos. Any disc. Letter or fax enquiry or typescript.

Tuam Herald and Western Advertiser

Herald Printing & Publishing Co, Dublin Road, Tuam, Co Galway. tel. day 093-24183 night 093-24251 fax 093-24478. Weekly (Wed.), 11,000. Editor: David Burke. News: Jim Carney.

Tullamore Tribune, The

Church Street, Tullamore, Co Offaly. tel. 0506-21152 fax 0506-21927. Weekly, 6,000. Editor: G. V. Oakley.

Tyrone Constitution, The

25-27 High Street, Omagh, Co Tyrone. tel. 08-01662-242721 fax 08-01662-243549. Weekly, 10,500. Editor: N. F. Armstrong.

Tyrone Times

see Morton Newspapers

UCD Alma Mater

Ryan Media, The Basement, 12 Hume Street, Dublin 2. 01-676-9538 fax 01-676-9538. Quarterly, 30,000. 0791-8747. Editor: Jackie Dawson
No other data supplied.

Ulster Farmer

Irish Street, Dungannon, Co Tyrone. tel. 08-018687-22557 fax 08-018687-27334. Weekly.

Ulster Gazette and Armagh Standard

56 Scotch Street, Armagh. tel. 08-01861-522639 fax 08-01861-527029. Weekly, 11,000. Editor: Karen Bushby.

Ulster Herald

John Street, Omagh, Co Tyrone. tel. 08-01662-2434444 fax 08-01662-242206. Weekly (Thurs.), 12,500. Editor: E. J. Quigley.

Ulster Star

12A Bow Street, Lisburn, Co Antrim BT28 1BN. tel. 08-01846-679111 fax 08-01846-602904. Weekly, 18,500. Editor: David Fletcher.

Waterford News & Star

25 Michael Street, Waterford. tel. 051-74951 fax 051-55281. Weekly, 16,000. Editor: Peter Doyle.

Western People, The

Francis Street, Ballina, Co Mayo. tel. 096-21188 fax 096-70208. Weekly, 28,000. Editor: Terry Reilly.

Wetmeath Examiner

19 Dominick Street, Mullingar, Co Westmeath. tel. 044-48426 fax 044-40640. Weekly, 13,250. Editor: N. J. Nally.

Westmeath Topic

see Meath Topic

Wexford Echo

see Echo

Wicklow People

Main Street, Wicklow. tel. 0404-67198 fax 0404-69937 or Main Street, Arklow. tel. 0402-32130 fax 0402-39309. See People Newspapers.

Writing for radio

Joe O'Donnell

THE FIRST PLAY written for radio was broadcast seventy years ago. *Danger*, by Richard Hughes, was set in pitch darkness at the bottom of a coal mine, during a power failure. It can be no coincidence that its first line was "The lights have gone out"! These words established the arena where the best radio drama has occurred ever since: inside the head of the listener.

Not all radio drama is specially written for the medium: a typical week's output on BBC or RTÉ might include drama serials, plays adapted from the theatre or from published fiction, situation comedies, soap operas, and comedy sketch shows. But radio at its most exciting is primarily evocative, and has its greatest impact through resonances provoked in the mind of the listener.

The writer for stage, television or film has a range of non-verbal devices with which to convey information—setting, costumes, gesture, facial expression, even colour. The radio dramatist relies entirely on what can be heard. This essentially breaks down into four elements: speech, sound effects, music and silence—this last a potent if often neglected element. But what may initially seem a limitation, applied imaginatively, becomes a liberating opportunity. Radio drama at its best is pure theatre of the head.

For my money, a milestone in the development of radio drama was *The War of the Worlds*, adapted from the novel by H. G. Wells and performed by Orson Welles' Mercury Theatre. Presented on 30 October 1938 in the form of an actuality broadcast, it convinced thousands that reports of the Martian landings were real. It was theatre of the head at its most potent. Other classics to study are Dylan Thomas's *Under Milk Wood*, Harold Pinter's *A Slight Ache*, and Samuel Beckett's *From an Abandoned Work*.

Although the flood of radio drama on RTÉ and BBC has diminished in recent years, anyone unfamiliar with the form will be astonished by the abundance and variety on both services. In the week in which this is being written RTÉ has over three hours and BBC has over 13 hours of drama. In one week!

Radio is still hospitable to the new writer. So how does one go about writing a radio play?

A good radio play is a good *play* first and foremost. Ideally the subject should be something which could not be done successfully in any other medium. The classic principles of structure apply equally to radio as to other forms of drama. One of the questions the radio writer might consider is whether the plot is exciting enough to make listeners want to find out how it develops: because listeners may not be attentive, they may switch on late, they may wander in and out of the room, they may be interrupted. They have no immediate visual frame of reference.

As to characters, although a good director will cast voices to exploit the range of timbre and pitch, it is helpful if the speech pattern of each character is distinctive. One of the problems for the listener is knowing which character is present and which is not. If a scene is overcrowded, listeners may find it hard to sort out who's who. It is difficult for the ear to differentiate between too many voices in a single scene.

It must always be clear where each scene is happening so effects and music must be chosen with care to provide not only additional sound texture but necessary information.

There is a standard format for presenting a radio script, but common sense will dictate that you keep a wide left hand margin in which nothing appears but the names of the characters who are speaking so that it is clear who is speaking at any given moment. In addition, you should distinguish clearly between the words the listeners are to hear, and all other directions, sound effects, music details and so forth. Usually it's not necessary to tell the actor how to say a line. The line should be written in such a way that *it* tells the actor how to say it. A cover sheet should give the name of the play, your name, address and phone number. A separate sheet should list the cast, together with a brief note on their characters.

Apart from plays, the openings for the writer are mostly limited to short pieces, the equivalent of the newspaper article, for such programmes as RTÉ's *Sunday Miscellany*, and, of course, short stories.

A short story is a short story whatever the medium and most short stories will work on radio, given the parameters of length. Most broadcast stories are 15 minutes long, which means between 1,900 and 2,000 words. Stories with a single point of view—i.e. told through the eyes of one character only—seem to work best. The story told in the first person singular seems particularly suited to radio as it lends an intimacy which works very well.

Stories and non-fiction pieces should be read aloud to see whether they flow easily. Does the story begin at a point where the audience will soon grasp the situation and know what the central conflict is? Does the story move, progressing from event to event and approaching a climax?

As you may not be reading it yourself, make it as foolproof as possible. Broadcast sentences should be short, conversational and uncomplicated. Their meaning should be lucid and proof against misunderstanding. The language should be concrete rather than abstract. Each sentence must have a plain meaning and lead to the next, so that the ear will take in the sequence which the eye cannot. Your listener cannot turn back the page to check out something which is unclear.

If statistics, numbers or any type of graphic representation is part of your submission, then you must seek an imaginative way around this.

Radio can also create a unique style of comedy. The *Goon Show* series has become a classic and the scripts of this and other series are published, and available on cassette. In the absence of the actual broadcast, there is no better way to get the feel of the medium than by listening critically to the now widely available cassettes.

But for an unforgettable audio experience seek out the sound recording of *The Muppet Show*, and listen to the track *The Great Gonzo Eats a Rubber Tyre to the Music of Rimsky Korsakov*. Now this is pure theatre of the head, guaranteed to blow your mind.

Joe O'Donnell is a freelance writer and director. Over twenty of his radio plays have been produced in Ireland, Britain, France and Germany. His latest, *Four Riders on the Rim of the Sea*, was selected as RTÉ's entry for the 1995 Prix Futura in Berlin.

Further Reading

The Way to Write Radio Drama by William Ashe (Elm Tree 1985).

Under Milk Wood by Dylan Thomas (Dent 1954).

The Hitchhiker's Guide to the Galaxy by Douglas Adams (Pan, 1982).

The Goon Show Scripts (Sphere, 1972).

The radio plays of Samuel Beckett in *Samuel Beckett: The Complete Dramatic Works* (Faber, 1986).

Radio drama and comedy available on cassette from BBC Enterprises, 80 Wood Lane, London W12 0TT.

Radio stations

Radio Telefís Éireann

Radio Centre, Donnybrook, Dublin 4. tel. 01-208-3111 fax 01-208-3080. Director of Radio Progamming: Kevin Healy. Managing Editor, Features & Arts Radio: Michael Littleton. Editor, Drama: Laurence Foster. Editor, Arts/Drama: Seamus Hosey. Editor, Features and Documentaries: Paddy Glackin. Special Development of Documentaries: Lorelei Harris. Commissioning Editor, Education: John Quinn. Commissioning Editor, Religion: John MacKenna.

Short stories

The bulk of Radio One's short-story requirements are drawn from the annual Francis MacManus Short Story Competition. The five winning stories are broadcast from December to March.

The Francis MacManus competition is open to people born or normally resident in Ireland. Stories, in English or Irish, should be written for radio and must not have been previously published in any medium. Typewritten entries of 1,850-1,950 are considered and should be submitted to the above address, clearly marked Francis MacManus Award, between 17 June and 16 September. The results are announced in late November of each year. The winning author in 1994 received £1,500. There were three runner-up prizes of £750, £500 and £250, plus a special prize of £1,000 sponsored by the Irish Congress of Trades Union to mark its centenary.

The best stories submitted outside of the MacManus competition, plus a limited number which appeal to the competition judges but are not awarded prizes, are broadcast at the end of the MacManus season at current rates of payment (£6.64 to £10.64 per minute, depending on number of previous acceptances).

An anthology based on the first eight years of the MacManus competition, *Prize-winning Radio Stories*, has been published by Mercier Press and is available from bookshops at £6.99.

Drama

Serials: regularly presented, generally in six 27-minute episodes, but most usually radio adaptations of published novels. Original radio drama serials are considered, preferably "middle of the road drama" with a strong narrative line and good characterisation, bearing in mind suitability for an Irish audience. "Almost anything that is good of its kind will have a reasonable chance of acceptance, but the further a play is removed from the middle of the road the better it has to be."

Children's plays

No children's plays were being produced at the time of writing, but discussions on this matter with the European Broadcasting Union are on-going and requirements may change in the near future.

Irish-language plays

Plays of 30, 45 or 60 minutes are considered.

One-off plays

Plays of 30, 45 or 60 minutes are presented, but the main demand is for shorter plays.

In addition, RTÉ administers the annual **P. J. O'Connor Awards** for writers new to radio drama and for amateur drama groups. In the writers' category, three awards, of £1,000, £750 and £500, are presented and each of the winning plays is produced. Six additional plays are selected for the Amateur Drama Radio Festival and their authors awarded £250 each. Radio plays of 30 minutes duration, in English or Irish, by Irish writers or writers resident in Ireland, will be considered. Only writers with a maximum of two hours radio drama professionally performed may enter. The deadline for entries is 12 November and the winners are announced in late February.

Non-fiction

There are a number of outlets at RTÉ Radio 1 for carefully targeted non-fiction submissions. *Sunday Miscellany* is a general interest magazine programme which considers scripts on all sorts of topical issues as well as personal reminiscences, short literary pieces and poetry. Scripts of 700 words or five minutes long should be sent to producer Lorelei Harris at the above address. *Voice Over* is a half-hour programme that can take the form of reportage, documentary or studio discussion. Topics recently covered include commercial travellers, the growth of golf and the amateur dramatic movement. Submit ideas in the first instance to programme adviser Bill Meek. Fifty- to ninety-second scripts with a spiritual theme are considered for *Matins*; submissions to religious programmes editor John MacKenna.

BBC Radio Northern Ireland

Broadcasting House, Ormeau Avenue, Belfast BT2 8HQ. tel. 08-01232-338000. Controller, Northern Ireland: Robin Walsh. Senior Producer, Drama: Pam Brighton. Editor, Current Affairs: Andrew Colman. Editor, News: Tom Kelly.

Like the four other regional radio centres in the BBC network, BBC Northern Ireland produces drama for Radio 3 and Radio 4. Its output includes original radio plays, radio dramatisations of novels and stage plays, series and serials, poetry, features and short stories. Irish writers may submit directly to the BBC's London headquarters, but given the huge volume of material submitted to London (250 scripts per week), you are more likely to receive a prompt reply from BBC Northern Ireland. Complete scripts for plays should be accompanied by a synopsis, together with a full cast list and brief notes on the main characters.

Radio 3

Drama Now: plays up to 75 minutes, dedicated to new and challenging work; *Studio Three*: plays up to 45 minutes, with exploratory and experimental use of sound.

Radio 4

The Monday Play (75 or 90 minutes) aims to provide an outlet for original writing on complex themes; *Saturday Plays* (75 or 90 minutes) are 'family' entertainment with a strong narrative line; *the Afternoon Play* (30, 45 and 60 minutes) is broadcast on weekday afternoons, largely original plays with a significant number of works by new writers; *Sixty Minute Series* (60-minute weekly episodes, three or four parts) are self-contained episodes but with continuing central characters, strong storylines and a bias towards detection; *Thirty Minute Serials/Series* (30 minute weekly episodes, two to eight parts) require a wide range of material, but it must have popular appeal, e.g. light comedy, romance, detective stories, thrillers; *Wednesday Afternoon Series* (45 minutes, three to six parts) are mostly original works which aim to provide a mix of serials and anthology series; *Short Story* (15 minutes) uses a substantial amount of new writing, but commissioned and published work as well; *Features* (normally 30, 45 and 55 minutes) cover a wide range of subjects, and it is always advisable to propose the subject before embarking on a script; *Poetry*—a variety of slots to cover both published and new work; *Drama for Younger Audiences*—following the removal of drama from Radio 5, Radio 4 will be broadcasting half-hour serials for young and family audiences and serialised readings of young people's fiction.

Writing for film and television

Philip Davison

LET US SAY that you have some lingering doubts about the screenplay you are about to submit for production funding. You have shown the work to several people whose judgement you trust. Their response is favourable generally, but you are a little surprised by the vagueness of the terms they use. No two of them offer the same suggestions. A few remarks strike a chord. You make a number of minor changes but these do not redress your doubts. What is to be done?

It might help to ask what does the actor want from your screenplay. You might read the screenplay again. Do not stop to make notes. You need to read it through with a cold, unblinking eye if you are to have a complete picture of what is actually on the page. At this stage the writer must contend with distortions that are the product of the creative process. The writer's perception of the screenplay may be coloured by the material that was ultimately rejected. He or she may still be preoccupied with the tortuous business of making the whole thing work.

Are you immediately arrested by the opening? Is it evident that there is something at stake as we progress, sentence by sentence, scene by scene? Is there a sense of completeness? The screenplay must be a good read. It should be at once lean and evocative.

Sometimes, the inexperienced screenwriter is hindered by his or her expectations of the medium. The camera figures too early in the process. I have found in my work with film students that often the most striking, most poignant images come from what are essentially exercises for radio. Why is this? Perhaps because there is no camera. Your task as screenwriter is to write the drama, not interpret it. Write for the audience, not for the camera. The camera will find its way. If you are a writer-director, write your script, then interpret as director. These are separate tasks.

It is often said that you should write about events and circumstances that are familiar to you—yes, but you should be stretching your knowledge, writing into the unknown.

Look again at your screenplay. What is the nature of the journey your principal character has undertaken? How has he or she grown? The sense of completeness I look for is not to be confused with answering every question. It may be that the story justifies itself by virtue of the questions it raises. In a confusing and contradictory world we look to drama and fiction to give us a perspective on the human condition, to give us clarity and insight. We get a chance to look at events in a context that hitherto has eluded us.

You have re-read your screenplay. You have a good ear for dialogue, a keen aptitude for drama, but you are not satisfied with the dialogue. You decide that the ending is also unsatisfactory. The root of these problems is usually inadequate character portrayal. Without full, rounded characters how can the writer create dilemmas that will test those characters and thereby allow them to reveal their true nature?

Conveying a sense of the physical can be difficult. Description of physical properties may be insufficient in itself. When we listen to dialogue we listen to the words, but also to the tone and to the rhythm of the exchange. We look at the posturing. The posturing may tell more than the words spoken. We take account of what is left unsaid. Can we measure the gap between what one character says and another desires to hear? Look again at the progression, scene by scene. What forces are at work? What appears to be happening? How does this differ from what is actually happening? Have you revealed the significance of events as they unfold? You are working in a demonstrative medium. You must tell your story in pictures and sound.

When starting out there is a tendency to fix what we might call the frame of the story too early. The writer is deciding at too early a stage what is to be depicted in the screenplay and what is to be left out. Consequently, the reader has little or no perception of life outside the script. The reader doubts that the character exists beyond the scenes on the page—apparently, our character has no family, doesn't need to work, has always held the same views, has never been a child, has had no other relationships, has no fears, no aspirations. What is needed here is a more thorough exploration of the character's life as a whole, an exploration of what Flannery O'Connor calls 'the mystery of personality'. What has made these people who they are? How have they reached this point in their lives?

With a greater breadth and greater depth, we can ensure that we step into their lives at a most telling moment. We can make more enlightened decisions as to what belongs in the screenplay and what we should leave out. The frame of the story now affords us that sense of completeness.

Use the standard format for screen drama (samples are readily available in books relating to the subject if you are not already familiar with it). The producer, director and actor expect to read a script in standard format. Pay close attention to the syntax. Long, unwieldy sentences can hinder the flow of a scene and send conflicting messages regarding the dramatic emphasis. Look again at the cuts, the transitions, the links you have forged. Audiences take full account of that which has transpired between any two consecutive scenes.

You cannot equate a good idea with a good script. You must have a structure that facilitates the forward movement of the drama if the one is to become the other. A structure that is working is a structure that is invisible. It, in turn, facilitates the credible options for our principal characters and allows us to reveal the nature of their relationships.

You have a bound copy of your screenplay in a manilla envelope. You have decided to drop it in by hand. It must be clear from the outset whether the submission is coming from the writer alone or from a team which would include the director and/or producer. If it is a team submission there may well be a requirement to submit additional information—a preliminary budget, notes on style, a video featuring previous work, etc. Clearly, it is unwise for the writer alone to attempt to furnish a budget. Nor should he or she elaborate on the style. If the drama demands a particular stylistic approach this should be evident in the screenplay. Presenting the additional information is essentially the work of the producer and director.

Finally, how do you ensure that your screenplay is read? Simply, you must submit a good story that is well told. You have always known that nothing less would suffice.

Philip Davison is a scriptwriter and script tutor at Dun Laoghaire College of Art and Design.

Television stations

Radio Telefis Éireann

Headquarters: Radio and Television Studios, Donnybrook, Dublin 4. tel. 01-208-3111 fax 01-208-3080. Director General: Joe Barry. Director of Television Programmes: Liam Miller. Assistant Director of Television Programmes: David Blake Knox. Group Head, Sports Programming: Tim O'Connor. Commissioning Editor, Independent Productions: Clare Duignan. Head of Agriculture: Joe Murray. Editor, Irish Language Programmes: Cathal Goan. Editor, Current Affairs: Peter Feeney. Editor, Young People's Programmes: (vacant). Editor, Religious Programmes: Father Dermod McCarthy.

The main opportunities for freelance scriptwriters are in RTÉ's drama department, where new writers are most likely to start out as contributors to ongoing series like *Glenroe* or *Fair City*. These are written by teams of scriptwriters, many of whom go on to do other types of TV drama. Writers wishing to contribute to either of these series should submit sample episodes to the relevant series producer.

RTÉ points to a strong tradition of one-off dramas in this country, as represented by its recent *Two Lives* presentation, a collection of nine films by established prose writers like Dermot Bolger and Joe O'Connor. But it is keen to develop more serials (i. e. three-to-six-part dramas) and is trying to encourage more scriptwriters in this direction.

Short Cuts, a scheme aimed at extending the range and scope of short-film-making and encouraging new talent in all areas of Irish film production, was launched in 1994, in conjunction with the Irish Film Board. The scheme is open to film-makers with "original ideas, visual flair and a fresh view of contemporary Ireland". At the time of writing, funding for up to six half-hour films was available, to a maximum of £30,000 per project. Full details of this scheme are available from the Independent Productions Unit at the above address.

RTÉ also runs workshops and seminars for promising beginners, with candidates being chosen by the drama department on the basis of work submitted or existing track record.

BBC Northern Ireland

Broadcasting House, 25-27 Ormeau Avenue, Belfast BT2 8HQ. tel. 08-01232-338000 fax 08-01232-338800. Controller: Robin Walsh. Head of Programmes: Pat Loughrey. Head of News & Current Affairs: Keith Baker. Editor, News: Tom Kelly. Chief Producer, Sport: Jim Neilly. Chief Producer, Agriculture: Veronica Hughes. Chief Producer, Features: Colin Lewis. Chief Producer, Music: David Byers. Chief Producer, Music & Arts: Ian Kirk-Smith. Head of TV Drama: Robert Cooper. Drama Script Editor: Niall Leonard. Chief Producer, Youth & Community Programmes: Fedelma McVeigh. Chief Producer, Education: Michael McGowan. Chief Producer, Religion: Bert Tosh. Chief Producer, Current Affairs: Michael Nairns.

The drama department at BBC Northern Ireland produces drama for both the BBC and ITV networks. Recent productions include *Shannongate*, a four-part comedy thriller for BBC1, written by Barry Devlin; *The Hanging Gale* by Alan Cubitt, a four-part adventure set during the Great Famine (produced for BBC1 in association with RTÉ and Little Bird); *A Man of No Importance*, a feature film starring Albert Finney and Brenda Fricker, also written by Barry Devlin (produced in association with Little Bird and Majestic); and *Life after Life*, a Screen Two film by Graham Reid, set and shot in Belfast.

BBC Northern Ireland is particularly keen to develop new drama series—"we will give our eye teeth for good quality, long-running series proposals"—soaps and sitcoms. Also, limited opportunities in serials or mini-series and single films.

Ulster Television

Havelock House, Ormeau Road, Belfast BT7 1EB. tel. 08-01232-328122 fax 08-01232-246695. Controller of Programming: A. Bremner. Commissioning Editor: Andrew Crockart. Head of News & Current Affairs: Michael Beattie. News Editor: Colin McWilliams. Director of Light Entertainment: Will Armstrong. Director of Arts: Bob Brien. Director of Gardening/Heritage: Ruth Johnston/Robert Lamrock.

Produces its own regular programmes on news and current affairs, sport, farming, education, music, light entertainment, arts, politics and industry, but not drama.

Independent companies

In addition to the TV stations, there are a number of independent film and video production companies listed in the following pages.

Film and video producers

Acme Story Co
Apartment 2, 90 Lr Drumcondra Road, Dublin 9. tel. 01-830-4665 fax 01-830-4665. Producer/Director: Rob Coyle.
Screen writing and feature film production, also pop and corporate video.

Alegro Animation
Broom House, 65 Mulgrave Street, Dun Laoghaire, Co Dublin. tel. 01-284-4373 fax 01-284-4376. Producer: Jimmy Murakami. Directors: Jimmy Murakami, Aidan Hickey.
Animation features and series. 'Tales of Terror', TV series based on classic stories.

Anner Productions Ltd
50 Upper Mount Street, Dublin 2. tel. 01-661-2244 fax 01-661-2252. Editor: Jorgen Andreason. Producers: Patrick Barron, Charlie Doherty. Director: Patrick Barron
'Harp of My Country', 'Cusack by Cusack', 'Dublins of the USA', 'Pet World'.

Bandit Films
9 Parliament Street, Dublin 2. tel. 01-671-5444 fax 01-671-4996. Producer: Paul Donovan. Director: Johnny Gogan.
Drama, full-length features about Dublin, "its people and their stories". 'The Bargain Shop', 'Stephen'.

Banter Productions
4 Donegal Street Place, Belfast BT1 2FN. tel. 08-01232-245495 fax 08-01232-326608. Directors: Petar Millar, Brendan Byrne, Simon Wood.
Documentaries, short dramas and videos. 'My St Louisa's Orchestra', 'Keep the Party Going', 'Dome of Delight'.

Barndoor Films
Shroove, Co Donegal. tel. 0504-266757. All functions: Sara Mackie.

BC Productions Ltd
4 New Row Square, Dublin 8. tel. 01-454-6578 fax 01-454-6578. Director: Bernadine Carraher. Producer: Patrick O'Sullivan.
'Changing Places' shorts series for UTV, 'W.B. Yeats Poetry 1910-1939', 'This is Dublin'.

Besom Productions
23-25 Shipquay Street, Derry City. tel. 08-01504-370303 fax 08-01504-370728. Director: Margo Harkin.
Single and series documentary and low budget drama.

Black (Cathal) Film & Video Productions
57 Ailesbury Grove, Dublin 14. tel. 01-298-8073 fax 01—298-8073. Producer/Director: Cathal Black. Director: Yvonne White.
TV and cinema drama and documentary. 'Wheels', 'Our Boys', 'Pigs'.

Black Coffee
13 Leahy's Terrace, Sandymount, Dublin 4. tel. 01-660-6168 fax 01-661-4810. Managing Director: Brendan Culleton.
Documentary and features. 'European Social History 1919 to 1939'.

Blue Light Productions
The Barracks, 76 Irishtown Road, Dublin 4. tel. 01-668-7781 or 01-660-7654 fax 01-660-4521. Producer: Brendan McCarthy. Director: Geraldine Creed.
Established film editing company which has recently turned to short drama and feature film production. 'Into the Abyss', 'The Stranger Within Me'.

Bluth, Don
Phoenix House, Conyngham Road, Dublin 8. tel. 01-679-5099 fax 01-679-5397. Managing Director: James Butterworth.
Animation studio making animated feature films, television series, interactive products. 'The Pebble and the Penguin'.

Bootleg Films Ltd
11 Castle Court, Booterstown Avenue, Co Dublin. tel. 01-288-1699 fax 01-676-0178. Producer/Director: Denis McArdle.
Drama, documentary, corporate, music inc. feature-length. Submit treatment; "Done

everything, will travel!"

Callister Communications Ltd
88 Causeway End Road, Lisburn, Co Antrim. tel. 08-01846-673717 fax 08-01846-673652. Producer: John Callister. Director: Colin McKeown

Camera Pen Ltd
10 River Lane, Shanganagh, Shankill, Co Dublin. tel. 01-282-7033 fax 01-280-6616. Producer: Marie Thérèse Duggan.
Drama, documentary, children's, arts, comedy, music; interested in stories of Ireland today, with universal themes. Any approach is acceptable.

Charlemont Films Ltd
8 Lower Baggot Street, Dublin 2. tel. 01-661-6790 fax 01-676-4681. Producer: Roger Greene.
Drama, documentary, sports, arts. 'St Patrick's and the Tiger' and 'Down for the Match' (both BBC), 'Five from Home' and 'The Greatest Field Game in the World' (both RTÉ and UTV), 'Silence would never do' (BBC and RTÉ). Submit treatment or complete pitch.

Chrysalis Television Ireland
57 University Street, Belfast BT7 1FY. tel. 08-01232-333848 fax 08-01232-438644. Director: Anne Stirling.
TV features and sports production. Post-production facilities.

Cinetel International
41 Floraville Avenue, Clondalkin, Co Dublin. tel. 01-459-3857 fax 01-459-3857. Producer/Director: Paul Irvine.
Drama, documentary, children's, sports, corporate. Submit treatment.

Ciotóg Films
75 The Coombe, Dublin 8. tel. 01-454-6201 fax 01-874-6305. Producer: Fiona Keane. Director: Paul Duane.
Ideas-based company with a strong interest in innovative new drama. 'Misteach Bhaile Atha Cliath (The Dublin Mystic)', 'Blind Alley'.

Circus Films
Meaney Avenue, Dalkey, Co Dublin. tel. 01-284-8115 fax 01-285-9977. Managing Director/Producer: Liam Cabot.
Music videos, music and current affairs documentaries, concert specials. 'Ethiopia—A Ter-

rible Beauty'.

Clingfilms
4 Windmill Lane, Dublin 2. tel. 01-671-3122 fax 01-671-8413. Producers/Directors: Paul Fitzgerald, Damien O'Donnell, John Moore, Harry Purdue.
Short films, music videos and commercials, feature films. 'Jack's Bicycle', 'He Shoots, He Scores'.

Corporate Video Associates
1 Beresford Place, Dublin 1. tel. 01-874-2388 fax 01-836-3246. Scripts: Mark Long. Producer: Dick Conroy. Director: Joe Lee.
Documentary, children's, business, corporate. Submit treatment.

Creative Television Pictures
23 Dartmouth Square, Dublin 6. tel. 01-660-0599 fax 01-660-0482. Producer: Noelle McCormack. Director: Tom McCormack.
TV commercials, documentaries and corporate videos.

Crescendo Concepts Ltd
88 Leinster Road, Rathmines, Dublin 6. tel. 01-497-4676 fax 01-497-4799. All functions: Louis Lentin.
Feature films, TV programmes (mainly arts documentaries and drama), corporate videos. Submit treatment.

Dagda
Foundation House, 12 Northumberland Avenue, Dun Laoghaire, Co Dublin. tel. 01-280-4966 fax 01-280-4973. Scripts: Noelle Quinn. Producers: Paul Bolger, Karen Scanlon. Director: Paul Bolger.
Animation, children's. In production: 'Pippi Longstocking', co-production with Svenskfilm (Sweden), Trickompany (Hamburg).

Davral Entertainment
55 Valleyview, Brackenstown Road, Swords, Co Dublin. tel. 01-840-2668. Director: David Ralph.
Established "to make the most commercially viable films possible and to take on the Americans at their own game". 'Our Hero's Footsteps' (action thriller).

DBA Television Ltd
7 Lower Crescent, Belfast BT7 1NR. tel.

08-01232-231197 fax 08-01232-333302. Producers: David Barker, Clem Lenehan. Directors: Damian Gorman, Carlo Gébler. *Single and series documentary. 'Plain Tales from Northern Ireland' (6x30 mins for BBC), 'Belfast Trilogy' (2x40 mins for BBC), 'Giving Out' (3x15 mins drama co-production with BBC). 'A Little Local Difficulty' (3x30 mins for BBC).*

de Buitléar, Éamon Ltd

Hillside House, Delgany, Co Wicklow. tel. 01-287-6094 fax 01-287-7626. Directors: Éamon de Buitléar, Caillí de Buitléar. Children's, drama, documentary, arts, sports, education, religion, nature, music, corporate, inc. feature-length. Documentaries for BBC, series for RTÉ, inc. 'Ireland's Wild Countryside'; Wildscreen Award for wildlife documentary. Exceptionally well equipped.

De Facto Film and Video

30 Chamberlain Street, Derry City, BT48 6LR. tel. 08-01504-260714 fax 08-01504-266757. Producer/Director: Tom Collins. *Features and documentaries, inc. 'The Bishop's Story', 'A Long Way to Go'.*

Destiny Films

18 Lower Kilmacud Road, Stillorgan, Co Dublin. tel. 01-288-5281 fax 01-283-4015. Producers: Jerry O'Callaghan, Maurice O'Callaghan, Grainne Ferris. Directors: Maurice O'Callaghan, Patrick Farrelly, Kate O'Callaghan. *Takes original ideas, scripts and develops them for the international marketplace, e.g. 'Broken Harvest', feature film about New York businessman recalling his childhood in 1950s Ireland.*

Devane (Dan)

18 Rock Street, Tralee, Co Kerry. tel. 066-27100. *Corporate videos.*

Dieva Ltd

Cassir, Inver, Co Donegal. fax 073-37253. Producer/Director: Dietrich Bohnhorst. Director: Eva Haussier. *Drama, comedy.*

Double Band Films

Crescent Arts Centre, 2-4 University Road, Belfast BT7 1NHD. tel. 08-01232-243331 fax 08-01232-236980. Producers/Directors: Michael Hewitt, Dermot Lavery. *Documentary, arts, lifestyle.*

Dovinia

Cuilí, An Daingean, Co Chiarraí. tel. 066-51000 fax 066-51991. Managing Director: Bosco O'Chonchuir. Producer: Niamh Ní Bhaoill. *Irish language TV programmes, inc. children's animation, documentary, music.*

Dreamchaser Productions

First Floor, 88-90 Townsend Street, Dublin 2. tel. 01-671-9000 fax 01-671-9008. Producer/Director: Ned O'Hanlon. Producer: Liam Cabot. Director: Maurice Linnane. *Documentary, music, TV series: 'Children of Chernobyl', 'U2: Rockumentary', 'Achtung Baby'; 'The Commitments in Concert', music videos for U2, Black Velvet, David Bowie.*

Dreoilín Productions

25 Walnut Close, Kingswood Heights, Dublin 24. tel. 01-451-9177. Managing Director: Brian Sheerin. Producer: Stephen Sheerin. *Documentaries on Ireland's culture and heritage. 'An Irish Hooley', 'A Feast of Irish Set Dancing', 'Roscommon—Remembered and Rediscovered'.*

Emdee Productions

The Stockyard, 20 Upper Sheriff Street, Dublin 1. tel. 01-874-1044. Scripts: Larry Masterson. *Documentary, sports, arts, LE, lifestyle, nature, music. Series: 'Waterways' (x24), 'From the Horse's Mouth' (x6), 'Written in Stone' (x6). Submit treatment or written pitch.*

Eo Teilifís

Baile Ard, An Spideal, Co na Gaillimhe. tel. 091-83500 fax 091-83611. Producer/Director: Máire Ní Thuathail. Script Editor: Carol O'Connor. *'Mise agus Pangur Ban', 'Pangur agus a Cháirde', 'Mire Mara'.*

Fand Productions

99 Rathgar Road, Dublin 6. tel. 01-490-7774 fax 453-7692. Director: Arthur Lap-

pin.

Feature films. 'In the Name of the Father', *'The Voyage of the Naparima', 'Jock' (twenties period film).*

Farrelly (Mary Breen) Productions

Ardmore Studios Complex, Herbert Road, Bray, Co Wicklow. tel. 01-286-2971 fax 01-286-6637. Scripts: Tracy Richardson. Producer: Mary Breen Farrelly.

Drama, education, arts, music, inc. feature-length. Feature films in production: 'Driftwood' and 'Sheltering Desert'. Submit treatment.

Ferndale Productions

4 Harcourt Terrace, Dublin 2. tel. 01-676-8890 fax 01-676-8874. Managing Director/Producer: Noel Pearson.

Feature Films, inc. 'Frankie Starlight', based on Chet Raymo's novel 'The Dork of Cork'.

Fileoir Productions

Danville Lodge, Kilkenny. tel. 056-21558. All functions: Kevin J. Hughes.

Drama, documentary, arts, inc. feature-length. 'The Flower and the Rabbit'. Mainly in-house story and project development.

Fís Thír Chonaill

Na Doirí Beaga, Leitir Ceannainn, Tír Chonaill. tel. 075-31354 fax 075-31405. Producer/Director: Muiris Mac Conghail. Producers: Cuimín Mac Aodha Bhuí, Liam Deane.

Documentaries in Irish for TV, children's.

Flying Fox Films Ltd

37 Queen Street, Belfast BT1 6ER. tel. 08-01232-244811 fax 08-01232-234699. Scripts: David Hammond. Producers: Catherine Gifford, Neil Martin.

Documentary, education, arts, music. 'Another Kind of Freedom' (Channel 4, 1 hr); 'Beyond the Troubles' (x3, Channel 4). Submit treatment or verbal pitch.

Forefront

Unit 10, Enterprise Centre, North Mall, Cork. tel. 021-302129 fax 021-302129. Producers/Directors: Joe McCarthy, Tony McCarthy.

Documentary, sports, corporate. 'Why Not Millstreet', documentary on 1993 Eurovision, 'On the Jazz Trail', documentary on 1993 Cork Jazz Festival. Submit written pitch.

Frontier Films

2 Northbrook Road, Dublin 6. tel. 01-497-7077 fax 01-497-7731. Producers/Directors: Kevin Heffernan, Joseph Farrell.

Music, quiz programmes for TV, drama and documentary. 'Blackboard Jungle', 'The Children of Lir', 'Megazone'.

Gabbro Productions Ltd

12 Morehampton Road, Donnybrook, Dublin 4. tel. 01-668-6276 fax 01-668-6858. Producer: Al Byrne. Directors: Gay Byrne and Al Byrne.

Videos and films.

Gaelcom

52 Glenageary Park, Dún Laoghaire, Co Dublin. tel. 01-285-9606. Producer: Liam Ó Murchú. Director: Denis O'Grady.

Documentary and light entertainment. 'No More the Bell Tolls', 'A Rich and Rare Land'. Submit script.

Gaelmedia

Na Forbacha, Co na Gaillimhe. tel. 091-592533 fax 091-592203. Scripts: Christy King; Producer: Edna Mac Namara Connolly; Director: Máire Ní Chonlain.

Drama, documentary, education, sports, arts, comedy, LE, lifestyle, religion, business/corporate, inc. feature-length. Submit treatment, written pitch or script.

Glass Machine Productions

27 Philipsburg Avenue, Dublin 3 and 14 Seaview Drive North, Portstewart, Co Derry. tel. 08-01265-833280. Producers/Directors: Dr Desmond Bell, Stephanie McBride.

TV documentary on Irish and other themes. 'Dancing on Narrow Ground' (rave culture in Northern Ireland), 'Germany's Ireland' (German images of Ireland).

Good Film Company, The

15 Vesey Place, Monkstown, Co Dublin. tel. 01-284-4881 fax 01-284-4882. Scripts : Katy McGuinness; Producers: Michael Garland and Katy McGuinness.

Drama, inc. feature-length. 'All Things Bright and Beautiful'. Submit treatment, written pitch or script.

Graph Films

12 The Elms, Donnybrook, Dublin 4. tel. 01-260-1333 fax 01-269-7270. Scripts, production, direction: Darragh Byrne; Producer: Adrian Lynch.

Documentary, corporate. Submit treatment. In-house production and post-production facilities for other producers. 'Love Songs of Connaught' (RTÉ '93), 'The Morrison Tapes' (series x4 on contemporary Irish emigration to the US, RTÉ '94); cultural programmes for public authorities and private industries.

Halford (Brian) Productions

31 Morehampton Road, Donnybrook, Dublin 4. tel. 01-668-4132 fax 01-668-4307. Director and producer: Brian Halford; Producer: Barbara Halford.

TV and cinema commercials, pop promos.

Holmes & Moriarty Productions

Mincloon, Rahoon, Galway. tel. 091-22855 fax 091-22514. Director and producer: Antony Sellers. Producer: Cecily Kelleher.

Documentary, drama.

Hummingbird Productions

The Old Barracks, 76 Irishtown Road, Irishtown, Dublin 4. tel. 01-660-4599 fax 01-660-4521. Scripts: Sarah Power; Producer: Nuala O'Connor; Director: Philip King.

Drama, documentary, education, arts, lifestyle, music. 'Christy' documentary on Christy Moore, 'A River of Sound' 7x40 min. series on Irish music from sources to confluence. Submit treatment or written pitch.

Imagine Ltd

22 Sandymount Green, Dublin 4. tel. 01-668-7855, 088-545017 fax 01-668-7947. Directors/Producers: Paul Howard and Kevin O'Connor.

Film, video and TV production and post-production. 'Dawn to Dusk', documentary on Dublin Airport, 'Birr Castle', on restoration of the largest telescope in the world.

Key Feature Productions

The Powerhouse, Pigeon Harbour, Dublin 4. tel. 01-668-7155 fax 01-668-7945. Producers: Michael E. Clyne, Michael Hayden; Directors: Stephen Collins and Michael Hayden.

Documentary, music, art, lifestyle. 'Celtic Grooves', documentary on fusion of traditional music and contemporary dance music.

Key Video

Ormond Multimedia Centre, 16-18 Lwr Ormond Quay, Dublin 1. tel. 01-872-3500 fax 01-8723348. Director: Aileen O'Reilly. Producer: Hilary Jones.

Children's programming and documentaries.

Lagan Pictures Ltd

7 Rugby Court, Agincourt Avenue, Belfast BT7 1PB. tel. 08-01232-326125 fax 08-01232-326125. Director: Stephen Butcher. Producer: Alison Grundle.

Drama, documentary, comedy, corporate. Have broadcast documentary and corporate. now concentrating on one-off and series drama. Submit written pitch.

Like It Love It Productions

Ardagh, Blackrock, Co Dublin. tel. 01-283-4490 fax 01-283-6420. Producers/Directors: Andy Ruane, Philip Kampff.

Light entertainment, specialising in game shows.

Liquid Films Ltd

33 Pembroke Road, Ballsbridge, Dublin 4. tel. 01-668-9491/ 01-660-8795 fax 01-668-4834. Producers: Nicholas O'Neill, Emma Scott. Directors: Gerard MacCarthy, Donal Ruane.

Drama inc. feature-length, documentary, music, commercials. 'Hugh Cullen', film about growing up in Northern Ireland during 1970s.

Little Bird

122 Lower Baggot Street, Dublin 2. tel. 01-661-4245 fax 01-660-0351. Managing Director: James Mitchell. Producers: Jonathan Cavendish, Brian Rafferty.

Film and TV drama, inc. feature-length. 'The Hanging Gale', 'A Man of no Importance'.

Lunar Video & Television

5-6 Lombard Street East, Dublin 2. tel. 01-677-9762 fax 01-671-0421. Scripts: Brian Molloy. Producers: Brian Molloy, Graham Molloy. Director: Ian McGarry.

Drama, documentary, comedy, music. St Patrick's Day special for Nashville Network, USA, 'An Evening with Niall Toibin' etc. Submit written pitch.

McGarry, The Production System

Heatherfield Lodge, 5 Barnhill Road, Dalkey, Co Dublin. tel. 01-285-9139 fax 01-284-9932. All functions: Ian McGarry.
Light entertainment, music. 'Secrets of Skiing' 1 and 2, Sandy Kelly series, Country at the Olympia. Submit treatment.

Marshall Film Productions

450 Ballyfermot Road, Dublin 10. tel. 01-626-3109. Producers/Directors: Alan Walsh, June Connell.
Low-budget action adventure drama.

Meade, Aiden Ltd

10 Orwell Park, Rathgar, Dublin 6. tel. 01-496-0533 fax 01-496-7693. All functions: Aiden Meade.
Documentary in 16 mm film and video. 'Gap of the North', about business survival in northeast of Ireland over past 25 years, 'Little Ireland', about Ireland as a tourist destination.

Mediawise

3 Lower Fitzwilliam Street, Dublin 2. tel. 01-676-8477 fax 01-676-8470. Producers/Directors: Andrew Kelly, Peter McNiff. Producers: Elaine Glynn, Bill O'Herlihy.
Documentary, corporate, in-flight programming.

Mercurian Productions

24 Bloomfield Avenue, Dublin 8. tel. 01-454-7210 fax 01-454-3722. Producer: Marina Hughes. Director: Martin Duffy.
Family/children's feature films. 'The Boy From Mercury', comedy set in Dublin in 1960.

Merlin Films

41 Fitzwilliam Place, Dublin 2. tel. 01-676-4460 fax 01-676-4368. Managing Director: Kieran Corrigan. Director: John Boorman.
Documentary, drama. International finance for film and TV productions as well as production facilities. 'The Treaty', drama about 1921 treaty negotiations, 'Journey to Knock' (comedy).

Midas Productions

11a Herbert Lane, Dublin 2. tel. 01-661-1384 fax 01-676-7825. Managing Director:

David Harvey. Producer: Mike Keane.
Documentary, corporate video. 'Crimeline' (two series for RTE), 'Hit the Road' (8x1hr for young people), 'Let's Do It' (5x30 mins on job creation).

Moo Moo International

35 Orangefield Drive, Belfast BT5 6DN. tel. 08-01232-673196 fax 08-01232-236743. Producers: Colm Hackett, Neil Perry. Directors: Brian-Henry Martin, Michael Burns.
Cross community film company producing documentary and drama. 'Cemetery Poetry, "the art of the graveyard poet", 'Grifter', futuristic police adventure.

Moving Still Animated

44 East Essex Street, Dublin 2. tel. 01-676-4921 fax 01-676-4921. Director: Tim Fernée. Producer: Nuala O'Toole.
Animation, children's, commercial, idents.

Nemeton

An Rinn, Dungarvan, Co Waterford. tel. 058-46499. Producer: Irial Mac Murchú. Directors: Irial Mac Murchú, Tadhg Ó Maoileoin.
Gaeltacht based company specialising in sports productions and Irish language programmes. 'Bua Nó Bás' (on hurling), 'Lifeline' (on Dungarvan/Waterford railway line).

Nocht TV

Coshclady, Bunbeg, Letterkenny, Co Donegal. tel. 075-32102. Producers/Directors: Mairéad Ní Ghallchóir, Aine Tummon.
Irish-language programmes for RTÉ, currently working on series of Irish language dramas, 'Snap'.

Northland Film Productions

Springrowth House, Springtown Industrial Estate, Balliniska Road, Derry BT48 0NA. tel. 08-01504-267616 fax 08-01504-363654. Producers/Directors: Joe Mahon, Denis Bradley.
Documentary, religious, drama. 'Seanachaí', dramatised ghost stories for BBC/RTE. Film crew hire.

Ocean Film Productions

The Powerhouse, Pigeon House Harbour, Dublin 4. tel. 01-668-7155 fax 01-668-7945.

Producer: Catherine Tiernan. Director: Frank Stapleton.

Drama, documentary. 'Parent Practice' (6 x 30 mins documentary series for RTE), 'The Feeling Soul' (one hour documentary with poet Nuala Ní Dhomhnaill for RTE).

Odyssey

Millbrook Studios, Rathfarnham Village, Dublin 14. tel. 01-493-2147 fax 01-493-9241. Producers/Directors: Sean Walsh, Justin Healy.

Drama, documentary. 'Ulysses the Series' (the life and times of James Joyce).

O'Leary (Ronan) Productions

23 Upper Mount Street, Dublin 2. tel. 01-676-6831 fax 01-676-5261. All functions: Ronan O'Leary.

Drama, inc. feature-length. 'Riders to the Sea', 'Diary of a Madman'. Submit treatment or written pitch.

Open Channel

5 Fitzwilliam Place, Dublin 2. tel. 01-676-1341 fax 01-676-1341. Director: Brendan Culleton.

Corporate videos, documentary, film, local TV production and training.

O'Sullivan Forde Productions

Ardmore Studios, Bray, Co Wicklow. tel. 01-286-2971 fax 01-286-6810. Producers: Morgan O'Sullivan, Ignatius Forde.

Drama for US and global markets. 'Scarlett', 'The Old Curiosity Shop' (in association with RHI).

Ox Pictures

1 Herbert Terrace, Herbert Road, Bray, Co Wicklow. tel. 01-286-8800. Director: Colum Kenny.

Pancom Ltd

23 Seapoint Avenue, Blackrock, Co Dublin. tel. 01-280-8744 fax 01-280-8679. Producer: Anabella Jackson. Director: Keith Nolan.

Drama, documentary, corporate, music. Multimedia production facilities. 'The First Shannon/Erne Boat Rally' (one hour documentary to celebrate re-opening of Ballinamore/Ballyconnell Canal). Submit treatment.

Paradox Pictures

6 Belvedere Place, Dublin 1. tel. 01-836-6868 fax 01-836-6868. Producers/Directors: Liam O'Neill, Declan Recks.

Drama, documentary, arts, corporate, music, inc. feature-length. Short films and pop videos, inc. 'The Big Swinger', 'Sunny's Deliverance', 'The Barber Shop', all winners of festival awards and placed with European and American broadcasters. Co-producing feature film 'Roseland' with British and German partners in 1995. Emerging and established writers welcomed: submit treatment.

Parallel Film Productions Ltd

4 Windmill Lane, Dublin 2. tel. 01-671-4344 fax 01-671-4151. Producers: Alan Moloney, Tim Palmer.

TV series, documentaries, feature films, inc. 'The Last of the High Kings' (supported by European Script Fund and Irish Film Board).

Parting Shots

Northern Visions Media Centre, 4-8 Lwr Donegall Street, Belfast BT1 2FN. tel. 08-01232-245495 fax 08-01232-326608. Producer: Marilyn Hyndman. Directors: David Hyndman, Marilyn Hyndman.

Documentary, feature films, inc. 'Product of the Troubles'.

Picture House, The

25 Herbert Place, Dublin 2. tel. 01-661-5437 fax 01-283-3879. Directors: Fintan Connolly, Hilary Dully.

Drama, TV series, documentary.

Pioneer Pictures

61 Rockmills, Strand Road, Derry City. tel. 08-0504-370019 fax 08-0504-363166. All functions: Paul Boyle.

Animation, documentary, children's, sports, arts, religion, corporate, music, current affairs. Submit treatment or written pitch.

Poolbeg Productions

9 Mount Street Crescent, Dublin 2. tel. 01-676-2521 fax 01-284-0958. Producers: Donald Taylor Black, James Hickey, Ivan Martin. Director: Donald Taylor Black.

Documentary features, inc. '100 Years of Cinema (Ireland)', for the BFI/Channel 4 documentary series to celebrate the centenary of film in 1995.

Premier Video Productions

Dublin Road, Cahir, Co Tipperary. tel.

052-41353. All functions: Brenda Kerins. *Corporate video and commercials.*

Prism Audio Visual Ltd

63 Kenilworth Square, Dublin 6. tel. 01-496-7450 fax 01-496-7581. Producer/Director: Roy Esmonde.
Commercials, documentary. 'Frank Browne', portrait of a song collector.

Quateru Film Ltd

65 Mulgrave Street, Dun Laoghaire, Co Dublin. tel. 01-284-4378 / 01-280-0753 fax 01-284-4376. Director: Jimmy T. Murakami.
Animated and live-action corporate, commercial and feature productions.

Quin Films Ltd

Coalbrooke, Thurles, Co Tipperary. tel. 052-54309. Producer/Director: David Quin.
Model animation for TV. 'Bunny' (pre-school series for children), 'Suzi' and 'Neddy' (both series of 52 x 10 mins programmes for children).

Radharc Films

6 Rock Road, Blackrock, Co Dublin. tel. 01-288-1839 fax 01-288-1939. Managing Director: Joseph Dunn. Producer: Peter Kelly.
Documentaries of social, religious and historical interest.

Radius Television

Glenageary Office Park, Dun Laoghaire, Co Dublin. tel. 01-285-6511 fax 01-285-6831. Director: David Collins.
Drama, music, magazine programmes for Irish and international markets. 'Sign of the Times', 'Up and Running', 'The Claddagh Story'.

Ravel Production Co Ltd

52 Mount Pleasant Square, Ranelagh, Dublin 6. tel. 01-496-2094 fax 01-496-2355. Director: Michael O'Sullivan.
Drama and documentary for RTE, Channel 4, UTV and BBC.

Red Factory Films

7 St Patrick's Avenue, Dalkey, Co Dublin. tel. 01-284-0513. Producer: Linda Hassett. Director: Séamus Carraher.
Documentary, inc. 'Whitefriar Street Sere-nade' about inner city Dublin.

Red Hen

Rookwood Lodge, Stocking Lane, Rathfarnham, Dublin 16. tel. 01-493-2797. Producer: Sinéad Lemass.
Drama, documentary, children's, comedy, inc. feature-length. New company headed by the producer of the award-winning 'Jack's Bicycle'.

Reel Image Productions

Leeson House, 22 Lower Leeson Street, Dublin 2. tel. 01-676-3355 fax 01-676-9282. Managing Director: Maureen Ryan. Producer: Cathy Donoghue. Director: Ken Flynn,
Corporate and training videos, plus European news agency service.

River Run Television Ltd

31 Percy Place, Dublin 4. tel. 01-660-4133 fax 01-660-4510. Contact: Paul Blanchfield.
Documentary, corporate, business, 'factual entertainment'. Submit treatment or written pitch.

Roebuck Moving Pictures

47 Lwr Albert Road, Sandycove, Dun Laoghaire, Co Dublin. tel. 01-284-4068 fax 01-284-4069. Directors/Producers: Tiernan MacBride, Pat Murphy.
Corporate, training and documentary, inc. 'Seán MacBride Remembers' (2 x 1hr TV series).

Roisín Rua Films

9 Parliament Street, Dublin 2. tel. 01-671-5444 fax 01-671-4996. Producer: Paul Donovan. Director: Orla Walsh.
Drama, documentary. 'The Visit', drama about prisoner's wife in Northern Ireland.

RTE Commercial Enterprises

Donnybrook, Dublin 4. tel. 01-208-2978 fax 01-208-2620. Managing Director: Conor Sexton.
Handles RTE's commercial activities. Catalogue of drama, documentary, light entertainment and animation work on request.

Russell Avis Productions

The White House, Strawberry Beds Road, Dublin 20. tel. 01-820-5318 fax 01-820-5946. Producer: Russ Russell. Directors:

Meiert Avis, Colum Maguire.
Feature films, TV drama, commercials.

Safinia

Glenageary Office Park, Dun Laoghaire, Co Dublin. tel. 01-285-6243 fax 01-285-6264. Producer: Rebecca Cox. Directors: Shay Healy, Declan Farrell.
Documentary, inc. tributes to Phil Coulter and Phil Lynott.

Samson Films

76 Irishtown Road, Dublin 4. tel. 01-667-0533 fax 01-667-0537. Producer: Michael Keegan. Director: Tim O'Neill.
Feature films and TV drama. 'The Disappearance of Finbar B' (supported by European Script Fund).

Scannáin Dobharchú

Srath na Corcra, Doirí Beaga, Co Donegal. tel. 075-32185 fax 075-32188. Producers/Directors: Máirín Seoighe, Mairéad Nic Ghéidí.
Irish language documentary, children's, drama, magazine programmes. 'Amharc! Amharc!' (children's programme), 'Murdar ar an Melrose' (historical drama).

ScothógFíse

Abha na Dála, Daingean Uí Chúis, Co Chiarraí. tel. 066-51606 fax 066-51606. Producers/Directors: Aodh O Coileáin, Cóilín O Scolaí.
Children's drama, documentary. 'An Sceach Gheal' (half hour modern drama), 'As Seo Amach' (six part comedy series for Network Two).

Setanta Studios Ltd

Ardmore Studios Complex, Herbert Road, Bray, Co Wicklow. tel. 01-286-2971 fax 01-286-6637. Scripts: Tracy Richardson. Producer: Mary Breen Farrelly.
Animation, children's, education, comedy, music. 'The Sign of the Fish', 'Eddy Suzette'. Associated with Mary Breen Farrelly Productions. Submit treatment.

Sin Sin! Teoranta

Cill Bhriocáin, Rosmuc, Co na Gaillimhe. tel. 091-74349. Producer/Director: Trevor Ó Clochartaigh.
Irish language courses and training videos. 'Celtica' (Celtic arts programme).

SOL Productions

Quarantine Hill, Wicklow. tel. 0404-67270 fax 0404-67153. Producers: Kevin Jacobsen, Bernard Kirby. Directors: Kevin Jacobsen, Seamus Byrne.
Documentary, drama, music.

Speers Film Production Co

65 Grosvenor Square, Dublin 6. tel. 01-496-7308 fax 01-496-0860. Producers: Jonny Speers, Dara McClatchie. Directors: Conor Horgan, Michael Colbert.
TV commercials.

Storm Productions Ltd

17 Conquer Hill Avenue, Clontarf, Dublin 3. tel. 01-833-1646 fax 01-833-1646. All functions: Hilary McLoughlin.
Drama and TV series and serials, inc. feature-length. Submit treatment or complete script.

Straight Forward Film and TV Production

Crescent Studios, 18 High Street, Holywood, Co Down. tel. 08-01232-427697 fax 08-01232-422289. Managing Director: Peter Morrow.
Documentary, inc. 'Greenfingers' (gardening co-production for BBC Northern Ireland and RTE) and 'Expedition Fire and Ice' (on an expedition to Iceland).

Strathin Enterprises

Strathin, Templecarrig, Delgany, Co Wicklow. 01-287-4769 fax 01-287-4769. Producer: Jim Sherwin. Directors: Jim Sherwin, Anne Sherwin.
Film, video, inc. documentaries on bereavement and 150th anniversary of death of Fr Ignatius Rice.

Telwell Productions

The Gate Lodge, Kerlogue, Wexford. tel. 053-45041 fax 053-45431. Managing Director: Barrie Dowdall.
Documentaries on social and educational matters, corporate and training videos. 'Ruby Backdrop', half hour documentary about Wexford Opera Festival.

Temple Films

4 Windmill Lane, Dublin 2. tel. 01-671-9313 fax 01-671-9323. Producers/Directors: Ed Guiney, Stephen Bradley.
Feature-length drama and television series.

'Ailsa', award-winning feature film by Joe O'Connor, directed by Paddy Breathnach. Especially interested in developing new Irish writers/directors. Submit written pitch.

Total Video

69 Pembroke Lane, Dublin 4. tel. 01-668-3535 fax 01-668-3535. Producer/Director: Paddy McClintock.

Video production company. Commercials, corporate and TV.

Treasure Film Ireland

Shamrock Chambers, 2-3 Eustace Street, Dublin 2. tel. 01-670-9609 / 670-9610 fax 01-670-9612. Scripts and production: Robert Walpole. Director: Paddy Breathnach.

Drama, Documentary, Music, inc. feature-length. 'The Long Way Home' by Joe O'Connor (1994), 'The Road to America' documentary (1993), 'A Stone of the Heart' drama, winner of special jury prize at 36th Cork Film Festival. Submit treatment or complete script.

Tyrone Productions

50 City Quay, Dublin 2. tel. 01-671-8811 fax 01-671-8501. Producers/Directors: John McColgan, Moya Doherty.

Light entertainment, documentary, drama. 'Riverdance—The Show', and documentary on life of Maureen Potter.

Vedanta Productions

77 Fairyhill, Bray, Co Wicklow. tel. 01-286-8790. Producers: Pat Shine, Audrey McMahon. Director: Pat Shine.

Social documentaries and children's programmes. 'No Frontiers', documentary on young Irish people working in other EU countries.

Vermilion Films

12 Abbey Street, Howth, Co Dublin. tel. 01-832-2294 fax 01-832-3517. Producer: Gerry Gregg. Director: Deirdre Dowling.

Drama, documentary, sports, arts, inc. feature-length. 'Recruits' (series for RTÉ on Gardaí), 'Slaying the Dragon' (documentary marking centenary of Irish Congress of Trade Unions).

Videoactive Ltd

ENG House, Tubbermore Road, Dalkey,

Co Dublin. tel. 01-285-4555 fax 01-285-5942. Producers/Directors: Leslie Graham, Eleanor Nelson.

Children's, sports, lifestyle. Over 200 hours of sport and young people's programmes transmitted by RTÉ, inc. 'Weekend Sport' (x 26). Submit treatment.

Volta Films

47 Lower Albert Road, Sandycove, Dun Laoghaire, Co Dublin. tel. 01-284-4068 fax 01-284-4069. Producers: Tiernan MacBride, Ina Gogan. Director: Pat Murphy.

Main purpose is to produce a feature film based on the life of Nora Barnacle, wife of James Joyce.

Brian Waddell Productions

Crescent House, 14 High Street, Holywood, Co Down BT18 9AZ. tel. 08-01232-427646 fax 08-01232-427922. Producers: Stephen Stewart, Lesley Black. Directors: Brian Waddell, Stephen Stewart.

Documentary series, inc. 'Gourmet Ireland', 'Hot Pursuits'.

Greg Wheeler Productions

9 Prince Edward Terrace Lower, Blackrock, Co Dublin. tel. 01-288-9969 fax 01-288-9911. Producer: Lucienne Purcell. Director: Greg Wheeler.

TV commercials.

Wild Acre Productions

Stratton House, Bishopstown Road, Cork. tel. 021-341483 088-531136 fax 021-342862. All functions: Declan O'Connell.

Documentary, arts, nature, corporate. RTÉ: Choral Festival '93 and 'The Sculpture Factory'; corporates: Nycomed Ireland and 'The Gas Interconnector'.

Wildgoose Films Ltd

Rockfort House, Rockfort Avenue, Dalkey, Co Dublin. tel. 01-285-9140 fax 01-285-3805. Producers: David Cabot, Liam Cabot. Director: David Cabot.

Documentary, arts, lifestyle, nature, corporate. 'Clare: the Nature of an Island', 'The Shannon-Erne Waterway', 'The Irish Country House', 'Death of the Fairies?'. Submit treatment or written pitch.

Wolf (Fred) Films

Bell House, Montague Street, Dublin 2. tel. 01-478-3199 fax 01-478-3696. Scripts: Eamonn Lawless. Producer: Michael Algar. Director: Gary Blatchford.

Children's, animation. 'Budgie the Little Helicopter', 'Teenage Mutant Ninja Turtles', 'James Bond jnr'. Submit treatment, written pitch or script.

Wolfhound Films

Heritage Mews, 16 Warners Lane, Dublin 6. tel. 01-660-0399 fax 01-660-6430. Managing Director: Conor Harrington. Producers: Conor Harrington, John Kelleher. *Feature films for an international audience. 'September', four hour mini-series based on Rosamunde Pilcher novel.*

Zanita Films

63 Lower Albert Road, Sandycove, Dun Laoghaire, Co Dublin. tel. 01-280-6524 fax 01-280-4903. All functions: Séamus Byrne. *Production, co-production and development.*

Writing for the theatre

Bernard Farrell

I NEVER SET OUT to be a playwright. I never thought there were any vacancies anyway. The theatre seemed to be well catered for by Leonard, Friel, Murphy, Kilroy, Keane—not to mention all the dead playwrights, the foreign ones, and, of course, Mr Shakespeare. So, although I always went to plays, it never crossed my mind that I should (or could) write one.

At the age of 15, all I knew was that I wanted to write. I began with poetry. At 16 I knew I wasn't a poet and began to write short stories. When I was 17 I had two stories published in the *Evening Press*. My literary future looked so bright that I decided henceforth to use a pseudonym, to avoid being mobbed in the streets.

Three years passed before I had another story published, and in that time I collected enough rejection slips to paper a wall. I had learned my first lesson—being a writer can break your heart.

However, if I had bothered to study the rejection slips I might have learned a few more valuable lessons. For many of the rejections told me that, although my plotting was questionable and my characterisation doubtful, my dialogue was excellent. In my despair, I never noticed this pointer towards working completely in dialogue (the theatre) and, instead, abandoned the short story form and launched into my new career as a novelist.

Six months later I was halfway through a novel that was boring me to death. But I would not let it go. Night after night I would attack it again, pushing it a few pages further down its boring path, determined not to let it best me. God knows what it would have done to me if I hadn't been saved by a friend who told me that he wanted to write a play.

He had already applied to join The Lantern Theatre Workshop, and he wanted me to come along with him because he knew that Theatre Folk spent all their time kissing, hugging and darling-ing each other—and he needed support. I went, knowing that it would be hell. It was heaven. The people were (reasonably) normal, and imbued with the philosophy that 'nothing is easy, but everything is possible'. Aspiring directors and actors were all given the chance to fail, and aspiring playwrights were allowed to make all their mistakes, on the stage.

The Lantern closed in 1977—the year I decided to write my first full-length play. I did not find it easy, but I found myself more comfortable than I had ever been before. And this brings me to my theory about the way

55

Lady Luck determines how we begin as writers. Our first instinct is that, for some reason (leave it to the psychoanalysts), we want to write. Now, each of us will do our best work in one particular medium—perhaps the poem, the play or the novel. And how early we hit on the right medium determines how quickly we will find satisfaction (and maybe even success).

I was lucky enough in 1977 to write a very successful first play, *I Do Not Like Thee Doctor Fell*, but I would point to a wall of rejection slips and a boring novel as evidence of how I worked in the wrong medium for so long. And thereafter, as I went on to write further plays, I would point to years of watching plays as my theatrical development. For as aspiring novelists must learn their trade by studying the novel, so aspiring play-wrights should (but often don't!) go to the theatre.

The secret of learning stage craft (and therefore play writing) is to go to plays and see HOW things happen. Don't just sit and watch the play—study how every successful effect has been achieved. And if the night is a failure, try to discover why. Was it poor direction or bad acting—or was the play over-written or lumbered by a structure that killed its intention?

Thus every visit to the theatre becomes a learning process, and you begin to notice, for example, how the playwright has allowed an actor enough time to change clothes between appearances, how he has managed to plausibly get his characters on and off the stage, how he has ended his first act on the kind of up-beat that will lure the audience back from their G&Ts after the interval.

I once met a doomed playwright who showed me a play with the first scene set in a cluttered garage and the second scene in a richly decorated lounge. I asked him how he saw this quick change being achieved. His reply (a familiar misconception) was that 'It's up to the director to do that'. Wrong. The first director of any play is the playwright—as he or she writes the play. The instructions you insert into the script tell the director how the play can be staged and you only gain this knowledge by going to the plays and, to a lesser degree, by reading published plays.

After that, if playwriting is your medium, you will be able to tell the play's story in dialogue. You should have a basic ability to do this, but practice (and rejection and heartbreak!) will gradually perfect it.

And don't think, as I did, that the theatre is a closed shop. There is always a search for new plays and playwrights, and you don't need to 'know someone'. When I decided to send my first play to the Abbey, I had to phone to find out how I would address the envelope!

Then it's down to determination, discipline—and more than a nod from Lady Luck. And, one day, you could be signing programmes in the foyer.

Bernard Farrell is one of Ireland's leading contemporary playwrights. His most recent play is *Happy Birthday Dear Alice*.

Theatre companies

Abbey Theatre, see National

Andrew's Lane Theatre
St Andrew's Lane, Dublin 2. tel. 01-679-5720 fax 01-679-7552. Scripts: Pat Moylan. Est 1989. Funding: Box office.
Commercial work preferred, approx. 2 hours running time. Submit synopsis and sample. 'Happy Birthday Dear Alice' by Bernard Farrell, produced by Red Kettle Theatre Co (see below).

Barnstorm Theatre Company
Desart Hall, New Street, Kilkenny. tel. 056-51266. Artistic Director: Philip Hardy. Est 1992. Funding: Box office, Arts Council, fund raising.
New Irish writing considered, approx. 2 hours. Phone or submit complete script.'One, Two, Three, O'Leary' by Bernard Farrell, 'Wild Harvest' by Ken Bourke.

Belltable Arts Centre
69 O'Connell Street, Limerick. tel. 061-419709 fax 061-418552. Artistic Director: Mary Coll. Funding: Box office, Arts Council.
New work considered, approx. 2 hours. Submit synopsis and sample.

Bickerstaffe Theatre
11 The Spires, Dean Street, Kilkenny. tel. 056-51254 fax 056-63559. Scripts: Richard Cook, Lynn Cahill. Est 1992. Funding: Box office, Arts Council, commercial sponsorship.
New work considered. Submit enquiry letter, synopsis and sample or complete script. 'Long Black Coat' by John Waters, 'Snow' by Michael West, 'True Lines' devised by John Crowley and actors.

Blue Raincoats Theatre Company
The Factory Performance Base, Lower Quay Street, Sligo. tel. 071-70431. Scripts: Malcolm Hamilton. Est 1991. Funding: Box office, Arts Council.
Open to suggestions, produces broad range of work, from Yeats to Joe Orton. Preferred running time: 20-30 mins. for lunchtime programme, or 2 hours. Query by phone first. 'Playboy of the Western World'.

Charabanc Theatre Company
c/o Ulster Hall, Linenhall Street, Belfast BT2 8AB. tel. 08-01232-234242 fax 08-01232-312969. Scripts: Carol Moore. Est 1983. Funding: Arts Council.
Community based material which puts women's experience to the fore, in one or two acts. Letter of enquiry. 'Vinegar Fly' by Nick Perry, 'A Wife, a Dog and a Maple Tree' by Sue Ashby.

Corca Dorca Theatre Company
11-12 Marlborough Street, Cork. tel. 021-278-326. Artistic Director: Enda Walsh. Est 1990. Funding: Box office, Arts Council.
Programme includes work devised in-house ('Inside Out' series) and adaptations of classics (Dickens, Moliére, Berkhoff), but also open to outside submissions, up to 90 mins. Submit written outline or phone to discuss. 'Ginger Ale Boy' by Enda Walsh.

Cork Opera House
Emmet Place, Cork. tel. 021-270022 fax 021-270357. Executive Director: Gerry Barnes. Est 1965. Funding: Box office, Arts Council, co-productions.
Considers new work—"no limits". Submit letter or synopsis and sample. 'The Art of Waiting' by Johnny Hanrahan, co-produced with Meridian (see below).

Down to Earth Theatre Company
Basement, 3 Beresford Place, Dublin 1. tel. 01-855-0339/855-1736. Artistic Director: Lynne Kinlon. Est 1991. Funding: Box office, commercial sponsorship, Fás.
Open to suggestions. Submit synopsis and sample. 'Pandora's Box', 'Down in the Dumps'.

Druid Theatre Company
Chapel Lane, Galway. tel. 091-68660 fax 091-63109. Scripts: Anne Butler. Est 1975.

Funding: Box office, Arts Council, Galway County Council & Corporation.
Considers new work of any type. Submit letter or synopsis and sample. 'Summerhouse' by Robin Glendinning, 'Silverlands' by Antoine O' Flatharta, 'Song of the Yellow Bittern' by Vincent Woods.

Dublin Theatre Festival Ltd
47 Nassau Street, Dublin 2. tel. 01-677-8439 fax 01-679-7709. Est 1957. Funding: Box office, Arts Council, commercial sponsorship.
Annual platform for new work by other companies, inc. 'The Ash Fire' by Gavin Kostick (Pigsback 1992), 'Brothers of the Brush' by Jimmy Murphy (Peacock 1993).

Feedback Theatre Company
8 Fitton Street, Morrison's Island, Cork. tel. 021-277258. Artistic Director: Pat Talbot. Est 1991. Funding: Box office, Arts Council, commercial sponsorship.
Considers anything in full length (2 hours) or one act (40 mins) form. Submit letter and/or synopsis and sample. 'Talbot's Box' by Thomas Kilroy, 'Bold Girls' by Rona Munro, 'Absent Friends' by Alan Ayckbourn.

Field Day Theatre Company
Foyle Arts Centre, Lawrence Hill, Derry BT48 7NJ. tel. 08-01504-360196 fax 08-01504-365419. Administrator: Colette Nelis. Est 1980. Funding: Box office, Arts Council, commercial sponsorship.
Considers new work of any kind. Preferred running time 2 hours. Submit complete script. 'The Madame Macadam Travelling Theatre', 'The Cure at Troy'.

Galloglass Theatre Company
30 Parnell Street, Clonmel, Co Tipperary. tel. 052-26797. Artistic Director: Theresia Guschlbauer. Est 1990. Funding: Box office, Arts Council, commercial sponsorship.
Open to suggestions, including children's shows and lunchtime theatre, 1 to 2 hours. Submit letter, synopsis and sample or complete script. 'Alice in Wonderland' (commissioned adaptation), 'Gulliver's Travels', 'Bailegangaire'.

Gate Theatre
Cavendish Row, Dublin 1. tel. 01-874-4368 fax 01-874-5373. Scripts: Anne Clarke. Est 1928. Funding: Box office, Arts Council.
Considers new work but, due to limited resources, script-reading process is protracted and theatre regrets that it cannot always give a detailed analysis of submitted plays or provide a service for new writers. Also, as the Gate does not possess a studio theatre, in producing new work it has historically tended to concentrate on new plays by established writers. Recent productions: The Pinter Festival (May 1994), 'Molly Sweeney' by Brian Friel (August 1994).

Garter Lane Arts Centre
5 and 22a O'Connell Street, Waterford. tel. 051-55038 fax 051-71570. Est 1984. Funding: Box office, Arts Council.
Generally stages work of other companies, inc. 'The Art of Waiting' (Meridian), 'The Vinegar Fly' (Charabanc).

Graffiti Theatre Company
50 Pope's Quay, Cork. tel. 021-505758 fax 021-505587. Scripts: Emilie Fitzgibbon. Est 1984. Funding: Arts Council, commercial sponsorship.
Considers work for young audiences and Theatre in Education. Preferred running time 1 hour. Submit letter or synopsis and sample. 'Infidel' by Roger Gregg, 'Fishy Tales' by Enda Walsh.

Hawk's Well Theatre
Temple Street, Sligo. tel. 071-62167/61526 fax 071-71737. Artistic Director: Maeve McCormack. Est 1982. Funding: Box office, Arts Council.
Considers new work of any kind. Preferred running time 2 hours. Submit letter or synopsis and sample. Recent programme consists largely of productions by other companies, e.g. 'The Art of Waiting' by Johnny Hanrahan (Meridian/Cork Opera House), 'Loco County Lonesome' by Pat McCabe (Co-Motion).

Iomhá Ildánach Theatre Company
The Crypt Arts Centre, Dublin Castle, Dame Street, Dublin 2. tel. 01-671-3387 fax 01-671-3370. Artistic Director: John O'Brien. Est 1985. Funding: Box office, Arts Council, commercial sponsorship.
Considers educational and/or devised work,

approx. 2 hours, but tends to commission new work rather than accept unsolicited material. Most productions, both stage and theatre-in-education, are devised by performers, a director and (if necessary) a writer. Submit letter or synopsis and sample. 'Single White Male' by Niall Ó Sioradáin, 'Lúnasa' devised by Iomhá Ildánach.

Island Theatre Company

Church Street, King's Island, Limerick. tel. 061-410433. Artistic Director: Terry Devlin. Est 1988. Funding: Box office, Arts Council.
Considers new work of up 1½ to 2 hours. Submit synopsis and sample or complete script. 'The Crunch' (adapted from Moliére by Mike Finn and Terry Devlin), 'The Tempest' (Dublin Theatre Festival '93).

Lyric Theatre

55 Ridgeway Street, Belfast BT9 5FB. tel. 08-01232-669660 fax 08-01232-381395. Artistic Director: Robin Midgley. Est 1968. Funding: Box office, Arts Council.
Considers new work of any kind. Submit enquiry letter or complete script. 'Pictures of Tomorrow' by Martin Lynch, 'Volunteers' by Brian Friel.

Machine, The

Lissadell, White Church Road, Rathfarnham, Dublin 16. tel. 01-493-9483. Scripts: Michael Scott. Est 1984. Funding: Box office, Arts Council.
Considers new work. Phone first or enquiry letter. 'The Hostage', 'Carousel', 'Columban Pageant'.

Macnas

Fisheries Field, Salmon Weir Bridge, Galway. tel. 091-61462 fax 091-63905. Scripts: Gary McMahon. Est 1986. Funding: Box office, Arts Council.
Most work is developed in-house, scripts occasionally commissioned from outside. Enquiry letter. 'Táin', 'Sweeny'.

Meridian Theatre Company

11-12 Marlborough Street, Cork. tel. 021-276837. Artistic Director: Johnny Hanrahan. Est 1989. Funding: Box office, Arts Council.
Aims to produce new or little known work, 2 hours with a maximum cast of 8. Submit

script, but allow 2 months for reading. 'The Art of Waiting' by Johnny Hanrahan, 'White Woman Street' by Sebastian Barry, 'The Rock Station' by Ger Fitzgibbon.

National Theatre Society

Abbey and Peacock Theatres, Lower Abbey Street, Dublin 1. tel. 01-874-8741 fax 01-872-9177. Scripts: Christopher Fitz-Simon. Est 1903. Funding: Box office, Arts Council, commercial sponsors.
Will consider new work, preferably full-length plays (2 hours) by Irish authors exploring Irish themes. Enquiry letter in the first instance, followed by synopsis and sample, possibly complete script thereafter. 'Asylum! Asylum!' by Donal O'Kelly, 'The Broken Jug' by John Banville, 'Brothers of the Brush' by Jimmy Murphy, 'The Bird Sanctuary' by Frank McGuinness.

Peacock see National

Pigsback Theatre Company

The Ormond Centre, 16-18 Ormond Quay Lower, Dublin 1. tel. 01-872-3500 fax 01-872-3348. Scripts: Jim Culleton. Est 1988. Funding: Box office, Arts Council. Considers new work. Submit letter, synopsis and sample or complete script. 'The Ash Fire' by Gavin Kostick, 'Buffalo Bill has gone to Alaska' by Colin Teevan.

Playwrights and Actors Theatre Company

9 North Frederick Street, Dublin 1. tel. 01-874-6089 fax 01-874-7583. Scripts: Kevin McHugh. Est 1984. Funding: Arts Council.
Considers new work. Submit letter or synopsis and sample. 'Oscar' by Senator David Norris.

Punchbag Theatre Company

6 Quay Lane, Galway (theatre) or 58 Dominick Street, Galway (admin). tel. 091-65422 fax 091-68642. Scripts: David Quinn, Brendan Murray. Est 1989. Funding: Box office, Arts Council, commercial sponsorship.
Policy is to produce 'new work by new voices'. Considers work of any type and length. Phone, write or submit complete script. 'Eclipsed' by Patricia Burke Brogan, 'The Life of Stuff' by Simon Donald.

Red Kettle Theatre Company

5 O'Connell Street, Waterford. tel. 051-79688 fax 051-57416. Artistic Director: Jim Nolan. Est 1985. Funding: Box office, Arts Council, commercial sponsorship.
Considers new work of any kind. Submit complete script. 'Happy Birthday Dear Alice' by Bernard Farrell.

Rough Magic Theatre Company

5-6 South Great George's Street, Dublin 2. tel. 01-671-9278 fax 01-671-9301. Est 1984. Funding: Arts Council.
All new work produced is commissioned. 'Down onto Blue' by Pam Boyd, 'Hidden Charges' by Arthur Riordan.

Siamsa Tire Theatre & Arts Centre

Town Park, Tralee, Co Kerry. tel. 066-23055 fax 066-27276. Administrator: Martin Whelan. Est 1974. Funding: Box office, Arts Council.
'Theatre without words'—doesn't use scripts. Will work with writers to develop ideas but most work is generated in-house. Phone or write in first instance. 'Samhain', 'Séadhna'.

TEAM Theatre Company

4 Marlborough Place, Dublin 1. tel. 01-878-6108 fax 01-874-8989. Scripts: Richard Seager. Est 1975. Funding: Arts Council, commercial sponsorship.
Most productions devised in-house but will work with outside writers. Preferred running time 1 hour 15 mins. Submit letter or synopsis and sample. 'The Well' by Ken Bourke, 'Monkey Puzzle Tree' by Maeve Ingoldsby.

Theatre Omnibus

Unit 12, Clare Business Centre, Francis Street, Ennis, Co Clare. tel. 065-29952 fax 065-21234. Scripts: Jean Regan, Bernard Dowd. Est 1981. Funding: Arts Council.
Considers new Irish writing for visual theatre, 90 mins. Enquire by letter in first instance. 'On Broken Wings' by Dermot Healy, 'Unlucky Wally—Twenty Years On' by Raymond Briggs.

Theatreworks

1 Richmond Cottages, Dublin 1. tel. 01-836-6076. Scripts: Laura Caffrey. Est 1994. Funding: Box office, Arts Council, commercial sponsorship, Irish Congress of Trades Union (ICTU).
Considers political and/or women's interest plays, 90 mins. Submit letter, synopsis and sample or complete script. 'These Obstreperous Lassies', May Day celebrations 1994 at Riverbank Theatre and Women's Community Theatres.

Wet Paint Arts

The Basement, 17 Herbert Street, Dublin 2. tel. 01-661-1757/8 fax 01-662-1595. Administrator: Sharon McGrane. Est 1985. Funding: Arts Council.
Considers new Irish writing, preferably youth orientated, 90 mins. Letter of enquiry. 'F', 'Tangles'.

Yew Theatre Company

Casement Street, Ballina, Co Mayo. tel. 096-71238 fax 096-71100. Scripts: Pierre Campos. Est 1987. Funding: Box office, Arts Council.
Will consider new work of any kind, 2 hours. Submit synopsis and sample. 'The Misfortunate Husband' (Molière adaptation).

Getting your book published

Jo O'Donoghue

IF YOU ARE an author seeking publication you may have a manuscript, a synopsis or 'treatment', or simply an idea. It is possible to sell any of these. Some of the variable factors are timing, originality, quality, and whether or not publishers have room on their lists or you find an editor who will go for your idea. Let no one tell you that luck is not a factor in getting published. However, there are some general guidelines that may help you to sell your product.

Fiction

Fiction is where the big money is but it is difficult for publishers to make it work in a small market like Ireland. Opportunities for serious writers of fiction are limited and are probably becoming more so, given the preference of most big publishing houses—and increasingly small houses as well—for 'sure' money-spinners that command big advances and are marketed as blockbusters.

It is difficult to get a first novel accepted—your second novel may be even more problematic unless your first has been either respectfully received or a commercial success—even if it is wildly original (will the readers understand it?) or stunningly good (who can agree on what good means?). But publishers do take on first novels; many of them harbour literary tastes even if they are frequently forced to stifle them in the interests of 'the market'.

Even more significant, hope springs eternal that the next unsolicited pile could yield a Roddy Doyle or Jennifer Johnston. On the other side of the fiction spectrum, works of 'popular', mass-market fiction—page-turners—have sometimes been commissioned over the past few years rather than written by talented unknowns, although one of the most successful, Patricia Scanlan, was just such an unknown.

In Ireland a certain number of publishers do risk literary fiction so it is worth trying them. Look in the 'Irish-published' or 'Just published' section of your bookshop to see who might be a likely target for your manuscript and use this information in tandem with your *Writers' Guide*. Be aware of the danger, however, of trying to imitate a successful formula (like the aforementioned Doyle or Scanlan). First of all, it is extremely difficult; secondly, there is no guarantee that the publishers in question will want to churn out twenty clones of success number one.

Non-fiction

The market for home-published non-fiction in Ireland is strong and likely to remain so. History, reportage, biography, human interest, politics, controversial issues (but beware Ireland's severe libel laws), cookery, lifestyle, health, religion are all good areas to investigate. I often think that competent writers might be better to look for an opening in non-fiction than to write mediocre fiction.

If you have a good non-fiction idea but no track record, check carefully whether there is any similar book on the market. Such a book need not rule yours out but may change the way you focus it. Ask yourself seriously who will buy this book. Do not delude yourself that everyone is interested in astro-physics just because you are. Neither do you have to convince the publishers that your book will appeal to all age groups and sections of the population. Publishers will often be impressed by a realistic, modest target audience that will be easy to reach rather than wish to spread their marketing operations thinly over the whole adult population. If there is any way you could encourage the sale of the book—for instance by having it put on a student book-list or by arranging with a company to give a copy free to every important customer—be sure to state this. A few hundred certain sales may make the difference between a 'yes' and a 'no, we'd love to but we don't think that it's commercial.'

Submitting your manuscript

It makes sense to make a phone call to the publishers you target to ascertain how the editor likes to receive manuscripts. This directory briefly describes the publishers' preferences where possible, but there's nothing like your own market research. Usually the receptionist or administrator will be able to help you. Most publishers favour, in the case of fiction, a synopsis, sample chapters (the first two, or else chapter one and a later chapter) and maybe a detailed character breakdown, although this last applies more to mass-market fiction than to 'serious' literature. I like to receive the whole novel.

For non-fiction it is normal to submit a detailed description of the project, a chapter breakdown, a sample chapter if you have written one and some comments on the marketability of the book. Your own CV may be a useful persuader, especially in the case of non-fiction. You should always send return postage: the most convenient for the publisher is a stamped addressed jiffy bag like the one in which you dispatch your manuscript, but stamps for the same amount as your package costs to post will be fine, or a cheque or postal order. When you make the exploratory phone call find out the name of the editor who will be dealing with your manuscript and put the name, correctly spelled, on the envelope.

Present your manuscript as carefully as possible. Use a good ribbon (or new toner cartridge) and uniform font and layout throughout. Be sure to double-space between the lines. Use your spell-check and ask someone whose literacy you trust to cast an eye over it. A messy manuscript will certainly prejudice any reader and this may be significant if you come into the near miss or near hit category. You don't need to worry about following publishers' house style at this stage, although if it makes your work easier and answers some questions for you, you might think about acquiring such a style sheet from your target publishers. A brief, formal cover letter is adequate; few publishers are impressed by hyperbole, whimsy or by long puffs supplied by your neighbour or grandfather.

Coping with non-response

Contrary to rumour, Irish publishers do generally read the slush-pile. However, because they tend to have small staffs, it may be a long time before you receive a decision or even a response. For my imprint, I respond only once to a submission—when I have reached a decision on it. You could try phoning your original contact in the publishing company if you have had no acknowledgement in two or three weeks—if only to establish that your MS arrived safely in the hands of the intended recipient. After that the time taken to reach a decision can vary greatly from publisher to publisher. If your idea or novel is 'red hot' you may hear within a few days; a few months (three to six) is more normal and much longer is common.

You will gain little from harassing the publisher, although a gentle reminder may bear fruit. It is your prerogative, of course, to ask for the return of your manuscript at any stage or simply to inform the publisher that you intend to submit it elsewhere. Impatience is understandable but try to bear in mind that yours is only one manuscript of many on a crowded desk in a busy working day.

Coping with rejection

Try to be both philosophical and practical, i.e. send your manuscript off again by the next post or take any advice the publishers give (they may be too busy to send any but the most formal rejection) and revise the work. If the rejection is categorical try your idea or manuscript on someone you know whose judgement you respect but who will not be afraid to offend you. Maybe you should stick to journalism or think about writing a biography rather than a novel. No work is ever wasted even if it is not published, and I have a personal theory that all novelists should have one novel that remains unpublished in a bottom drawer until it is discovered by a postgraduate researcher after their death, auctioned for a vast sum and published as juvenilia.

Literary agents

Literary agents have long been part of the publishing world in the UK and US but, probably because of the size of the country, they have not been necessary in Ireland. It is usually easy for authors to make contact with publishers or editors because publishing companies here are small. Funds are scarce for the big advances or escalating royalties that an agent might negotiate for you. It is often quite difficult to get agents to put you on their books: they will have to be convinced of the publishability of your efforts; this applies especially to 'big-name' or well-regarded agents. Many Irish authors have London agents, even those who are published in Ireland. There is only one agent in Dublin, Jonathan Williams (listed under Editors and indexers), and he deals with both Irish and London publishers, and will also sell rights abroad.

You may survive perfectly well without an agent if you manage to find a publisher for your work but if you are not good at figures and resent time given to haggling about subsidiary rights, an agent might be a good idea for you. In general, I feel that Irish publishers are likely to consider a manuscript submitted by the author just as seriously as one submitted by an agent, but this is certainly not the case in London.

Jo O'Donoghue is commissioning editor with Marino, the new imprint of the Mercier Press; previously she was with Poolbeg.

Book publishers

Not all the publishers here will consider unsolicited manuscripts; many are one-person or spare-time outfits. The listings should be used intelligently, and do not obviate the usefulness of research in a library or bookshop, where the character and scope of the publishers' lists will become clearer. Membership of CLÉ (the Irish Book Publishers' Association or Cumann Leabharfhoilsitheoirí na hÉireann), CLAI (Children's Literature Association of Ireland) or IEPA (Irish Educational Publishers' Association) is indicated at the end of the main data. The section in italics indicates the number of staff, the sort of books (and series titles) published, the preferred approach by writers, and whether a standard contract form is used. Finally (in roman type) there are details of the publisher's representation and/or distribution in Ireland and overseas to give an idea of marketing reach. Most but not all publishers answered our questionnaire.

Abbey Books

Holy Cross Abbey, Thurles, Co. Tipperary.

Able Press

Able Public Relations, 35 Sandymount Avenue, Dublin 4. tel 01-269-2803. Director: Francis Xavier Carty. ISBN prefix 0-906281-.

A 'very occasional' small publisher of 16 years' standing. Unsolicited manuscripts are not considered.

Adare Press

White Gables, Ballymoney Hill, Banbridge, Co Down.

Anna Livia Press

21 Cross Avenue, Dun Laoghaire, Co Dublin. tel. 01-280-3211 or 01-280-6954 fax 01-280-5127.

This imprint has been inactive for some time, and writers should check its present state before submitting work.

Anvil Books

45 Palmerston Road, Dublin 6. tel. 01-497-3628. Publisher: Rena Dardis.

Staff of 2. History, biography, sociology, politics. Most active nowadays under its subsidiary imprint The Children's Press, which we list separately.

APCK

Association for Promoting Christian Knowledge, Church of Ireland House, Church Avenue, Dublin 6. tel. 01-496-6981 fax 01-497-2865.

Appletree Press

19-21 Alfred Street, Belfast BT2 8DC. tel. 08-01232-243074 fax 08-01232-246756. Director: John Murphy. Editor, Irish interest and non-fiction: Douglas Marshall. Editor, cookery and gift books: Pat Scott. Marketing: David Ross. Publicity: Claire Skillen. Production: Paul McAvoy. 40 titles in 1993; ISBN prefix 0-86281- (old: 0-904651-); Clé.

Staff of 19. Irish-interest gift books, guide books, history, music, humour, criticism and stationery. Series: Appletree Pocket Guides and Little Cookbooks each featuring the cuisine of a different country or region. Submit letter with synopsis and specimen chapter.

Ireland: own distribution; Britain: Derek Searle Associates; Europe excl. Scandinavia: Clark McNeish; Scandinavia: Anglo Nordic Agencies; N. America: Irish Books & Media; Australia: Peribo; New Zealand: David Bateman; S. Africa: Struik Book Distributors.

Aran Books

Aran Book Publishing Group Ltd, 46 Charnwood, Bray, Co Wicklow. tel. 01-284-2493 fax 01-284-2493. Director and editor, children's and non-fiction: Cecily Golden. Editor, adult list: Pat O'Loughlin. Marketing and publicity: Tony Cafolla. 6 titles in 1993; ISBN prefix 1-897751-; Clé, CLAI.

This company has been much less active recently and its current state should be checked before any material is submitted. Staff of 2. Best known for children's and young adults' adventure and fantasy. Submit letter with synopsis and specimen chapters(s). Contract follows recommendations of Society of Authors and Irish Writers' Union.

Ireland: Eason and own distribution; Britain: Central Books; Europe: Agence Cazenave, Madrid; N. America: Irish Books & Media; Australasia: S. & M. Story, Bundaberg, Queensland.

Argenta Publications

19 Mountjoy Square, Dublin 1. tel. 01-874-8796 fax 01-874-8797. Director: Uinseann Mac Eoin.

Athol Books

10 Athol Street, Belfast BT12 4GX. 3 titles in 1993; ISBN prefix 0-85034-.
Political and social campaigning.

Attic Press

29 Upper Mount Street, Dublin 2. tel. 01-661-6128 fax 01-661-6176. Director: Róisín Conroy. Marketing: Maeve Kneafsey. 23 titles in 1993; ISBN prefix 1-85594-. Clé.
Staff of 5. Specialises in adult and teenage fiction, women's studies, history and practical reference books by and about women, including controversial subjects. Series: Bright Sparks (young adult), Queer Views (gay and lesbian). Annual diary. Basement Press is Attic's general division, with emphasis on the fresh and irreverent. Submit letter, synopsis and specimen chapter. Own standard contract.

Ireland: Gill & Macmillan; Britain (rep. & distrib.) Turnaround; N. America: Book People and Irish Books & Media.; S. Africa: Trade Winds.

Authentik

Authentik Language Learning Resources, 27 Westland Square, Dublin 2/ tel. 01-677-1478 fax 01-677-1196.

Avelbury

56 South William Street, Dublin 2. tel. 01-679-6635 fax 01-679-2973. Manager: Attracta Flattery.
Books for the education market.

Ballinakella Press

Whitegate, Co Clare. tel. 061-927030 fax 061-927030. All functions: Hugh W. L. Weir. 3 titles in 1993; ISBN prefix 0-946538-.
Staff of 2. Irish topography, history, biogra-phy, guide books (Weir's Guides imprint), true stories and facsimile reprints. Series: Irish Biographies, Irish Family People and Places, Irish County Houses. Submit letter with specimen chapter or pages. Own contract form.

Ballydesmond Publications

Ballydesmond, Co Cork

Basement Press see Attic Press

Beehive Books see Veritas

Beyond the Pale Publications

PO Box 337, Belfast BT9 7BT. tel. 08-01232-645930. Contact: Bill Rolston. 3 titles in 1993; ISBN prefix 0-9514229-.
No full-time staff. Books on the North focussed on issues of conflict, political identity and human rights. Submit letter only in first instance. Own contract form.

Ireland: own distribution; Britain: Turnaround; Europe: Missing Link, Bremen. N. America: Irish Books & Media.

Blackstaff Press

3 Galway Park, Dundonald, Belfast BT16 0AN. tel. 08-01232-487161 fax 08-01232-489552. Director and editor: Anne Tannahill. Marketing: Lawrence Greer. Publicity: Liam Carson. Production: Wendy Dunbar. 24 titles in 1994; ISBN prefix 0-85640-; Clé.
Staff of 8. Poetry and prose anthologies, biography, memoirs, cookery, educational, fiction, limited editions, history, politics, humour, natural history, photographic, poetry. Recently (UK) Small Publisher of the Year, and in 1995 this company became wholly owned by the Antrim printing company W. & G. Baird. Submit letter with synopsis, sample chapter and return postage. Own contract form based on Clark's Publishing Agreements.

Ireland, Britain and world except USA, Australia and S. Africa (distrib.): Gill & Macmillan; Britain: Mainstream Publishing; Europe: Michael Geoghegan; N. America: Dufour Editions, Irish Books & Media; Australasia: Keith Ainsworth Pty; S. Africa: Trade Winds Press.

Blackwater Press see Folens
Boglee Books see Clegnagh
Bookmark see Ossian Publications
Boole Press
AIC Ltd, 26 Temple Lane, Dublin 2. tel. 01-679-7655 fax 01-679-2469. Director: Paulene McKeever. Editor: Dr John Miller. Marketing: Niav Miller. 2 titles in 1993. ISBN prefix 0-906783-.
Staff of 2. Also publishes as Hamilton Press. Scientific, medical and technical, inc. conference proceedings. Own contract form.

BPP
3 Rosemount Park, Newtownabbey BT37 0NL.

Braid Books
69 Galgorm Road, Co. Antrim BT421AA.

Brandon
Brandon Book Publishers Ltd, Cooleen, Dingle, Co Kerry. tel. 066-51463 fax 066-51234. Director and editor: Steve Mac-Donogh. Assistant Editor: Peter Malone. Marketing and publicity: Linda Kenny. Production: Berni Goggin. 14 titles in 1993; ISBN prefix 0-86322-; Clé.
Staff of 6. General: fiction and non-fiction of national and international appeal. Series: Brandon Originals. Known writers with a track record should submit an outline; new writers should submit synopsis, author profile and specimen text. Own contract form.
Ireland: Gill & Macmillan distribution; Britain: Turnaround Distribution (stockholding and repping); N. America: Irish Books & Media (stockholding some titles).

Brehon Publishing
4 Upper Ormond Quay, Dublin 7. tel. 01-873-0101 fax 01-873-0939. All functions: Bart D. Daly.
Law books.

Brookside see New Island
Burning Bush Publications
134 Ballynahinch Road, Lisburn, BT27 5HB.

Butterworths
Butterworth Ireland Ltd, 26 Upper Ormond Quay, Dublin 7. tel. 01-873-1555 fax 01-873-1876. Director: Gerard Coakley. 10 titles in 1993; ISBN prefix 1-85475-.
Staff of 9. Specialising in books on Irish law and tax. Series: Irish Planning Law and Practice, Tax Guide, Irish Income Tax, Irish Conveyancing Precedents, Tax Accounts, Capital Tax Accounts, VAT Accounts, Landlord and Tenant Law. Meets potential authors to discuss ideas. Own contract.
Ireland: Own distribution; Britain, Europe and India: Butterworths London; N. America: Butterworths USA and Butterworths Canada; Australasia: Butterworths Sydney; S. Africa: Butterworths

Carbad
Seomra 7, 6 Sráid Fhearchair, Baile Átha Cliath 2. Director: Liam Mac Cóil. 1 title in 1993
Irish-language books.

Careers & Educational Publishers
Lower James Street, Claremorris, Co Mayo (Editorial: 193 Ard Easmuin, Dundalk, Co Louth). tel. head office 094-62093 / 71398. tel. editorial 042-35705 fax 042-35705. Director and editor: Eamonn P. O'Boyle. Marketing: B. C. O'Boyle. Publicity: Christina Martin. Production: William J. O'Keeffe. 2 titles in 1993; ISBN prefix 0-906121-.
Careers, education, training, cookbooks, local history, biography, religion. Also uses Heritage Books imprint. Submit letter with synopsis or specimen chapter or pages. Clé contract.
Ireland: Eason; N. America: Irish Books & Media.

Carmelite Publications
St Teresa's, Clarendon Street, Dublin 2.

Causeway
6 Murray Street, Belfast BT16DN.

Cecil Press
8 Cecil Street, Limerick. tel. 061-410964. Publisher: Flann O'Connor.
Only the publisher's own poetry at present, but plans to put out editions of rare classics.

Celtpress
Celtales, Kindlestown Hill, Delgany, Co Wicklow. tel. 01-287-3026 fax 01-287-3026. Director, editor, marketing, production: Colin Vard. Publicity: Ciara Vard. 5 titles in 1993; ISBN prefix 1-897973-; CLAI.

Has been inactive lately, and writers should check present position before submitting material. Staff of 2. Young people's fiction. Series: Key to the Past on women in Irish history, and Princess Finola on Celtic mythology in modern language. Submit complete manuscript.

Children's Poolbeg see Poolbeg

Children's Press, The

45 Palmerston Road, Dublin 6. tel. 01-497-3628. Publisher: Rena Dardis.

Children's and young adults' books of higher than average quality. This is an imprint of Anvil Books which is listed separately.

CITIS

2 Rosemount Terrace, Booterstown Avenue, Co Dublin. tel. 01-288-6227 fax 01-288-5971. Editor: Donal Murphy.

Civil engineering books.

Clegnagh Publishing

Clegnagh House, Mosside, Armoy, Ballymoney, Co Antrim BT53 8UB. tel. 08-012657-51625. Director: C. A. Moffett. Editor: J. D. C. Marshall. 1 title in 1993; ISBN prefix 0-9512941-.

No full-time staff. Archaeology, history, prose and poetry. Boglee Press: schoolbooks. Submit letter, full manuscript or proposal and return postage. Own contract negotiable.

Clóchomhar, An

13 Gleann Carraig, Baile Átha Cliath 13. tel. 01-832-4906. Editor: Stiofán Ó hAnnracháin. 6 titles in 1993.

No full-time staff. Books in Irish of academic research, general interest, modern fiction and poetry. Submit letter.

Ireland: ÁIS.

Cló Iar-Chonnachta

Indreabhán, Conamara, Co na Gaillimhe. tel. 091-93307 fax 091-93362. Director, editor and production: Micheál Ó Conghaile. Co-editor: Nóirín Ní Ghrádaigh. Marketing and publicity: Deirdre O'Toole. 21 titles in 1993; ISBN prefix 1-874700-; Clé.

Staff of 4. Irish-language poetry, novels, history, songs and books for children; dual-language books and translations. Some poetry and song titles issued simultaneously with cassette tapes. Submit letter and manuscript. Own contract form.

Ireland: ÁIS; Britain: Connolly Publica-

tions; N. America: Chulainn Publications, Denver, CO and Irish Books & Graphics, NY; Australasia: Roibeard Mac Eoin, Sydney.

Coiscéim

Cosanic Teo, 127 Bóthar na Trá, Dumhach Trá, Baile Átha Cliath 4. tel. 01-269-1889 fax 01-260-0794. 25 titles in 1993.

Irish-language general list, heavy on poetry, light on children's books.

Ireland: ÁIS.

Collins Press

Collins Bookshop, Carey's Lane, off Patrick Street, Cork. tel. 021-271346 fax 021-275489. All functions: Con Collins. 2 titles in 1993; ISBN prefix 1-898256-; Clé.

To date has published mostly non-fiction and mainly of Cork interest. Is expanding list to books of wider interest. Submit letter with synopsis and specimen chapter. Own contract form.

Colourpoint Press

Omagh Business Complex, Gorbrush, Omagh, Co Tyrone BT78 5LS. tel. 08-01662-249494 fax 08-01662-249451. Director and marketing: Sheila Johnston. Editor, transport, school texts, history: Norman Johnston. 2 titles in 1993; ISBN prefix 1-898392-; Clé.

Specialises in educational texts for NI curriculum, also on transport and history. No fiction. Submit letter briefly specifying experience and qualifications on subject, with outline and specimen chapter(s). No phone calls. Own contract.

Columba Press, The

93 The Rise, Mount Merrion, Blackrock, Co Dublin. tel. 01-283-2954 fax 01-288-3770. Director, editor and production: Seán O'Boyle. Marketing and publicity: Cecilia West. 25 titles in 1993; ISBN prefix 1-85607- (old: 0-948183-); Clé.

Staff of 7. General religious books, especially pastoral, spiritual, theological and catechetical. Under Gartan imprint: Irish-language books and those of general Irish cultural interest. Submit letter with contents, synopsis and sample chapter. Own contract form.

Ireland and Britain: Columba Book Service; Europe (reps): Books for Europe; N.

America: XXIIIrd Publications, Mystic, CT; Australasia: E. J. Dwyer.

Cork University Press

University College, Cork. tel. 021-276871 fax 021-273553. Chairman: Professor Desmond Clarke. Publisher: Sara Wilbourne. Marketing and publicity: Anne Lee. Production: Eileen O'Carroll. 10 titles in 1993; ISBN prefix 1-85918- (old: 0-902561-); Clé. *Staff of 5. Established in 1926. Publishes books of interest to the academic community worldwide. Submit letter with synopsis and specimen chapter. Own contract form.*
Ireland: Robert Towers; Britain: Central Books.

Corrymeela Press

Corrymeela House, 8 Upper Crescent, Belfast BY7 1NT. tel. 08-01232-325008 fax 08-01232-315385. Director: Revd Trevor Williams. Marketing: Alan Evans. Production and publicity: Norman Richardson. 5 titles in 1993; ISBN prefix 1-873739-. *Books on conflict, peace, justice and reconciliation in Ireland; social, political and theological reflections; liturgy, poetry, music. Submit letter and synopsis.*

Cottage Publications

15 Ballyhay Road, Donaghadee, Co Down BT21 0NG.

Country House see Town House

Daybell, Christopher

Wychwood, Carrickbrennan Road, Monkstown, Co Dublin.

December Publications

157 University Street, Belfast BT7 1HR. tel. 08-01232-231913. fax 08-01232-331380.

Dedalus Press

24 The Heath, Cypress Downs, Dublin 6W. tel. 01-490-2582. Director: John F. Deane. 11 titles in 1993; ISBN prefix 1-873790-, 0-948268- (old)
New poetry by Irish writers, and poetry in translation, preferably by Irish translators. Series: Dedalus Editions and Icarus. Dedalus also produce the Peppercanister books for and by Thomas Kinsella. Submit letter with specimen page and stamped return envelope. Own contract form.
Ireland: own distribution; Britain and

Europe: Password.

Dé Danann Press

7C Avalon, Burrow Road, Sutton, Dublin 13. tel. 01-839-0007 fax 01-839-0007. Director: P. Fitzpatrick.
Publishes only books and portfolios of Jim Fitzpatrick's artwork.

Dissident Editions

71 Ballyculter Road, Downpatrick, Co Down. tel. 08-01396-881364. Director: Frederik Wolff. Editor, poetry: Tom Matthews. Editor, philosophy: Anthony Weir. 1 title in 1993; ISBN prefix 0-9520451-.
Anti-christian works of cultural and philosophical dissidence, misanthropy, rational pessimism and the politics of suicide. Submit letter only.

DO Publications

20 New Cabra Road, Dublin 7.

Dolmen Press see Smythe

Dominican Publications

42 Parnell Square, Dublin 1. tel. 01-873-1355 fax 01-873-1760. Director and editor: Austin Flannery OP. Marketing: Mary Kavanagh. Publicity: Kathleen O'Connor. Production: Bernard Treacy. 6 titles in 1993; ISBN prefix 1-871552- (old: 0-907271-, 0-9504797); Clé.

Dreamland Publications

33 Dublin Road, Enniskillen, BT74 6HN.

Drumlin Publications

Nure, Manorhamilton, Co Leitrim. tel. 072-55237 fax 072-55663. Director, marketing, publicity and production: Betty Duignan. Editor: Proinnsías Ó Duigneáin. 3 titles in 1993. ISBN prefix 1-873437-.
Staff of 1. Local, social and family history. Submit specimen chapter or complete manuscript.
N. America: Irish Books & Media.

Dublin Institute for Advanced Studies

School of Celtic Studies, 10 Burlington Road, Dublin 4. tel. 01-688-0748 fax 01-688-0561.

Dublin Travellers' Education & Development Group

46 North Great Charles Streeet, Dublin 1.

Duffry Press

Enniscorthy, Co Wexford.

Dundalgan Press

Francis Street, Dundalk, Co Louth. tel. 042-35376/34013 fax 042-32351. Editor: G. Gormley.

History, architecture, crafts.

Eason

Eason & Son Ltd, 66 Middle Abbey Street, Dublin 1. tel. 01-873-3811 fax 01-873-3545. Director: Gordon Bolton. ISBN prefix 1-873430- (old: 0-900346-); Clé.

Publishing wing of major distributor, wholesaler and bookshop chain. Tourists' picture books and the Irish Heritage Series of illustrated booklets by experts on a number of subjects.

Eblana Editions see Gandon

Economic & Social Research Institute

4 Burlington Road, Dublin 4. tel. 01-676-0115 fax 01-668-6231. Director: Professor K. A. Kennedy. Editor: Mary McElhone. Marketing, publicity and production: John Roughan. 15 titles in 1993; ISBN prefix 0-7070- (old: 0-901809-).

Staff of 60 carries out research both independently and for other organisations. Apart from quarterly and biennial economic reviews, ESRI publishes in the series: General Research, Policy Research and Broadsheets. Most material is generated by the staff; non-staff authors should normally submit complete manuscripts.

Distribution from the Institute direct.

Education Bureau see Paraclete

Educational Company

47-49 Queen Street, Belfast BT16HP.

Educational Company of Ireland

Ballymount Road, Walkinstown, Dublin 12. tel. 01-450-0611 fax 01-450-0993. Director: Frank Maguire. Editor: Oisín Mulcahy. Production: Paul Cullen. 38 titles in 1993; ISBN prefixes ECI: 0-86167- (old: 0-90180-), Longman, Browne & Nolan: 0-7143-, Talbot Press 0-8545-.

Staff of 38. Primary and post-primary schoolbooks for ages 4 to 18. Own contract form. Submit letter with synopsis and/or specimen

chapter or pages. Some backlist titles under Longman, Browne & Nolan and Talbot Press imprints.

Ellis Publications

36 Taney Crescent, Dublin 14.

Elo Publications

47 Reuben Avenue, Dublin 8

Emperor Publishing

27/29 Washington Street, Cork. tel. 021-275429 fax 021-270559. Director and marketing: J. A. O'Conor. Editor: K. O'Conor. Publicity: M. McCarthy. Production: J. Sharkey. 19 titles in 1993; ISBN prefix 1-874338-.

Staff of 5. Popular romantic and nostalgic fiction for women and 'executive-style' fiction for men. Submit manuscript and letter.

Ireland: Eason; Britain: Bookpoint; Australasia: Keith Ainsworth.

Era-Maptec

5 South Leinster Street, Dublin 2. tel. 01-676-6266 fax 01-661-9785. Director: Paul Kidney. Marketing: Elizabeth Deegan. Production: Gary Bowes. 15 titles in 1993.

Staff of 25 producing maps, guides, atlases, charts and posters. The company operates a sophisticated computer map-making system.

ESRI see Economic & Social

Estragon Press

Coomkeen, Durrus, Co Cork. tel/fax 027-61186. Directors: John McKenna, Sally McKenna.

Staff of two. Publish annual guides—'Bridgestone 100 Best' books and Bridgestone Good Food Guide etc.

Ireland: Gill & Macmillan.

European Foundation for the Improvement of Living and Working Conditions

Loughlinstown Ho., Shankill, Co Dublin

Exemplar Publications

4 Baltrasna, Ashbourne, Co Meath. tel. 01-835-0663 fax 01-835-2514.

Education books.

Fallon, C. J.

Lucan Road, Palmerstown, Dublin 20. tel. 01-626-5777 fax 01-626-8225. Director: Henry McNicholas. Editor: Niall White. Production: Maurice Ledwidge. 60 titles in 1993; ISBN prefix 0-7144-; IEPA.

Staff of 36. Core and supplementary textbooks for primary and post-primary schools, also under the imprint School and College Publishing.

Farmar, A. & A.

78 Ranelagh Village, Dublin 6. tel. 01-496-3625 fax 01-497-0107 e-mail 102021.150 @compuserve.com. Directors: Tony and Anna Farmar. ISBN prefixes 1-899047- (old: 0-9509295-). 7 titles last year.

Staff of 3. Leisure, food, wine, travel, Irish classics. Commission publishing of business and social history.

Ireland: Brookside (representative Butler Sims). Britain: Central Books (representative Ion Mills).

FET see Fortnight Educational Trust

Field Day Publications

Foyle Arts Centre, Old Foyle College, Lawrence Hill, Derry BT48 7NJ. tel. 08-01504-360196 fax 08-01504-365419. Administrator: Colette Nelis. No titles in 1993; ISBN prefix 0-946755-.

Has one full-time employee.Best known for its Anthology of Irish Writing *co-published with Faber & Faber in Britain and with Norton in USA. Submit letter.*

Fish Publishing

Durrus, Bantry, West Cork. tel. 027-61355 fax 027-61355. All functions: Tim Rowe and Clem Cairns. 1 title in 1993; ISBN prefix 0-9523522; Clé.

Staff of 2. Short-story anthologies, adult and children's fiction. Submit full manuscript with letter and stamped addressed return envelope. Own contract form.

Ireland: Eason.

Friar's Bush Press

24 College Park Avenue, Belfast BT7 1LR. tel. 08-01232-327695.

History, photo books.

Flyleaf Press

4 Spencer Villas, Glenageary, Co Dublin. tel. 01-280-6228 fax 01-283-0670. All functions: James Ryan. ISBN prefix 0-9697806-

Books on genealogy.

Foillseacháin Inis Gleoire

14 Fitzwilliam Avenue, Belfast BT72HJ.

Foilseacháin Ábhair Spioradálta

Eaglais an Chroí Naofa, An Corrán, Luimneach.

Folens

Broomhill Business Park, Tallaght, Dublin 24. tel. 01-451-5311 fax 01-451-5308. Director, marketing and publicity: John O'Connor. Editor, post-primary, third-level and adult Blackwater titles: Anna O'Donovan. Editor, primary and children's Blackwater titles: Deirdre Whelan. Production: Jim Kearns. 100 titles in 1993; ISBN prefix 0-7099-.

Staff of 70. Primary and post-primary schoolbooks in all subjects; academic titles on politics, accountancy and languages. The Blackwater Press imprint publishes on politics, sport, fiction, humour, medical and general. Submit letter with synopsis and specimen chapter.

Ireland: Eason, Argosy, Hughes & Hughes; Britain: Folens UK distribute their own education titles.

Fortnight Educational Trust

7 Lower Crescent, Belfast BT7 1NR. tel. 08-01232-236575 fax 08-01232-232650. 2 titles in 1993; ISBN prefix 0-9509081-.

Booklet supplements to Fortnight *magazine, and books promoting understanding of social, political, economic and cultural issues relevant to Northern Ireland. Submit letter.*

Four Courts Press

Kill Lane, Blackrock, Co Dublin. tel. 01-289-2922 fax 01-289-3072. Director and editor: Michael Adams. Marketing, publicity & production: Ronan Gallagher. 10 titles in 1993; ISBN prefixes 1-85182- (old: 0-906127-); Clé.

Staff of 1. Spiritual and religious titles including a series of Bible commentaries (Navarre Bible); also scholarly books on theology, philosophy, church history and Celtic Studies series. Submit letter and short synopsis. Own standard contract.

Ireland: Gill & Macmillan distribution; Britain: Andrew Russell; N. America· Diana Bickerton (rep.) and International Specialized Book Service, Portland, OR (stockholding).

Friar's Bush Press

24 College Park Avenue, Belfast BT7. tel. 08-010232-327695.

Has published excellent local studies and a series of collections of old photographs. Seems to be less active currently, and writers should check its state before submitting material.

Gallery Books

The Gallery Press, Loughcrew, Oldcastle, Co Meath. tel. 049-41779 fax 049-41779. Director, editor & publicity: Peter Fallon. Marketing: Patricia Nicol. Production: Jean Barry. 15 titles in 1993; ISBN prefix 1-85235- (old: 0-904011- and 0-902996-).

Staff of 2. Established in 1970, Gallery is a leading literary publisher with more than 300 titles—mostly poetry and plays from emerging and established writers—and a reputation for high quality. Submit letter with biographical note and sample. Plays that have been professionally produced only. No fiction. Own contract form.

Ireland: own distribution; Britain and Europe: Password.

Gandon Books

Gandon Irish Art Books, Oysterhaven, Kinsale, Co Cork. tel. 021-770830 fax 021-770755. Director, editor and production: John O'Regan. Publicity and marketing: Nicola Dearey. 20 titles in 1993; ISBN prefix 0-946641-.

Specialises in books on art and architecture, editing, designing and producing such books for other publishers as well as for its own imprints, which included Gandon Editions and Eblana Editions, the 'Works' series on Irish artists, the Art Monographs series and Portfolio, an annual review of modern art. Submit letter and synopsis first or (artists) telephone. Offers a one-page standard contract.

Ireland: own distribution; Britain and Europe: Central Books; Co-publishes with British and US houses.

Gartan see Columba Press

Geography Publications

24 Kennington Road, Templeogue, Dublin 6W. tel. 01-456-6085. Director: William Nolan. Marketing: Teresa Nolan. 3 titles in 1993; ISBN prefix 0-906602-.

No full-time staff. Specialises in regional history, geography and biography. Series: County History and Society. Own contract. Submit letter with synopsis.

Gill & Macmillan

Goldenbridge, Dublin 8. tel. 01-453-1005 fax 01-454-1688. Director: Michael Gill. Editors, educational: Hubert Mahony, Ailbhe O'Reilly. Editor, professional: Finola O'Sullivan. Editor, trade & academic: Fergal Tobin. Editors, general: Michael Gill & Eveleen Coyle. Marketing: Peter Thew. Publicity: Eveleen Coyle. Production: Mairead O'Keefe. 85 titles in 1993; ISBN prefix 0-7171-; Clé, IEPA.

Staff of 42. General, academic and professional books, and educational for secondary level. Associated in the Macmillan group with publishing companies throughout the world. Submit letter with synopsis and/or specimen chapter. Own contract form. Provides warehousing, invoicing and delivery services to a number of other Irish publishers.

Ireland: own distribution; UK excl. religion titles: Oldcastle Books; UK religious: A. Guy Taylor; Australia: Macmillan Company of Australia; Europe: Michael Geoghegan, London; Hong Kong, China, Thailand, Taiwan, Philippines: Macmillan Publishers (China); Japan: Macmillan Suppan KK; New Zealand: Macmillan & Co; Singapore, Indonesia, Brunei: Pansing Distribution, Singapore; West Indies and Caribbean: Macmillan Caribbean.

Glen Publications

Clonmel, Co Tipperary.

Goldsmith Press, The

Newbridge, Co Kildare. Fax 045-34648. Director: Vivienne Abbott. Marketing: Ber Smyth. 3 titles in 1993; ISBN prefix 1-870491-.

Also under Kavanagh Press imprint. Irish poetry, art, culture, and translations of poetry. Commissions work only: no unsolicited manuscripts, please. Own contract form.

Greystones Books

Caulside Drive, Antrim BT412RS.

An imprint used by the printers W. & G. Baird of Antrim, now owners of the Blackstaff

Press.

Guildhall Press

41 Gt James Street, Derry BT48 7DF. tel. 08-01504-264413.

A job-creating co-op which has produced a number of books of popular local studies.

Gulliver Books

Ditton House, 34 Fitzwilliam Street Upper, Dublin 2. tel. 01-676-3783. fax 01-661-8163. Director: Patrick Fitzgerald. 7 titles in 1995.

Publish Chronicle of Ireland *series.*

Gúm, An

44 Sráid Uí Chonaill uacht., Baile Átha Cliath 1. tel. 01-873-4700 fax 01-873-1140. Director: Caoimhín Ó Marcaigh. Editors: Dónall Ó Cuill and Máire Nic Mhaoláin. Publicity: Seosamh Ó Murchú. Production: John Dixon. 50 titles in 1993; ISBN prefix 1-85791-; Clé and IEPA.

Staff of 14. Publishing arm of An Roinn Oideachais (State Department of Education). Publishes books in Irish, particularly for children including co-editions of illustrated books for younger children.

Hamilton Press see Boole Press

Health Promotion Unit

Dept of Health, Hawkins House, Dublin 2.

Heritage Books see Careers & Educ.

HMSO

16 Arthur Street, Belfast BT14GD.

Humbert Publications

34 Eaton Square, Dublin 6W.

Humphreys, Tony

Leadington, Midleton, Co Cork.

Icarus see Dedalus

IIS see Institute of Irish Studies

IMS (Publications)

3 Beaumont Place, Cork. tel. 021-295208, and 62 Castle Byrne Park, Blackrock, Co Dublin. tel. 01-288-7578.

Has produced handbook on house buying and building and an events guide.

Inné Teo.

Dún Chaoin, Trá Lí, Co Chiarraí.

Institiúid Teangeolaíochta Éireann

31 Plás Mhic Liam, Baile Átha Cliath 2.

Institute of European Affairs

8 North Great Georges Street, Dublin 1.

Institute of Irish Studies

The Queen's University of Belfast, 8 Fitzwilliam Street, Belfast BT9 6AW. tel. 08-01232-245133 ext. 3386 fax 08-01232-439238. Editor: B. M. Walker. Assistant Editor: K. M. Newmann. 18 titles in 1993; ISBN prefix 0-85389-; Clé.

Academic press specialising in Irish history, biography, archaeology, art, language and cultural traditions. Series include the Ordnance Survey Memoirs of Ireland and Place-names of Northern Ireland as well as a periodical, The Irish Review. *First contact by letter only. Contract by exchange of letters.*

Republic trade orders to Robert Towers, 2 The Crescent, Monkstown, Co Dublin; Northern Ireland trade orders to Jane Crosbie, 89 Clifton Road, Bangor, Co Down BT20 5HY.

Institute of Public Administration

Vergemount Hall, Clonskeagh, Dublin 6. tel. 0-269-7011 fax 01-269-8644. Director: Jim O'Donnell. Editor: Tony McNamara. Marketing and publicity: Eileen Kelly. Production: Kathleen Harte. 11 titles in 1993; ISBN prefix 1-872002-.

Staff of 8. Public administration, government, politics, economics, health, law, public affairs and social administration. Submit letter and synopsis. Own standard contract form.

Interchurch Group on Faith and Politics

8 Upper Crescent, Belfast BT71NT.

Irish Academic Press

Kill Lane Blackrock, Co Dublin. tel. 01-289-2922 fax 01-289-3072. Director and editor: Michael Adams. Marketing, publicity, production: Martin Healy. 18 titles in 1993; ISBN prefix 0-7165-; Clé.

Staff of 4. Academic books in the humanities, particularly history, politics, militaria, art, architecture and music. Series: Irish Legal History, Irish Musical Studies. The Round Hall Press (see entry) is an associated company specialising in law books. Submit letter with short synopsis or contents page. Own standard contract.

Ireland: Gill & Macmillan Distribution; Britain: Joanne Legg at Frank Cass Publishers; N. America: Diana Bickerton (promotion) and International Specialized Book Services, Portland, Oregon (stockholding).

Irish Commission for Justice and Peace

169 Booterstown Avenue, Co Dublin.

Irish Council for Civil Liberties

35-36 Arran Quay, Dublin 7

Irish Law Publishing

15 Rathclaren, Killarney, Bray, Co Wicklow.

Irish Management Institute

Sandyford Road, Dublin 16. tel. 01-295-6911 fax 01-295-5150. Manager: Alex Miller.

Irish Science Fiction Association

14 Ardagh Park, Blackrock, Co Dublin.

Irish Times, The

Irish Times General Services, 10-16 D'Olier Street, Dublin 2. tel. 01-679-2022 fax 01-679-7991. Manager: Brenda McNiff.

Irish Political Studies

PSAI Press, College of Humanities, University of Limerick. tel. 061-333644 fax 061-338170. Secretary: Dr Nicholas Rees. Editors: Dr Vincent Geoghegan and Richard English. 1 title in 1993; ISBN prefix 0-9519748-.

Island Publications

132 Serpentine Road, Newtownabbey, Co Antrim BT36 7JQ. tel. 08-01232-778771. Director: Michael Hall. 6 titles in 1993; ISBN prefix 0-9514194-.

Series of pamphlets aimed at increasing popular awareness of the shared historical, cultural and social heritage of the peoples of 'our two islands', particularly of Ireland and of Northern Ireland. Does not consider submissions.

Justice Books

Fernhurst, Hillside Road, Greystone, Co Wicklow. tel. 01-287-4245. All functions: Derry Kelleher.

Self-publisher of socialist-republican books.

Kavanagh Press see Goldsmith

Kells Publishing

John Street, Kells, Co Meath. tel. 046-40117 / 40255, 088-526692 fax 046-41522. Director: Jack Fitzsimons. 3 titles in 1993. *Publishes the 'Bungalow Bliss' series of house designs.*

Kennys or KG

Kennys Bookshops & Art Galleries Ltd, High Street, Galway. tel. 091-62739 fax 091-68544. Director and publicity: Conor Kenny. Editor: Desmond Kenny. Marketing: Maryse Collins. 2 titles in 1993; ISBN prefix 0-906312-.
Local history, poetry, fiction. Submit letter. Ireland: Eason.

Killeen Fine Eds see Three Spires

Kingdom Books

56 Newtownpark Avenue, Blackrock, Co Dublin.

Kingstown Press

5 Marine Road, Dun Laoghaire, Co Dublin. tel. 01-280-3684 fax 01-280-5127. Director, publicity and production: Henry J. O'Hagan. Editor and marketing: Joe O'Donoghue. 7 titles in 1993; ISBN prefix 1-898101-; Clé.
Staff of 3. Novels, poetry, business and technical. Submit letter only. Own contract form. Ireland: Eason; Britain: Media Publications.

Lafferty Publications

IDA Tower, Pearse Street, Dublin 2. tel. 01-671-8022 fax 01-671-8240. Director: Michael Lafferty. Publisher: Paul Byrne. Reports manager: Carol Molloy. Marketing and publicity: Rupert Bowen. 35 titles in 1993; ISBN prefix 0-948394- (old: 0-9508473-).
Staff of 100. Main business is subscription newsletters for the international financial services industry and business management; books are one-off research studies on banking, finance, investment and credit and information technology. Submit letter and synopsis. Own standard contract.
Distribution by direct mail from Dublin, but there is a company Lafferty Australia Pty and a representative office for Asia in Singapore.

Lagan Press

PO Box 110 4AB, Belfast. All functions:
Patrick Ramsey.

*A small but conscientious literary publisher
whose focus seems to be on Ulster writers and
poets.*

Lapwing Publications

1 Ballysillan Drive, Belfast BT14. tel. 08-
01232-391240. All functions: Dennis and
Rene Greig. 8 titles in 1993; ISBN prefix
1-898472-.

*Staff of 2. Small books of contemporary Irish
poetry selling at £2 each. Submit twenty poems with letter. Offers 50 complementary copies in lieu of royalty.*

Distributor: "None; no-one wants it".

Léirmheas Publications

PO Box 3278, Dublin 6. tel. 01-497-6944.
ISBN prefix 0-9518777-.

Libra House

4 St Kevin's Terrace, Dublin 8. tel. 01-454-
2717. Editor: Cathal Tyrell.

Trade, transport, travel.

Lilliput Press, The

4 Rosemount Terrace, Arbour Hill, Dublin 7. tel. 01-671-1647 fax 01-671-1647. Director and editor: Antony Farrell.
Marketing and publicity: Amanda Bell.
Production: Mari-aymone Djeribi. 20 titles in 1993; ISBN prefix 1-874675- (old:
0-946640-). Clé.

*Staff of 3. Mainly non-fiction, but good fiction
may be considered. (Auto)biography, history,
criticism, literature, regional and Irish interest, current affairs, ecology, simple scientific
material, letters, diaries, pamphlets. Series:
ETCH pamphlets. Submit letter, synopsis and
specimen chapters.*
Ireland: Gill & Macmillan distribution;
Britain: Central Books, Ion Mills; N.
America: Irish Books & Media.

LiterÉire Publishers

114 Ballinclea Heights, Killiney, Co Dublin.

Longman, Browne & Nolan see Educational Company of Ireland

MacDonnell Whyte

102 Leinster Road, Dublin 6. tel. 01-497-
7449 fax 01-497-7440. Director: David
MacDonnell. 1 title in 1993; ISBN prefix

0-9517095-.
*Specialises in philately and postal history.
Series: Stamps of Ireland.*
Ireland: Eason; Britain: Vera Trinder;
Europe: David Feldman, Geneva; N.
America: Subway Stamp Co, New York.

Marino Books see Mercier Press
Martello Books see Mercier Press
Mentor Publications

43 Furze Road, Sandyford Industrial Estate, Dublin 18. tel. 01-295-2112/3 fax 01-
295-2114. Director: Daniel McCarthy.
Production: Margaret O'Driscoll.

*12 staff. Educational books, mainly for secon-
dary schools. Submit letter. Own contract
form.*

Mercier Press

PO Box 5, 5 French Church Street, Cork.
tel. 021-275040 fax 021-274969. Marino
Books: 16 Hume Street, Dublin 2. tel. 01-
661-5299 fax 01-661-8583. Director: John
Spillane. Editor, Mercier Press: Mary Fee-
han. Editor, Marino Books: Jo
O'Donoghue. Publicity: Anne O'Donnell.
24 titles in 1993; ISBN prefix Mercier: 1-
85635-; Marino: 1-86023; Clé.

*Staff of 11. Folklore, history, politics, current
affairs, general Irish interest, religion. Marino Books imprint (earlier called Martello)
covers popular and literary fiction, books for
children and teenagers, general non-fiction,
guides, lifestyle, spirituality. Mercier: submit
letter, synopsis and contents page if appropriate; Martello: letter and complete manuscript
if available. Own contract form.*
Ireland: own distribution; Britain: rep.
Ion Mills, Oldcastle Books, distrib. Central Books; Europe: rep. Michael
Geoghegan; N. America: Dufour Editions, Irish Books & Media; Australasia:
Keith Ainsworth.

Monarch Line

32 Booterstown Avenue Co Dublin. tel.
01-283-1336.

Theatre books and plays.

Monos New Publishing

24 Railpark, Maynooth, Co Kildare. tel.
01-628-5012 or 01-627-2609. Directors:
Vincent Doyle and John Drennan.

Specialises in work by unemployed people.

Morrigan Book Company

Morigna Mediaco Teo, Killala, Co Mayo.
tel. 096-32288. Director: G. Kennedy. ISBN
prefix 0-907677-.

Irish mythology, local history, heritage, environment. Series: Heritage Maps and Guides (25 titles) are produced in association with local groups. Submit letter with stamped return envelope.

Ireland: Eason (books), own distribution (guides); Tory Island: NW Regional Tourism, Aras Reddin, Sligo.

Moyola Books

Hill House, Owenreagh, Draperstown, Co Londonderry BT451AA.

Moytura Press

4 Arran Quay, Dublin 7. tel. 01-872-2373 / 872-3923 fax 01-872-3902. Director: Gerard O'Connor. Editor: David Givens. Marketing: Marian O'Reilly. Publicity: Karen McGrath. Production: Emer Ryan. 20 titles in 1993; ISBN prefix 1-871305-; Clé.

Staff of 8 between Moytura and the associated Oak Tree Press (see entry). Irish-interest fiction and non-fiction. Submit letter with synopsis. Own contract form.

Ireland: Gill & Macmillan Distribution; Britain: Central Books (stockholding).

MP Publications

49 Wainsfort Park, Dublin 6W.

MW Publications

333 Crumlin Road, Belfast BT147EA.

National Cartoon Company of Ireland

St Josephs, Portland Row, Dublin 1. tel. 01-855-1290 fax 01-855-1291. Directors: V. P. Koziell, G. O'Rourke.

National Gallery of Ireland

Merrion Square West, Dublin 2. tel. 01-678-5450 fax 01-661-9898. 3 titles in 1993; ISBN prefix 0-903162-; Clé.
Educational books on art.

National Library of Ireland

Kildare Street, Dublin 2. tel. 01-661-8811 fax 01-676-6690. Director: Dr Pat Donlon. Editing, marketing and publicity: Noel Kissane. 2 titles in 1993; ISBN prefix 0-907328-; Clé.

Has published 25 titles including booklets and document collections of literary and cultural interest, including facsimiles of items in the Library's collection.

Ireland: Eason, Argosy; N. America: Syracuse University Press.

Neidpath Publishing

4 Dunluce Park, Portballintrae, Bushmills, Co Antrim.

New Island Books

2 Brookside, Dundrum Road, Dublin 14. tel. 01-298-9937 fax 01-298-2783. Director and marketing: Edwin Higel. Editor: Dermot Bolger. Publicity and production: Bairbre Drury Byrne. 9 titles in 1993; ISBN prefix 1-874597; Clé.

Staff of 1 full-time. Mainly non-fiction, literary and political, including both present-day writers and neglected ones of the past. Also uses Brookside imprint. Submit letter and synopsis with stamped return envelope. Own standard contract.

Ireland: Edwin Higel; Britain: Password.

O'Brien Press, The

20 Victoria Road, Rathgar, Dublin 6. tel. 01-492-3333 fax 01-492-2777. Publisher: Michael O'Brien. Editorial director: Íde Ní Laoghaire. Publicity: Mary Webb. Production: Chenile Keogh. 42 titles in 1993; ISBN prefix 0-86278- (old: 0-905140-); Clé.

Staff of 7. Twenty years' established, a general publisher of books for adults and children of all ages, as well as educational books. Submit letter and sample chapters. Own contract form.

Ireland and Britain: Gill & Macmillan Distribution; Europe: Michael Geoghegan; N. America: Dufour Editions; Australasia: Keith Ainsworth; S. Africa: Trade Winds Press.

Oak Tree Press

4 Arran Quay, Dublin 7. tel. 01-872-2373 /872-3923 fax 01-872-3902. Director: Gerard O'Connor. Editor: David Givens. Marketing: Marian O'Reilly. Publicity: Karen McGrath. Production: Emer Ryan. 20 titles in 1993; ISBN prefix 1-872853-; Clé.

Staff of 8 between Oak Tree Press and its associated Moytura Press (see entry). Law, business, accountancy and finance for practi-

tioners, students and laymen in Ireland and the UK. Series: Irish Studies in Management and the Enterprise Series. Is associated with Cork Publishing which published account-ancy journals. Submit letter with synopsis. Own contract form.
Ireland: Gill & Macmillan Distribution; Britain: Central Books (stockholding).

Officina Typographica
University College Galway.

Oisín Publications
4 Iona Drive, Dublin 9. tel. 01-830-5236 fax 01-830-7860. Director: Liam Ó hOisín. Marketing: Seán Ó hOisín. Publicity: Brian Ó hOisín. Production: Nóirín Ó hOisín. 7 titles in 1993.

Ollav Healer Publications
9 Brunswick Park, Bangor, Co Down BT20 3DR. tel. 08-01247-473362. Director: Dennis Cassidy.
No full-time staff. Has produced biography and a novel.

On Stream Publications
Currabaha, Cloghroe, Blarney, Co Cork. tel. 021-385798 fax 021-385798. Director: Roz Crowley. 6 titles in 1993; ISBN prefix 1-897685-.
Staff of 1. Local history, food and wine, personal stories and corporate histories. Will consider subsidy publishing, but editorial and design decisions rest ultimately with the publisher. No fiction. Submit letter with synopsis and specimen chapter. Own contract form.

Ossian Publications
PO Box 84, 40 McCurtain Street, Cork. tel. 021-502040 fax 021-502025. All functions: John Loesberg.
Staff of 4. Irish and Scottish traditional music; general music, instruction and information, songbooks, tunebooks. The Bookmark imprint covers poetry, colouring, humour. Submit letter with synopsis and specimen pages. Own contract form.
Ireland and Europe: own distribution; Britain: Ossian UK, Graham Dixon, Music Exchange, Music Sales (all stockholding); N. America: Ossian USA (mail-order) and Music Sales (stockholding); Australasia: Noreen Ralph (mail order and stockholding).

Pallas Publications
PO Box 50, Pallaskenry, Co Limerick.

Paraclete Press
Mission Research & Publications, 169 Booterstown Avenue, Unit 3, Co Dublin. tel. 01-288-1789 fax 01-283-4307. Director: Revd Brian Gogan CSSp. 1 title in 1993.
No full-time staff. Series: Spiritan Roots. Also publishes under Education Bureau imprint.

Parkgate Publications
19 Montague Street, Dublin 2. tel. 01-475-8778 fax 01-475-0758. Director: Paul Hannon. Editor: Emily Dillon. 2 titles in 1993; ISBN prefix 0-9523109-.
Staff of 2. Memoirs of Anglo-Irish interest, business histories and illustrated books. Submit letter with 100-word synopsis.
Ireland: own distribution; Britain: Stockbridge Books and Pencorp Books.

Pavee Point Publications
46 N. Great Charles Street, Dublin 1.

Peppercanister see Dedalus

Poolbeg
Poolbeg Group Services Ltd, Knocksedan House, 123 Baldoyle Industrial Estate, Dublin 13. tel. 01-832-1477 fax 01-832-1430. Publisher and chairman: Philip MacDermott. Editor, Poolbeg: Kate Cruise O'Brien. Editor, Children's Poolbeg: Nicole Jussek. Editor, Torc: Zoë O'Connor. Editor, Salmon Poetry: Jessie Lendennie. Production: Gerard O'Rourke. 65 titles in 1993; ISBN prefix 1-85371-; Clé.
Staff of 17. Poolbeg largely fiction, Torc current affairs, Salmon poetry, Children's Poolbeg children's books. Submit letter with specimen pages or chapter. Own standard contract.
Ireland: own distribution; Britain: Fourth Estate; N. America: Dufour and Irish Books & Media; Australasia: Keith Ainsworth.

Práta
66 Bóthar Adelaide, Baile Átha Cliath 2.

Queen's University of Belfast
see Institute of Irish Studies

Real Ireland Design
27 Beechwood Close, Bray, Co Wicklow.

Relay

Tyone, Nenagh, Co Tipperary. tel. 067-31734. Director: Donal A. Murphy. 4 titles in 1993; ISBN prefix 0-946327-.

4 staff. Local history, biography, reference. Intends to publish children's books. Submit synopsis and specimen chapter. Own contract.

Roberts Rinehart Publishers

Main Street, Schull, Co Cork, and PO Box 666 121 2nd Avenue, Niwot, Colorado 80544, USA. tel. 028-28622 fax 028-28618. Director and editor: Jack van Zandt (Ireland). Editor and production: Rick Rinehart (USA). Editor, children's titles: Toni Knapp (USA). Marketing and publicity: Shelley Daigh (USA). 40 titles in 1993; ISBN prefix 0-911797-, 0-916567-, 1-57098-, 1-879373-; Clé, ABA, Publishers Association (USA).

Staff of 8. The Irish (and European) office of an American publisher, which originates its own titles here as well as selling those from USA. Irish and Irish-American interest, natural history, photography, history, biography, art, architecture, travel, politics, current affairs, young adult fiction, children's picture and activity books. Submit letter, synopsis and specimen. Own standard contract.

Ireland: Town House (orders to Gill & Macmillan); Britain and Europe: Airlift Book Company; N. America: own imprint and Publishers Group West; Australasia Bateman; S. Africa: Trade Winds.

Roinn Oideachais see Gúm

Round Hall Press, The

Kill Lane Blackrock, Co Dublin. tel. 01-289-2922 fax 01-289-3072. Director: Michael Adams. Editor: Eilish Maguire. Marketing, publicity and production: Terri McDonnell. 10 titles in 1993; ISBN prefix 1-85800- (old: 0-947686-).

Staff of 2. Associated with Irish Academic Press (see entry), and specialising in law books and journals. Series: Annotated Statutes. Submit letter and short synopsis. Own standard contract.

Ireland: Gill & Macmillan distribution; Britain: Joanne Legg at Frank Cass Publishers; N. America: Diana Bickerton

(rep.) and International Specialized Book Service, Portland, Oregon.

Royal Irish Academy

19 Dawson Street, Dublin 2. tel. 01-676-2570 fax 01-676-2346. Director: Patrick Buckley. Editor: Barbara Young. Marketing: Hugh Shiels. 6 titles in 1993; ISBN prefix 1-874045- (old: 0-901714-); Clé, Society for Scholarly Publishing.

Publishing staff of 5. Academic books of Irish interest: language, history, archaeology, sciences. Series: Irish Historic Towns Atlas, Medieval Dublin Excavations, Proceedings of RIA, New History of Ireland ancillary volumes, Dictionary of Medieval Latin from Celtic Sources ancillary volumes.

Sagart, An

Tigh na Sagart, An Daingean, Co Chiarraí. tel. 066-51104. Director and production: P. Ó Fionnachta. Editors: K. McCone, R. Ó hUiginn. Marketing and publicity: T. Furlong. 8 titles in 1993; ISBN prefix 1-870684-.

No full-time staff. Apart from journals, An Sagart publishes liturgical and devotional books in Irish, books on Irish language and literature. Series: Maynooth Studies, Léachtaí Cholm Cille, Dán agus Tallann.

Distribution: ÁIS.

Sáirséal Ó Marcaigh

13 Bóthar Crioch Mhór, Baile Átha Cliath 11. tel. 01-837-8914. Editor: Caoimhín Ó Marcaigh.

Salmon Poetry see Poolbeg

Sanas Press

PO Box 4056, Dublin 4.

Samovar Press

63 Ardagh Park, Blackrock, Co Dublin. tel. 01-288-1164. Contact: Louis Hemmings. 1 title in 1993; ISBN prefix 1-874136-.

No full-time staff. A 'samizdat' firm with a christian bias, publishing poetry, short stories and Christians for Freedom of Conscience series.

School and College see Fallon

Signal Press

17 Millview Court, Malahide, Co Dublin. *Books on transport.*

Skylark Books

Baltrasna, Ashbourne, Co Meath.

SLS Legal Publications

Faculty of Law, Queen's University, Belfast BT7 1NN.

Smythe, Colin

PO Box 6, Gerrards Cross, Bucks SL9 8XA, England. tel. 00-44-1753-886000 fax 00-44-753-886469. Director: Colin Smythe. 15 titles in 1993; ISBN prefixes Dolmen 0-85105-, Smythe 0-86140-, 0-900675-, 0-901072-.

The only firm not based in Ireland that we feel justified in listing. Smythe, with a staff of two, specialises in Irish literature, criticism, drama, poetry, folklore and history. Series: Irish Literary Studies, Ulster Editions and Monographs, Irish Drama Selections, Irish Dramatic Texts, Princess Grace Irish Library (inc. Lectures). Stocks and reissues books under the Dolmen Press imprint. Submit letter with synopsis and sample chapter. Own contract.

Ireland: Hibernian Book Services, 93 Longwood Park, Dublin 14; Britain: own distribution; N. America: Dufour.

Sporting Books

4 Sycamore Road, Mount Merrion, Co Dublin. tel. 01-288-7914 fax 01-288-7914 / 288-7347. All functions: Raymond Smith. 2 titles in 1993; ISBN prefix 0-9517804-.

Books on sport, particularly Gaelic games and the Turf as well as the Hurling and Football Annual. Submit letter on concept and short synopsis. Own standard contract.

Ireland: Eason, News Bros and WNS, Belfast.

Stress Books

121 Kingshill, Salthill, Galway. tel. 091-28838. Director: J. K. Burns.

Books, from popular to professional levels, on stress, 'life science' and religions.

Talbot Press see Educational Co of I.

Teagasc

19 Sandymount Avenue, Dublin 4. tel. 01-668-8188 fax 01-668-8023. Director: Dr Pierce Ryan. Editor, scientific publications: Dr Con O'Rourke. Editors, semi-technical and popular: John Keating and Michael Miley. Production: Frank Fegan. 25 titles in 1993; ISBN prefix 0-848321-; Irish Association of Learned Journals.

Teagasc is the state agriculture and food development authority. With a staff of 8 it publishes mainly periodicals, but also research, technical and popular reports, manuals and monographs and a few books. Work is commissioned from authors.

Third House

3 Victoria Road, Holywood, BT18 9BA.

Three Spires Press

Blackrock Village, Cork. Director: Pat Cotter. 3 titles in 1993; ISBN prefix 1-873548-.

Mainly poetry, with a Munster bias; the Killeen Fine Editions imprint is for hand-bound limited editions of poetry mainly by established writers. Does not consider unsolicited work. Verbal contracts.

Ireland: own distribution; Britain: Central Books.

Tír Eolas

Newtownlynch, Doorus, Kinvara, Co Galway. tel. 091-37452. Director and other functions: Anne Korff. Co-editor: Jeff O'Connell. ISBN prefix 1-873821-; Clé.

Guides, maps, books of topography, archaeology, history, ecology and environment. No fiction. Submit letter and synopsis.

Ireland rep.: Fergus Corcoran; Britain: Colin Smythe.

Topaz Publications

10 Haddington Lawn, Glenageary, Co Dublin. tel. 01-280-0460.

Law books.

Torc see Poolbeg

Tower Books

13 Hawthorn Avenue, Ballincollig, Co Cork.

Town House

THCH Ltd, Trinity House, Charlston Road, Ranelagh, Dublin 6. tel. 01-497-2399 fax 01-497-0927. Editing, marketing and publicity: Treasa Coady. Production: John McCurrie. 15 titles in 1993; ISBN prefixes 0-948524-, 0-946172-; Clé.

Staff of 3. The imprints Town House and Country House are used for appropriate titles.

Illustrated non-fiction, fiction, biography, TV tie-in books, general reference, art and antiquities. Submit letter with synopsis and 3-4 chapters. Contract adapted from Penguin's.
Ireland: Gill & Macmillan; Britain: BRAD; N. America: Roberts Rinehart.

Ulster Historical Foundation

Balmoral Buildings, 12 College Square East, Belfast BT1 6DD. tel. 08-01232-332288 fax 08-01232-239885. Director: Dr Brian Traynor. Marketing, publicity, production: Shane McAteer. 6 titles in 1993; ISBN prefix 0-901905-.

Books on Ulster history, including educational, genealogy, biography. Series: Gravestone Inscriptions. Submit letter only.
Ireland: Eason (NI) and own distributor; Britain: Mary Campbell; N. America: Blair's Book Service.

Veritas

7-8 Lower Abbey Street, Dublin 1. tel. 01-878-8177 fax 01-878-6507. Director: Father Sean Melody. Editor: Fiona Biggs. Marketing: Myra Delaney. Publicity: Maeve O'Byrne. Production: Tom Griffin. 25 titles in 1993; ISBN prefix 1-85390- (old: 0-86217-, 0-905092-, 9-01810-); Clé.

Staff of 10. Publisher to the Irish Hierarchy. Standard rituals, liturgical books, catechetical texts and general religious books including theology, scripture, marriage and family, prayer, biography, counselling and mariology. Series: Oscott. Children's books under the Beehive Books imprint. Submit synopsis and/or specimen chapter or pages. Own contract form.
Ireland: Veritas Wholesale, 8 Hanover Quay, Dublin 2, and Columba Press; Britain: Veritas Book & Video Distrib., Lower Avenue, Leamington Sap, Warwicks W31 3NP; N. America: Ignatius Press, San Francisco, CA; Australasia: Charles Paine Pty, Parramatta, NSW; Malta: Liberija Taghlim Nisrani, Sliema.

Weir's Guides see Ballinakella Press

White Row Press

135 Cumberland Road, Dundonald, Belfast BT16 0BB. tel. 08-01232-483586. Director: Jim Carr. Editor: Peter Carr. 1 title in 1993; ISBN prefix 1-870132-.

No full-time staff. General and local interest. Submit letter, synopsis, specimen chapter and stamped addressed envelope. Uses PA contract.

Whyte, Ian

Ian Whyte (Ireland) Ltd, 27 Upper Mount Street, Dublin 2. tel. 01-676 7228 fax 01-676-7229. Director: Ian Whyte. 1 title in 1993; ISBN prefix 0-9506415-.

Catalogues and handbooks of Irish postage stamps, Irish postal history. Series: Collecting Irish Stamps and Stamps of Ireland. Submit letter with synopsis and/or specimen pages.
Ireland: Eason; Britain: Vera Trinder; Europe: Lindner; N. America: Harry Edelmann.

Windows Publications

Auburn, Stagella, Cavan.

Wolfhound Press

68 Mountjoy Square, Dublin 1. tel. 01-874-0354 fax 01-872-0207. Director and editor: Seamus Cashman. Editor: Susan Holden. Marketing: Ciara Considine. Production: Jenna Dowds. 13 titles in 1994; ISBN prefix 0-86327-.

Staff of 8. Fiction, children's fiction, literary and general trade titles. Submit synopsis with stamped addressed envelope. Own standard contract form.
Ireland: Gill & Macmillan distribution; Britain: Ion Mills sales manager; Europe: Michael Geoghegan sales. N. America distribution: Dufour; Austalia distribution: Keith Ainsworth.

Yes Publications

10-12 Bishop Street, Derry. Director: L. Connor.
Books of poetry and peace studies.

Zeus Publishing

38 Leeson Place, Dublin 2. tel. 01-661-6360 fax 01-661-9298. Editor: J. Burke.
Offshoot of a design business.

Zircon Publishing

Scarriff Bridge, Ballivor, Co Meath. tel. 0405-46089 fax 0405-46089.
Has produced a book on chairing meetings.

Publishers by subject

This is an index by subject and special readership area to the main publishers listed on pages 65-80. Few publishers specialise absolutely, and many will consider or put out an occasional book on a subject for which they are not well known, so this listing is only indicative rather than exhaustive.

Academic
Cork University Press
Folens
Gill & Macmillan
Institute of Irish Studies
Irish Academic Press
Royal Irish Academy
Smythe

Accountancy
Oak Tree

Agriculture
Teagasc

Anthologies
Blackstaff
Gill & Macmillan

Archaeology
Royal Irish Academy
Institute of Irish Studies
Tír Eolas
Town House

Architecture
Gandon
Irish Academic Press
Nat. Gallery of Ireland

Art
Gandon
Institute of Irish Studies
Irish Academic Press
National Gallery
Town House
Wolfhound

Banking
Lafferty

Biography
Attic
Ballinakella
Blackstaff
Blackwater (Folens)
Brandon
Geography
Gill & Macmillan

Institute of Irish Studies
Irish Academic Press
Lilliput
O'Brien
Parkgate
Town House
Ulster Hist. Found.
Wolfhound

Business
Lafferty
Oak Tree

Celtic studies
Four Courts

Children's Books
Aran
Beehive (Veritas)
Celtpress
Children's Press
Cló Iar-Chonnachta
Gúm
Marino (Mercier)
Poolbeg
O'Brien
Roberts Rinehart
Wolfhound

Computer science
Aran

Cookery
Appletree
Blackstaff
Careers & Educational
Farmar
Gill & Macmillan
Mercier

Corporate history
Farmar
Gill & Macmillan
Parkgate

Current affairs
Lilliput
Mercier

Torc (Poolbeg)

Diaries
Appletree
Attic
Inst. of Public Admin.
Wolfhound

Ecology
Lilliput
Tír Eolas

Economics
Econ. & Soc. Res. Inst.
Inst. of Public Admin.

Education
Blackstaff
Careers & Educational
Wolfhound

Fantasy
Aran

Folklore
Mercier
Smythe

Fiction
Attic
Blackstaff
Blackwater (Folens)
Brandon
Emperor
Marino (Mercier)
Moytura
O'Brien
Poolbeg
Town House
Wolfhound

Finance
Lafferty
Oak Tree

Gaeilge see Irish

Gay and lesbian
Attic

Genealogy
Ballinakella
Roberts Rinehart
Ulster Hist. Found.

Geography
Geography
Tír Eolas

Gift books
Appletree
Gill & Macmillan
Town House

Government
Inst. of Public Admin.

Guides
Appletree
Ballinakella
Brandon
Gill & Macmillan
Marino (Mercier)
Morrigan
Tír Eolas
Wolfhound

History
Appletree
Ballinakella
Blackstaff
Colourpoint
Farmar
Geography
Gill & Macmillan
Irish Academic Press
Lilliput
Mercier
O'Brien
Royal Irish Academy
Smythe
Tír Eolas
Ulster Hist. Found.
Wolfhound

Human rights
Beyond the Pale
Brandon

Humour
Appletree
Blackstaff
Blackwater (Folens)
Mercier

Irish language
Carbad
Clócomhar

Cló Iar-Chonnachta
Coiscéim
Gartan (Columba)
Gúm
Sagart
Sáirséal Ó Marcaigh

Languages
Royal Irish Academy

Law
Butterworths
Inst. of Public Admin.
Oak Tree
Round Hall

Literary criticism
Appletree
Lilliput
Smythe
Wolfhound

Literature
Lilliput
New Island
Smythe
Wolfhound

Medical
Boole
Blackwater (Folens)

Music
Appletree
Beyond the Pale
Irish Academic Press
Ossian

Mythology
Morrigan

Nature
Blackstaff
Roberts Rinehart
Tír Eolas

Northern Ireland
Beyond the Pale
Blackstaff
Corrymeela
Fortnight
Institute of Irish Studies
Island
Ulster Hist. Found.

Photographs
Blackstaff
Eason
Gill & Macmillan

Roberts Rinehart
Wolfhound

Plays
Gallery
Smythe

Poetry
Blackstaff
Dedalus
Gallery
Goldsmith
Lapwing
Salmon (Poolbeg)
Samovar
Smythe
Three Spires
Wolfhound

Politics
Athol
Beyond the Pale
Blackstaff
Blackwater (Folens)
Inst. of Public Admin.
Irish Academic Press
Irish Political Studies
Mercier
New Island

Public relations
Able Press

Religion
Careers & Educational
Columba
Dominican
Four Courts
Gill & Macmillan
Mercier
Samovar
Veritas

School books
Colourpoint
Educational Co of Ireland
Fallon
Folens
Gill & Macmillan
Gúm
Mentor

Science fiction
Aran

Sciences
Boole
Royal Irish Academy

Social questions
Athol
Attic
Beyond the Pale
Cork University Press
Econ. & Soc. Res. Inst.
Inst. of Public Admin.
Lilliput

Sport
Blackwater (Folens)
Gill & Macmillan
O'Brien
Sporting Books

Wolfhound

Stamps
Irish Philately
MacDonnell White
Whyte, Ian

Tax
Butterworths
Oak Tree

Technical
Boole

Topography
Ballinakella
Morrigan
O'Brien

Tír Eolas

Transport
Colourpoint

Women's studies
Attic
Gill & Macmillan

Young adults
Attic
Marino (Mercier)
O'Brien
Poolbeg
Roberts Rinehart
Wolfhound

Publishers by ISBN prefix

International Standard Book Numbers are explained on p. 134 and the address of the ISBN Agency which assigns numbers is on p. 142.

Ireland shares prefixes 0 and 1 with UK and US publishers. The next group of 2 to 7 digits identifies the publisher, the last identifies the book.

0-7070-	Economic & Social Research Inst.
0-7099-	Folens or Blackwater
0-7143-	Longman, Browne & Nolan (Ed.Co)
0-7144-	Fallon, C. J.
0-7165-	Irish Academic Press (old I.Univ. P.)
0-7171-	Gill & Macmillan
0-848321-	Teagasc
0-85034-	Athol Books
0-8545-	Talbot Press (Educ. Co of Ireland)
0-85105-	Smythe (Dolmen Press)
0-85389-	Institute of Irish Studies
0-85640-	Blackstaff Press
0-86140-	Smythe, Colin
0-86167-	Educational Company of Ireland
0-86217-	Veritas (old)
0-86278-	O'Brien Press
0-86281-	Appletree Press
0-86322-	Brandon
0-86327-	Wolfhound Press
0-900346-	Eason (old)
0-900675-	Smythe (Gregory coll. works)
0-901072-	Smythe (AE coll. works)
0-901714-	Royal Irish Academy (old)
0-9018-	Educational Co. of Ireland (old)
0-901809-	Econ. & Social Research Inst. (old)
0-901905-	Ulster Historical Foundation
0-902561-	Cork University Press (old)
0-902996-	Gallery (old)
0-903162-	National Gallery of Ireland
0-904011-	Gallery (old)
0-904651-	Appletree Press (old)
0-905092-	Veritas (old)
0-905140-	O'Brien Press (old)
0-906121-	Careers & Educational Publishers
0-906127-	Four Courts Press (old)
0-906281-	Able Press
0-906312-	KG (Kennys, Galway)
0-906602-	Geography Publications
0-907271-	Dominican Publications (old)
0-907328-	National Library of Ireland
0-907677-	Morrigan Book Company
0-911797-	Roberts Rinehart
0-916567-	Roberts Rinehart
0-946172-	Town House or Country House
0-946327-	Relay
0-946538-	Ballinakella Press
0-946640-	Lilliput Press (old)
0-946641-	Gandon
0-947686-	Round Hall Press (old)
0-948183-	Columba Press (old)
0-948268-	Dedalus Press (old)
0-948394-	Lafferty Publications
0-948524-	Town House, Country House
0-9508466	Flyleaf Press

0-9508473-	Lafferty Publications (old)
0-9520451-	Dissident Editions
0-9504797-	Dominican Publications (old)
0-9506415-	Whyte, Ian
0-9509081-	Fortnight Educational Trust
0-9509295-	Farmar (old)
0-9512941-	Clegnagh Publishing
0-9514194-	Island Publications
0-9514229-	Beyond the Pale Publications
0-9517095-	MacDonnell Whyte, Irish Philately
0-9518704-	Sporting Books Publishers
0-9519748-	Irish Political Studies
0-9523109-	Parkgate Books
0-9523522-	Fish Publishing
0-9697806-	Flyleaf Press
1-57098-	Roberts Rinehart (USA)
1-85182-	Four Courts Press
1-85235-	Gallery Books
1-85371-	Poolbeg
1-85390-	Veritas
1-85475-	Butterworth
1-85594-	Attic or Basement Press
1-85607-	Columba Press
1-85635-	Mercier Press
1-85791-	Gúm, An
1-85800-	Round Hall Press
1-85918-	Cork University Press
1-86023-	Martello Books (see Mercier)
1-870132-	White Row Press
1-870491-	Goldsmith Press
1-870684-	Sagart, An
1-871305-	Moytura Press
1-871552-	Dominican Publications
1-872002-	Institute of Public Administration
1-872853-	Oak Tree Press
1-873430-	Eason
1-873548-	Three Spires Press / Killeen
1-873790-	Dedalus Press
1-873821-	Tír Eolas
1-874045-	Royal Irish Academy
1-874136-	Samovar Press
1-874338-	Emperor Publishing
1-874597-	New Island Books
1-874675-	Lilliput Press
1-874700-	Cló Iar-Chonnachta
1-879373-	Roberts Rinehart
1-898101-	Kingstown Press
1-897685-	On Stream Publications
1-897751-	Aran Books
1-897973-	Celtpress / Celtales
1-898256-	Collins Press
1-898392-	Colourpoint
1-898472-	Lapwing Publications
1-899047-	Farmar

Copyright

There are a lot of confused ideas about copyright, but essentially it is simple. The right to copy (particularly to print, publish, perform or broadcast) any work belongs to the person who created it, which with literary works means the person who wrote it; but if the work was commissioned by someone else for a fee, or written as part of the writer's employment, then the copyright belongs to the commissioner or employer. There is no form of registration, but the formula "© John Smith 1995" is internationally recognised as claiming (not proving) copyright. Other elaborate warnings are sometimes used to discourage people from photocopying or other breaches of copyright, but strictly they are unnecessary. Neither facts nor information can be copyright, but the form of words in which they are given can be.

Assignment of rights

Copyright is a possession that can be sold outright or partially 'assigned' or leased. A book's author usually assigns copyright to a publisher in return for royalties for as long as the publisher keeps the book in print, but often retains at least a share of subsidiary (serial, film, broadcasting, translation) rights. When you sell an article or story to a magazine, you are normally taken to be assigning 'serial rights' only, but you can specify 'first serial rights', leaving you free to sell the second to another publication, or the book rights to a publisher.

Even if it has been sold or assigned, copyright subsists only until the end of the seventieth year after the death of the original writer (or after first publication, if the author died first), though in the UK the change from fifty to seventy years to conform with the European standard has not yet been made. After that, works are 'in the public domain' and may be freely copied and published. But beware: an editor or translator may establish copyright in a later *edition* of a copyright work, or in an edition of a work that is already in the public domain. Thus if you dramatised a Dickens novel or wrote a shortened version of it for schools, you would be establishing a new copyright. The printed image of a work in the public domain may itself be the publisher's copyright, so be careful about publishing facsimiles. An edition, adaptation, translation, reproduction or performance of a work not yet in the public domain is a breach of copyright, and to publish anything of this sort you should first obtain the right to do so from the copyright owner.

Quoting copyright work

If you want to quote from a copyright work (or reproduce artwork, photograph or music) you should obtain permission from the copyright owner, and it is normal to do so via the publisher unless another address is given. It is usual to charge a fee for such a permission and/or to seek an acknowledgement. The fee will vary according to the extent of the work being quoted and the potential sale or value of the work it is to be reproduced in.

However, copyright is not infringed by 'fair dealing' in reasonable quotations for teaching (if the original work was not written for teaching purposes) or research purposes or for criticism. 'Reasonable' may be taken to mean not more than 400 words from a book for instance, or a number of shorter quotations together not exceeding 800 words. Such reasonable quotations from a poem or other short work should not exceed a quarter of the whole. Permission must be got for every piece, however short, to be used in an anthology, but if it is published for educational or critical purposes *and* most of the other material in it is not copyright, then quoting reasonable extracts may be seen as fair dealing.

Libel

If in your writing you lower some living person in the estimation of right-thinking people—that is damage their reputation—you may be guilty of libel, even though what you say may be true, since the truth may be hard to prove. You can publish a libel without knowing or even having heard of the person you defame, for instance by an unfortunate coincidence of name and other details of a fictitious character. The defence that a passage is fair comment in the public interest, made without malice, is not easy to establish. You may say that someones *opinion* is lunatic or criminal, but you must not say or imply that *he* is a lunatic or criminal. A reviewer may hold a book up to ridicule (within reason), but not its author.

Defamation or libel law is extremely complicated; lawyers and even judges will differ in interpretation of it, while juries are notoriously unpredictable, and disproportionally high damages and legal costs are often involved. More than with most legal disputes, if is safer to keep out of court, and safest of all to avoid defaming living people in the first place. Publishing an apology or denial (for instance in the periodical where the libel was published), may help your case particularly where the libel was unintentional, but obviously this is not so easy when the libel is in a book, and care is needed since an apology might be seen as an admission of harm done. A complainant may seek to get an offending book or periodical withdrawn from sale, and if this happens the publisher should be careful to stipulate that the complainant will repay the costs and consequential loss if the libel suit eventually fails.

There are moves afoot to reform the legislation, but it is likely always to remain a minefield to the writer. In fact the writer, publisher and seller (for instance a bookshop) of a libel are held equally responsible for it and, since a publisher might be seen as wealthier than a writer and a big book distributor wealthier than either, they are likely to be the first targets of a libel suit. The result is that publishers are very wary of anything that might seem libellous, and Eason has been known to refuse to handle books that author and publisher thought were safe. Most publishers expect authors to indemnify them against libel damages in their contracts, but this is to frighten the author into being careful, since such indemnity might seem dubious in law, quite apart from suggesting that the publisher did not himself take proper care.

Writers of biographies, of books on crime, current affairs and politics should take great care, and even seek legal advice if in doubt—though lawyers are inclined to be over-cautious to protect themselves.

Tax

A writer, even a spare-time one, is subject to income tax on what he earns but may set his expenses as a writer against his earnings, as with any other form of self-employment. If expenses are more than revenue, the tax men might not allow you to set the loss against other income on the basis that your writing is a hobby rather than a business activity. Obviously, since they tax profits, you should insist that they should also make allowance for deficits, particularly as income from writing can vary wildly from year to year. A novel may take three years to write, and most of its royalties will be received in one year, long after the expenditure on research, stationery, typing and so on. Revenue from outright sales of copyright is regarded as income rather than capital. Capital allowances can be claimed, for instance for a computer, but not deducted from revenue; for this you need professional advice.

Tax exemption

However the Finance Act of 1969 allows people resident in the Republic total exemption from income tax on earnings (even from abroad) from 'original and creative works of cultural or artistic merit' if this relief is properly claimed and officially allowed.

The writer must apply to the Revenue Commissioners on one of two forms, Artists 1 (claiming that some published work or works are generally recognised as of cultural or artistic merit) or Artists 2 (submitting a particular published work for a decision on whether it conforms with the requirements). There have been some peculiar decisions because of different understandings of the word 'cultural' and opinions as to what has artistic merit. Although it is believed that the tax authorities consult the Arts Council, who do not themselves give grant aid to biographies, histories and such works, even a book of children's doggerel has been known to gain exemption though recent new regulations have excluded schoolbooks. Some appeals against the Commissioners' decisions have been successful.

So if you are likely to earn substantial sums from writing, it is well worth obtaining the forms and the guidelines provided with them. A number of best-selling authors, including some who produce fiction of questionable cultural or artistic merit, have settled in Ireland because of this provision.

Publishers

There is no special legal formality required of a publisher except for the provision of free copies of his products to certain 'statutory deposit libraries' (explained on page 142) and the observance of copyright and libel law as outlined above. Various non-compulsory forms of 'registering' a book's publication are dealt with under 'Producing a book' (p. 119) and 'Marketing a book' (p. 133), with addresses on p. 142.

Any person, company or other body can publish a book, periodical or whatever, and is subject to the ordinary laws of the land in respect of trading, contracts, employment, tax and so on. The Value Added Tax on books is currently zero in Ireland and the UK, and 21% on periodicals and stationery in the Republic. It is to the advantage of a publisher to be registered for VAT, since the tax on purchases can then be reclaimed, while there is little or no VAT to be charged and accounted for on what is sold.

Grant aid may be sought from the Arts Council to assist the publication of work of artistic merit, in addition to the other help provided by state agencies to small or new businesses, but the Councils look for a track record and/or good future prospects, and grants or interest-free loans are not paid until the publisher's tax affairs are certified as in good order. See Arts Council under 'Organisations'.

Censorship

Although the Censorship of Publications Act of 1929 and Censorship of Publications Board remain in being in the Republic, the latter has been remarkably inactive since the banning of *The Joy of Sex* in 1987. The Act prohibits the sale of obscene material, and the Board may arbitrarily ban an obscene publication from sale for twelve years, though there is an appeal mechanism. Another Act prohibits literature on abortion. Increasing conformity with European law (particularly in respect of homosexuality) has no doubt had some effect, and the criterion of what is acceptable in terms of pornographic writing has clearly shifted very considerably in recent years, but publishers should be aware that the pendulum could swing the other way at any time.

Publishing agreements

Most writers' guide books provide a specimen contract or agreement but, when it comes to the crunch, such model forms of wording can be of little help to the writer. What happens in reality is that the publisher offers his own printed agreement form with some details inserted by hand, and asks the writer to sign it. To ask for changes in some of the inserted details—dates, periods, percentages, amounts—may be possible, but to demand rephrasing of clauses might be seen as unreasonable. Instead of retiring to consult with his solicitor, the publisher might well back off altogether, seeing such a demanding writer as likely to be more trouble than he is worth.

Goodwill and mutuality

In reading and trying to understand the provisions of a publishing agreement and—more difficult and often more important—in working out what eventualities it does *not* cover, the writer might well feel a sense of unreality because, more than with most other sorts of contract, such an agreement must essentially rest on mutual goodwill rather than on watertight wording. If the parties fall into dispute, the written provisions and clauses, however carefully drafted, are likely to be of little help to either of them, for it would probably cost more to try and enforce them in a court of law—or for solicitors to negotiate compensation for a breach—than could ever be gained. A writer may find himself in the position that he can legally force a firm to publish his book, but does anyone want his work to be put out by an unwilling publisher who is likely to skimp on every expense and project something less than enthusiasm? Equally a publisher may be in a position to insist that an author give him the typescript of some book by a certain date, but no contract formula yet devised can ensure that the typescript will be a good or saleable one, and so the writer could force the publisher to reneg on the agreement without technically being in breach of its terms himself.

Contract by letter

The best and most practical way of varying or extending the terms of an agreement with a publisher without fuss is to do so by letter, which has the immense advantage that terms can be expressed in plain language and in a friendly tone. All that is necessary to make such terms just as legally binding as any in a formal contract is to obtain a reply to the letter agreeing with what it says.

For instance the following note from an author would successfully add a clause, modify two others and delete a fourth without making the process sound too complex or threatening.

Dear Publisher, I return the two copies of the agreement duly signed. One point (publication date) needs to be added and two clauses (translation and next-book option) modified. My agreement to all the terms is subject to your confirmation that you will publish the book within one year of receipt of the final typescript; that you will not exercise your rights under clause 6 d (assignment of translation rights) without first obtaining my written agreement to a sample of the proposed translation extending to no less than a thousand words; and finally that the option given in clause 12 (that I must offer you first refusal of my next two books) refers only to works of fiction and would not, for instance, be taken to refer to the school text-book I'm currently working on. When returning my copy of the agreement, would you please enclose a note agreeing to the three points set out above? In addition you will note that I have deleted clause 6e in both copies of the agreement since it seems irrelevant and could also be confusing. When signing the agreement, could you please initial the deletion as I have done?

Yours sincerely,   John Author.

The main general points to look for in a publishing agreement are:

Reciprocity

Whatever one party agrees to do to the advantage of the other party should be equitable in terms of value and/or time. An important constituent element of any contract is that there should be a 'consideration' (a payment or other benefit) in return for whatever is supplied or done. If a contract does not provide for such a fair balance of advantages between the parties it may be claimed to be wrongful, unenforceable or even extortionate.

Providing for failure

It is better to make provision for reasonable failure by either party to fulfil the conditions of the agreement—e. g. the author taking longer to complete the typescript than expected, or the publisher proving unable to price the book below a certain amount—than to imply that the whole contract becomes void because of some such minor infraction. When drafting and reading an agreement, consider the worst case as well as the best, and allow for both.

Rejection

So much depends on the quality of writing in a book, that publishers must provide in agreements for the rejection of material that they feel does not come up to reasonable standards. This may mean that a writer puts a lot of time and effort into writing something that can be rejected in a moment at the publisher's whim. Recognising this, it may be equitable to provide for some form of minimum or 'rejection' fee.

Indemnity

Some publishers have a clause in their agreements whereby the author indemnifies them against damages for libel or breach of copyright. Such a clause might well be hard to enforce, since the law counts printers, publishers and distributors just as responsible as authors for what they sell, and no private agreement can take that responsibility away. The clause is really there to frighten the author and make him take his responsibility seriously.

Extra work

It is generally the author's responsibility to obtain copyright permissions for reproducing illustrations or quotations. Bear in mind that this might be quite an onerous, expensive and time-consuming task, and make sure that it is properly covered by fees or royalties. Sometimes an agreement will also require the author to provide an index or other material of that sort. If you don't have experience of indexing, make sure you find out how much work is involved, or what a professional indexer would charge for the job before agreeing to do it. It is in your publisher's interests to help you by showing you what is needed and how to accomplish it.

Advances on royalties

In London and New York it has become fashionable for writers to boast of the size of their advances from publishers, and the writer whose book has been accepted may suppose he has a right to some such payment 'up front'. Generally with new authors this is not so. The publisher is committing risk capital to setting, printing and binding the book with no certainty that these expenses will be recouped and he may not be able to add to them. If the publisher offers an advance, then it is usually payable on delivery of the manuscript. If none is offered none should be expected.

Time

It is usually better to put some fixed term on an agreement so that it can be renegotiated after a period. Don't forget that things—including your point of view—can change. The history of literature abounds with authors who assigned their rights for ever or for an indefinite period in exchange for a lump sum or royalty that seemed generous at the time, and lived to see a publisher or agent make a fortune out of their work, while they earned little or nothing from it. On the other hand a publisher must be given enough time to cultivate a demand for an author's work, and this might involve publishing his first books at a loss, and being sure that his rights will continue in force long enough for him to see his first investment paying off.

Quantities

The author has a right to know the number of copies of his book produced by the publisher, since he will earn royalties on their sale, and must know the extent of his potential earnings. It is in the publisher's interest to be explicit about quantities, since a frequent cause of dispute is the author's suspicion that the publisher is not paying royalties on all the copies he sells. If the original print run (and any reprints, and how many free copies were sent out as samples or for review) is stated and known, then there can be no dispute about the number remaining in stock and therefore the number sold.

Amounts

Look for clarity in expressing royalties or other percentages. Some agreements specify the payment of a 10% royalty on the sales of a book, but do not specify what this is a percentage of. Is it of the selling price of the books, of the discounted price that the retailer pays the wholesaler or that the wholesaler pays the publisher, or is it 10% of the revenue the publisher realises after paying certain expenses? On a book priced at £10 the author might receive anything from £1 to a few pence per sale, depending on how such a royalty is calculated. In many agreements the home sales royalty may be specified as a percentage of the selling price, while the foreign rights royalty may be a percentage of 'receipts', meaning of the net amount that the original publisher receives from the foreign publisher, and this may result in a very inequitable deal for the author.

Format and design

It is the publisher's business how he publishes a book—in what format, at what price, whether first in cased form and later in paperback and so on—but all these things and style of marketing are of great interest to the author too, since they will enhance or restrict his earnings. Since it helps the publisher to have the author's ideas and collaboration in marketing (particularly a book for a specialist market), it is better for both parties to be open about their desires and intentions, and to work together, each acknowledging the other's particular experience and knowledge, and trying to reconcile differences.

Openness

In the nature of things authorship is a lonely business, and it is all too easy for lonely people to forget that others—publishers, reviewers, the public—are no less human and fallible, and no less well-intentioned. The author of a book is like the parent of a child and, like a parent, inclined to resent criticism of his offspring, whether or not justified, or to feel slights or insults where none was intended. At the worst, writers may develop a sort of mild paranoia and feel that the publisher or the book trade is out to cheat them. Just as authors should recognise that such feelings are inevitable and probably unjustified—since no publisher will stay in business long if he cheats his own authors—publishers too should be aware of how writers might see them, and go out of their way not to give excuse for such doubts. Unless author and publisher are partners, they are nothing.

Writing in the community

Brian Leyden

THE WRITER in our society remains a romantic figure. Writers are remote, obsessive souls at the mercy of their dreams and memories and broken love affairs. They are people of searching intellect and generous emotion. Above all, they are strongly individual pilgrim strangers in the world.

They do not, for example, get together on a Wednesday night for two hours, after they have put the children to bed, to read and discuss their work with the other members of a night class or writers' group—allowing a ten minute break for coffee and biscuits. They do not ask a well known author or dramatist to conduct an all-day workshop for their benefit. And no true writer will be caught near any place or event where face-painting is likely to take place.

Such remarkable individuals may exist. The maverick talents, the wilful outsiders—"the ones who never yawn or say a commonplace thing but burn, burn, burn," as Jack Kerouac would have it; a rare and zealous few who explode into our consciousness with a brilliant first novel or other debut.

A more probable arrival in print is the product of slow, tenacious labour of the sort that builds skill, style and reputation over a period of years. John McGahern once told the members of a writers' workshop that they should look on writing as the dullest business in the world. Glamorous was not a word that sprang to mind as he prepared to rewrite the one story for the fifty-seventh time.

This is the reality most writers will experience. Like all other trades there is an apprenticeship to be served; and an apprenticeship is probably not a strong enough description. It is more like serving time in a boot-camp for new recruits on some hell-bent mission to greatness. What has to be faced is an assault course of arts festival fringe events, literary weekends, writers' weeks, summer schools, writers' group workshops, back-room readings, submissions to broadsheets, submissions to short-story and poetry competitions or to regional anthologies. For anyone who writes because they just can't help it, this route to recognition can be a demanding, demoralising and even terrifying experience.

Worse still is the level of prejudice encountered. A creative individual may be working full-time at his or her craft but is very often technically unemployed. And as the arts in our society have been judged a non-essential occupation, you don't go into this business in the first place if you seriously wish to support a family. Despite all these handicaps, there has been an increase in the number of arts festivals and arts centres around the country, and a colourful flowering of many other arts-related projects. Most draw funding from the one source, the government agency FÁS; an institution with, ironically, a problem where the arts are concerned.

In the 1980s the government introduced through FÁS the first Social Employment Schemes, a move engineered to create a ripple in the vast standing pool of the long-term unemployed. The schemes were essentially targeted at corner boys, shopping mall panhandlers, habitués of the betting shop and all those judged to be entrenched in the welfare system. For a period of twelve months they would be press-ganged into road sweeping, wall building and other community improvements.

It was soon spotted by desperate arts administrators and organisers that these Social Employment Schemes could be used as a source of funding for their work. All you had to do was introduce the word 'community' into your submission and the funding for personnel as scheme workers and a materials grant soon followed. Arts festival organisers, drama groups, writers' groups, the editors and publishers of money-starved literary journals all tapped into this life-saving resource.

A world of run-down rooms, un-heated temporary accommodation, smudged photocopying and all things lacking the decorum of the more established and privileged arts institutions came into being. Here were women with wild hair and sweatshirts, men with thin tongues darting along roll-ups, travellers and new-agers with dogs on strings, college graduates, idealists and an army of perceived loafers, spongers, and deviant drug users, all lifted from the live register and operating under the banner of community arts.

When the first Social Employment Schemes were introduced I was jobless and writing compulsively. I loved the whole notion of being a writer, but I was living in Leitrim and however fanciful my imagination the west bank of the Shannon was no Paris. I didn't know that in the next county a dedicated and respected writer, Dermot Healy, was working with a writers' group made up of people like myself. My departure from the wilderness came when I won the RTÉ Francis McManus Short Story Award. Soon after, Dermot Healy contacted me to say he would like to print the story in issue one of a literary journal he was preparing for publication.

The idea of a literary journal first came up at a writing workshop in the Sligo Youth Contact Centre, and once more when the writers' group moved to the Markievicz Centre for the Unemployed. Each year the group gave a public reading and the standard of writing, in Dermot Healy's view, called for publication. He was also aware of a further crop of talented new writers as he read manuscripts in his capacity as judge for the Allingham

Festival short-story competition, the George A. Birmingham short-story award in Westport, and the Cootehill Festival competition in Cavan. Also active in the area was Leo Regan, the Arts Education Officer with Sligo VEC, and the editor of the literary journal *Flaming Arrows*. Through Leo Regan and the VEC, funds were found to cover the printing costs of the first issue of a journal with a separate literary identity to be called *Force 10*.

In the process of contacting writers scattered about the region, Dermot Healy established links with the Killybegs writers' group, the Moylurg writers' group in Co Roscommon and a further concentration of writers in Co Mayo. While trawling the northwest for material he concluded that *Force 10* should be more than a literary journal; it would be a visual and social document of the region. Photographs would be included and painters such as Sean MacSweeney were approached. There would be first-person interviews to celebrate over-looked lives and voices. More established writers like Leland Bardwell, Michael Mullen, Francis Harvey and Francis Stuart were invited on board to balance any suggestion that this was a purely provincial endeavour.

Inevitably the first issue had a regional bias and mostly local sales. The plan was to produce a twice-yearly journal, but this did not happen. Finance was the problem. One year later the journal had FÁS funding through a Social Employment Scheme and a hired crew of ten. There was a remarkable in-put of very fine poetry, special features on crafts, spiritual healing and mental health. A third issue followed soon after. Lar Cassidy of the Arts Council wrote to say the publication was one of the best regional magazines he had ever seen. But in the editorial introducing issue three, Dermot Healy is no longer able to contain his frustration.

He points out that certain people felt it was unbecoming for a writers' group to be based in a Centre for the Unemployed—as if unemployment were somehow contagious. Other lessons learned were that a regional magazine should not call itself a regional magazine. A geographical location is suspect. Any journal based outside Dublin is immediately labelled 'local history'. And if you want to be taken seriously you must avoid any mention of FÁS. "FÁS is a more colourful version of the term unemployed. It implies obligation on behalf of the public to be laudatory towards the artistic efforts of a group who are a public liability." The magazine takes on the character of a charity and will be reviewed with benevolent condescension. If it gets reviewed at all. Money and public relations seemed to set the agenda in the literary review columns of the Dublin newspapers.

Force 10 continued without this rubber stamp of critical approval. The Arts Council did row in with grant aid, and the journal has weathered through to issue six. There is a new SES team in place to continue the work. The terms of employment on these schemes are gradually improving, though a certain stigma still attaches. Distribution remains a problem though circulation has increased through a system of Dublin, Belfast and Cork based head-hunted editors. To confirm the path-finding status of *Force 10*, several of its former contributors have since been published in book form.

Of course there were hiccups and breakdowns in communication over the years, but through this one literary enterprise a cross-pollination of the arts was achieved. Literary competitions attached to festivals were used to source material. Photographers and artists found a publishing outlet, and there were exhibitions of original photographs that went on tour to coincide with the literary launches. Isolated writers' groups were drawn into a network that stretched along the Western seaboard from Donegal via Sligo to Belmullet. Each group was ready to host the other for a night of readings, music and after hours speak-easy shenanigans. Two Samuel Beckett plays were staged as *Force 10* productions, and there were follow-on writers' workshops under the title Force 10 in Mayo. The concept of writing in the community is not really applicable. What was established was a community of writers.

Brian Leyden's collection of short stories, *Departures*, is published by Brandon. He was the Irish contributor to *The Alphabet Garden*, a collection of European short stories launched simultaneously in twelve countries and published here by Brandon.

Writers' groups

The following groups are believed to meet regularly to discuss their work. New writers' groups are starting up all the time, and established ones are disbanding. If no writers' group for your area is listed, check with your local arts centre or arts officer (listed after the writers' groups) or your library. If you draw a blank, maybe you should start a group yourself? In addition to writers' groups, a number of local writing workshops and courses are run, usually tutored by an established writer and with the emphasis on pratical instruction. The timing, location, and duration of these courses vary from term to term and from year to year. For up-to-date information refer to a local guide to evening classes (Wolfhound publishes a guide to evening classes in Dublin, the Mercier Press publishes one for Cork), the adult education department of your local college or university, your local Vocational Education Committee or, again, your arts centre or library.

Antrim

Harmony Hill Creative Writing Group, c/o Harmony Hill Arts Centre, Lisburn, Co Antrim. Contact: Hazel Armstrong, 08-01846-662445.

Belfast Writers' Group, 20 Drumcree Place, Newtownabbey, Co Antrim BT37 9JA. Contact: 08-01232-862997.

City Writers, c/o Linen Hall Library, Donegall Square North, Belfast. Contact: Patricia Gore, 08-01232-242338.

Conway Mill Writers' Group, Conway Mill Education Centre, 5-7 Conway Street, Belfast. Contact: Elsie Best, 08-01232-242338.

Divis Writers' Group, Divis Community Centre, 9 Ardmullan Place, Belfast. Contact: Dolores Walshe.

Shankill Writers' Group, Shankill Women's Centre, 79 Shankill Road, Belfast. Contact: Sally Paul, 08-01232-240642.

Armagh

Armagh Writers, 8 Woodford Heights, Armagh BT60 2DY.

Carlow

Carlow Writers' Group, c/o 1 Strawhill Villas, Carlow. Contact: Deirdre Brennan, 0503-31485.

Cavan

Cootehill Writers' Group, c/o Arts Festival Committee, Cootehill, Co Cavan. Contact: Kay Phelan.

Clare

Adult Literacy Group, 25 Cusack Road, Ennis, Co Clare. Contact: James Whyns.

Killaloe Writers' Group, Boru Lodge, Killaloe, Co Clare. Contact: Emma Cooke.

Kilshanny Writers' Group, Carrowkeel, Kilshanny, Co Clare. Contact: John Doorty.

North Clare Writers' Group, Main Street, Ennistymon, Co Clare. Contact: Jacki Hersey, 065-71258.

Shannon Writers' Group, c/o 135 Cluain Airne, Shannon Town, Co Clare. Contact: Jean Murphy.

Cork

Carrigaline & District Writers' Group, Kiely Estate, Belgooly, Co Cork. Contact: Carmel Murphy, 021-770783.

Cork City Writers' Group, City Library, Cork. Contact: Thomas McCarthy.

Cork Prison Writers, Cork Prison, Cork. Contact: Catherine Coakley, 021-503277.

Cork Women's Poetry Circle, 22 Mount Oval, Rochestown, Cork. Contact: Maura Bradshaw, 021-895046.

Great Island Writers' Group, 20 Assumption Place, Cobh, Co Cork. Contact: Mary Grannell.

Midleton Writers' Group, 3 Beechwood Court, Youghal Road, Midleton, Co Cork. Contact: Betty Duffy, 021-613355.

Northside Writers' Group, 134 Farranferris Avenue, Cork. Contact: Denis Leahy, 021-394432.

The Women's Writers' Group, 82 Rathmore Terrace, Richmond Hill, Cork.

Contact: Hannah Cleary, 021-272036.

Derry

Derry Writers' Group, Verbal Arts Centre, Cathedral School Building, London Street, Derry BT48 6RQ. Contact: Sam Burnside.

Flowerfield Writers' Workshop, c/o Flowerfield Arts Centre, 185 Coleraine Road, Portstewart, Co Derry. Contact: Chris Audley, 08-01265-833959.

Donegal

Gleneely Writers' Group, Aghatubbrid, Gleneely, Lifford Post Office, Iniseoin, Co Donegal. Contact: Brid Walsh.

Killybegs Writers' Group, Church Road, Killybegs, Co Donegal. Contact: Barbara Parkinson.

Letterkenny Writers' Group, c/o Gallagher's Hotel, Letterkenny, Co Donegal. Contact: Brian Smeaton, 074-51013.

Letterkenny Writers' Group for Women, c/o The Women's Centre, Rainey's Yard, Letterkenny, Co Donegal. Contact: Helen Summors, 074-24985.

Ramelton Writers' Group, The Rectory, Ramelton, Co Donegal. Contact: Brian Smeaton.

Down

Newtownards Creative Writing Group, Ards Arts Centre, Town Hall, Newtownards, Co Down. Contact: Hugh Robinson, 08-01247-816753.

Newry Creative Writing Group, Adult Education Centre, Downshire Road, Newry, Co Down. Contact: Gerard Doherty, 08-01247- 69359.

Dublin

Balbriggan Writers' Group, Balbriggan Library, Georges Square, Balbriggan, Co Dublin. Contact: Trish McKeown.

Ballymun Writers, 77 Eamonn Ceannt Tower, Ballymun, Dublin 11. Contact: Pat Tierney.

Ballymun Writers' Group, Ballymun Library, Ballymun Road, Dublin 11. Contact: Kay Dennis, 01-842-1890.

Dollymount Writers' Group, 21 Dollymount Park, Clontarf, Dublin 3. Contact: Anne Marie Daly.

PARC Writers' Group, Parents Alone Resource Centre, 325 Bunratty Road, Coolock, Dublin 17. Contact: Noreen Byrne.

Dublin Writers' Workshop, South William Bar, South William Street, Dublin 2. Contact: Jean O'Brien.

Dundrum Writers' Group, College of Commerce, Main Street, Dundrum, Dublin 14. Contact: Pauline Brady, 01-494-5392.

Poetry Plus, 35 Mulgrave Street, Dun Laoghaire, Co Dublin. Contact: Liam Cox.

Fertile Quill, 31 Pine Valley Avenue, Rathfarnham, Dublin 16. Contact: Noreen McCrossan.

Fingal Writing Group, c/o 52 Cromcastle Court, Kilmore, Dublin 17. Contact: Ruth Regan, 01-847-1510.

Finglas Writers' Group, Fingal Centre for the Unemployed, St Helena's Resource Centre, St Helena's Road, Finglas, Dublin 11. Contact: Orla O'Connor.

Finglas West Writers, c/o Scoil Ide, Cardiffsbridge Road, Finglas West, Dublin 11. Contact: Áine O'Kelly.

Klear, St Mary's National School, Grangepark View, Raheny, Dublin 5. Contact: Cathleen O'Neill, 01-831-6255.

Malahide Writers' Group, 27 Chalfont Place, Malahide, Co Dublin. Contact: Paddy Ryan.

Onion Field Literary Circle, Richard Crosby's Pub, Ranelagh, Dublin 6. Contact: Paul Kenny.

Prison Writers, c/o Teachers' Unit, Mountjoy Prison, North Circular Road, Dublin 7.

Riversdale Writing Group, VEC, Corduff, Blanchardstown, Dublin 15. Contact: John Minahan.

Oasis Literary Group, 41 Balally Court, Sandyford, Dublin 16. Contact: Nora Connolly.

Skerries Writers' Group, 33 Shenick Avenue, Skerries, Co Dublin. Contact: Marie Bashford Synott.

Swords Writers' Group, 13 River Valley View, Swords, Co Dublin. Contact:

Peadar Mac Bradaigh.

Jobstown Writers' Workshop, c/o West Tallaght Resource Centre, Tallaght, Dublin 24. Contact: Cynthia Fogarty, 01-452-5788.

Priory Writing Group, c/o Priory School, Tallaght, Dublin 24. Contact: Marie Gahan.

Women's Writers' Group, 76 Stillorgan Wood, Stillorgan, Co Dublin. Contact: Ivy Bannister.

Writers' Island, 3 Desmond Street, South Circular Road, Dublin 8. Contact: Colm Quilligan.

Galway

Barna Adult Education Writing Group, Knocknagreine House, Furbo, Co Galway. Contact: Louise Martin, 091-92365.

Clifden Writers' Group, Cleggan, Co Galway. Contact: John Durning.

Galway Writers' Workshop, Auburn House, Fairhill, Galway. Contact: Jessie Lendennie, 091-62587.

Inisbofin Writers' Group, Forum, Inisbofin Island, Co Galway. Contact: Aileen Murray.

Kinvara Writers' Group, Ballyvaughan Road, Kinvara, Co Galway. Contact: Pam Gleming.

Letterfrack Writers' Group, c/o Connemara West Centre, Letterfrack, Co Galway.

Moycullen Writers' Group, Moycullen Community Centre, Moycullen, Co Galway. Contact: Vincent Gormally.

Tuam Writers' Group, Gateswide, Impala Lodge, Bermingham Road, Tuam, Co Galway. Contact: Kevin Dwyer.

Kerry

Dingle Writers' Group, Dingle, Co Kerry. Contact: Michael Fanning.

Listowel Writers' Group, St Patrick's Hall, Listowel, Co Kerry.

Moyvane Writers' Group, Moyvane, Co Kerry. Contact: Gabriel Fitzmaurice.

Tralee Writers' Group, Rosboultra, 43 Meadowlands, Tralee, Co Kerry. Contact: Padraig Mac Fheargusa.

Kildare

Celbridge Writers' Group, c/o Gateway Bookshop, Celbridge, Co Kildare. Contact: Colette McCormack.

Cill Dara Writers' Group, Inshalla, 55 Woodlands, Naas, Co Kildare. Contact: Mae Leonard, 045-76644.

Maynooth Writers' Group, Maynooth Library, Maynooth, Co Kildare. Contact: Stuart Lane.

Kilkenny

Kilkenny Writers' Group, Arts and Education Office, Ormond Road, Kilkenny. Contact: Proinsias Ó Drisceoil.

Mooncoin Writers' Group, Riverine, Chapel Street, Mooncoin, Co Kilkenny. Contact: Edward Power.

Thomastown Writers' Group, Legan, Thomastown, Co Kilkenny. Contact: Eliza Dear.

Laois

Stradbally Writers' Group, Tullamoy, Co Laois. Contact: Vera McHugh.

Leitrim

Knocknarea Writers' Group, Dromahair, Co Leitrim. Contact: Isobelle Connolly.

Limerick

Limerick Poetry Workshop, 11 Aylesbury, Dooradoyle, Limerick. Contact: Ciaran O'Driscoll, 061-301881.

Newcastle West Writers' Group, c/o The Tallyhoe Pub, Newcastlewest, Co Limerick. Contact: Helen Foley, 069-62737.

Raheen Writers' Group, Springdale, Raheen Road, Raheen, Limerick. Contact: Gerard Brilley.

Longford

Granard Writers' Group, Newtownbond, Ballinalee, Co Longford. Contact: Mary O'Reilly, 043-71179.

The Barbican Writers' Group, 22 Fair Street, Drogheda, Co Louth. Contact: Susan Connolly or Michael Holohan, 041-33946.

Louth

Dundalk Writers' Group, Town Hall, Dundalk, Co Louth.

Mayo

Ballyhaunis Writers' Group, c/o Ballyhaunis Chamber of Commerce, Bally-haunis, Co Mayo.

Ballina Writers' Group, c/o The Mortgage Store, Ballina, Co Mayo. Contact: Bernie Jackson, 096-70394.

Ballinrobe Writers' Group, Ballinrobe, Co Mayo. Contact: Bridie Molloy.

Castlebar Writers' Group, Linen Hall Arts Centre, Linenhall Street, Castlebar, Co Mayo. Contact: Iarla Mongey, 094-24115.

Castlebar Women Writers, Linenhall Arts Centre, Castlebar, Co Mayo.

Charlestown Writers' Group, Murray's Pub, Charlestown, Co Mayo. Contact: Gerry Murray.

Kiltimagh Writers' Group, Main Street, Kiltimagh, Co Mayo. Contact: David McCreevy.

Louisburgh Writers' Group, Louisburgh, Co Mayo.

Westport Writers' Group, Knockranny, Westport, Co Mayo. Contact: Ger Reidy or Mary Carr, 098-25657.

Roscommon

Moylurg Writers, Frybrook Lodge, Mill Road, Boyle, Co Roscommon. Contact: Ann Joyce, 079-62186.

Roscommon Abbey Writers, 'Greenfields', Mount Prospect. Contact: Peggy Sims, 0903-25126.

Tulsk Writers' Group, Kelly's Bar, Tulsk, Co Roscommon. Contact: Nora Beirne.

Sligo

Force Ten Writers' Group, Marcievicz Centre for Unemployed, The Village, High Street, Sligo. Contact: Dermot Healy, 071-42925.

Northwest Writers One, The Arts Office, Abbey Street, Sligo. Contact: Leo Regan, 071-45844.

Tipperary

Clonmel Writers' Circle, 1 Summerhill, Hill Drive, Clonmel, Co Tipperary. Contact: Diarmuid O'Keefe.

Nenagh Writers' Group, c/o Nationwide Building Society, Nenagh, Co Tipperary. Contact: Mr O'Brien.

Tyrone

Lough Shore WEA Writers' Group, c/o Fitzduff's, Loughshore, Co Tyrone. Contact: Ann Murphy, 08-012487-37211.

Waterford

Initials Writers' Group, c/o Downes Pub, Thomas Street, Waterford. Contact: Ann Farrell, 051-55290.

Westmeath

Athlone Writers' Group, c/o Athlone Library, Athlone, Co Westmeath. Contact: Gearoid O'Brien, 0902-92166.

Granard Writing Group, Kilmore Street, Co Westmeath. Contact: Breda Sullivan.

Wexford

Wexford Community Writing Group, c/o Wexford Arts Centre, Cornmarket, Wexford. Contact: Anne Heffernan, 053-23764.

Writers' Workshop, Wexford Arts Centre, Cornmarket, Wexford. Contact: Denis Collins, 053-23764.

Wicklow

Arklow Writers' Group, Alec Building, Wexford Road, Arklow, Co Wicklow. Contact: Sarah Heaney, South Quay, Arklow.

Ashford Writers' Group, Ballylusk Lodge, Ashford, Co Wicklow. Contact: Richard Bury.

Bray Writers' Workshop, Mayfair Hotel, Bray, Co Wicklow. Contact: Kathy O'Sullivan, 01-282-8748.

Arts centres & arts officers

Cavan
Arts Officer: Caitriona O'Reilly, Cavan County Council, The Courthouse, Cavan. tel. 049-31799.

Clare
Arts Officer: Eugene Crimmins, Clare County Council, Ennis, Co Clare. tel. 065-21616.

Cork
Triskel Arts Centre, Tobin Street, Cork. Contact: Liz McEvoy, tel. 021-272022/3.

West Cork Arts Centre, Old Bank House, Skibbereen, Co Cork. Contact: Jackie Butler, tel. 028-22090.

Donegal
Arts Officer: Traolach Ó Fionnain, County Library, Letterkenny, Co Donegal. tel. 074-21968.

Dublin
Project Arts Centre, 39 East Essex Street, Dublin 2. Contact: Fiach MacConghail, tel. 01-671-3327.

City Arts Centre, 23/25 Moss Street, Dublin 2. Contact: Sandy Fitzgerald, tel. 01-677-0643.

Arts Officer: Jack Gilligan, Dublin Corporation, Cumberland House, Fenian Street, Dublin 2. tel. 01-667-9611.

Arts Officer: Cliodhna Shaffrey, Dun Laoghaire Corporation, Town Hall, Dun Laoghaire, Co Dublin. tel. 01-280-6961.

Arts Officer: Rory O'Byrne, Fingal County Council, Parnell Square, Dublin 1. tel. 01-872-7777.

Arts Officer: Geena Kelly, South Dublin County Council, Parnell Square, Dublin 1. tel. 01-451-5804.

Galway
Nun's Island Arts Centre, 47 Dominic Street, Galway. Contact: Michael Diskin, tel. 091-65886.

Arts Officer: James Harrold, Galway County Council, County Buildings, Prospect Hill, Galway. tel. 091-63151.

Kerry
St John's Arts & Heritage Centre, Listowel, Co Kerry. Contact: Joe Murphy, tel. 068-22566.

Siamsa Tire, Tralee, Co Kerry. Contact: Martin Whelan, tel. 066-23049.

Arts Officer: Liz Culloty, County Library, Moyderwell, Tralee, Co Kerry. tel. 066-21111.

Kildare
Arts Officer: Monica Corcoran, Kildare County Council, Emily Square, Athy, Co Kildare. tel. 045-31109.

Kilkenny
Arts Officer: Margaret Cosgrave, Kilkenny Co Council, County Hall, John's Street, Kilkenny. tel. 056-52699.

Laois
Arts Officer: Muireann Ni Chonaill, County Hall, Portlaoise, Co Laois. tel. 0502-22044.

Limerick
Belltable Arts Centre, 69 O'Connell Street, Limerick. Contact: Mary Coll, tel. 061-319866.

Arts Officer: Sheila Deegan, Limerick Corporation, City Hall, Merchant's Quay, Limerick. tel. 061-415799.

Louth
Arts Officer: Brian Harten, Dundalk UDC, Town Hall, Dundalk, Co Louth. tel. 042-32276.

Mayo
Linenhall Arts Centre, Linenhall Street, Castlebar, Co Mayo. Contact: Marie Farrell, tel. 094-21769.

Arts Officer: John Coll, The Courthouse, The Mall, Castlebar, Co Mayo. tel. 094-24444.

Meath
Droichead Arts Centre, Schules Lane,

Bellscourt, Drogheda, Co Meath. Contact: Paul O'Hanrahan, tel. 041-33946.

Monaghan

Arts Officer: Somhairle Mac Conghaile, Monaghan County Council, The Courthouse, Monaghan. tel. 047-82211.

Sligo

Hawk's Well Arts Centre, Temple Street, Sligo. Contact: Maeve McCormack, tel. 071-62167.

Model Arts Centre, The Mall, Sligo. Contact: Sheila McSweeney, tel. 071-63513.

Waterford

Garter Lane Arts Centre, 5 O'Connell Street, Waterford. Contact: John Baraldi, tel. 051-55038.

Westmeath

Midland Arts Centre, Austin Friar Street, Mullingar, Co Westmeath. Contact: Brian Harten, tel. 044-43308.

Wexford

Wexford Arts Centre, Cornmarket, Wexford. Contact: Dennis Collins, tel. 055-23764.

Arts Officer: Máire Hearty, Wexford County Council, County Hall, Wexford. tel. 053-23799.

Festivals & summer schools

Most festivals boast some sort of literary or drama programme, and many summer schools not ostensibly on writing may be of interest to writers, but we list only those of specific interest here. Approximate dates are given. Bord Failte publishes a calendar of all festivals, and a detailed calendar of literary events is published in the April issue of *Books Ireland* magazine.

Boyle Arts Festival, Roscommon (July/August)

Poetry and fiction readings, workshops, storytelling, theatre and music. Festival Co-ordinator: Fergus Ahern, Greatmeadow, Boyle, Co Roscommon. tel. 079-63085.

Children's Literature Summer School, Dublin

Organised by ICBT and CLAI, this is open to anyone professionally or personally interested in children's books and writing. Irish Children's Book Trust, Irish Writers' Centre, 19 Parnell Square, Dublin 1. tel. 01-872-1302.

Clifden Community Arts Week, Galway (September)

Writers' workshops, readings, lectures, music and exhibitions. Brendan Flynn, Clifden Community School, Clifden, Co Galway. tel. 095-21184.

Cootehill Arts Festival, Cavan (August)

Street theatre, literary readings, writing workshops, music and art exhibitions. Kay Phelan, tel. 049-52321, or Anne Tully, tel. 049-53341.

Cúirt, Galway (March/April)

Predominantly poetry festival, but has expanded recently to include general literature. Varied programme of readings, with a special platform for unpublished poets to read their work. Michael Diskin, Galway Arts Centre, 47 Dominick Street, Galway. tel. 091-65886.

Éigse Carlow (May)

International arts and crafts festival; exhibitions, music, pageantry, drama workshops, busking, poetry and storytelling.

Bev Carberry, Pembroke Studios, Pembroke, Carlow. tel. 0503-41562.

Galway Arts Festival (July)

Theatre, parades, music, children's events, street theatre. Fergal McGrath, tel. 091-63800.

Goldsmith Summer School, Longford (June)

Prominent lecturers, traditional music and debate in celebration of Oliver Goldsmith. Sean Ryan, Battery Road, Longford. tel. 065-71051.

Hewitt (John) International Summer School, Antrim (July)

Seminars, lectures and readings, plus music, walks and excursions. Director, John Hewitt Summer School, St MacNissi's College, Garron Tower, Carnlough, Co Antrim. tel. 08-01266-44247.

Hopkins (Gerard Manley) International Summer School, Monasterevin (June)

Lectures by Hopkins scholars, poetry workshops, competitions and readings. Visiting writers, artists and critics from Europe, USA, Canada, Russia and Australia. Elaine Murphy, Monasterevin, Co Kildare. tel. 045-21715.

International Writers' Course, Galway (July)

On writing fiction and poetry, for undergraduates and graduates. Instruction and seminars by eminent Irish authors. Seamus O'Grady, Summer Schools, University College, Galway. tel. 091-24411.

Irish Theatre Summer School, Dublin (July)

Study of texts and performance in acting workshops at the Gaiety School of Acting, for drama and theatre-studies students. Seona Mac Reamoinn, USIT, 19-21 Aston Quay, Dublin 2. tel. 01-677-8117.

James Joyce Summer School, Dublin (July)

Lectures, seminars and social programme. Helen Gallagher, Dept of Anglo-Irish Literature, UCD, Belfield, Dublin 4. tel. 01-706-8480.

Kilkenny Arts Week (August)

Emphasis on classical music, but also literary events and theatre. Sheila Deegan, Kilkenny Arts Week, 1 William Street, Kilkenny. tel. 056-63663.

Parnell Summer School, Rathdrum (August)

All aspects of Irish history, literature and politics in the Parnell ancestral home at Avondale. Maire Tobin, Lissadell, 78 Heathervue, Greystones, Co Wicklow. tel. 01-287-4124.

Samhlaíocht Chiarraí, Tralee (March/April)

Kerry's Easter arts festival. Offers 'Poets' Platform'—five 'unknowns' are invited to read alongside more established poets on the basis of poems submitted prior to festival. Samhlaíocht Chiarraí, c/o Siamsa Tíre Theatre, Tralee, Co Kerry.

Scríobh, Sligo (August/September)

Literary readings and writing workshops. Orna MacSweeney, Model Arts Centre, The Mall, Sligo. tel. 071-63513.

Sligo Arts Festival (September)

Readings, theatre, concerts, exhibitions. B. Ferguson, Sligo Arts Festival, Stephen Street, Sligo. tel. 071-69802.

Swift (Jonathan) Seminar, Maynooth (June)

Lectures and debate. Aoife Kerrigan, Dept of English, St Patrick's College, Maynooth, Co Kildare. tel. 01-708-3667.

Synge Summer School, Wicklow (June)

Lectures and debate. Irene Parsons, Whaley Lodge, Ballinaclash, Rathdrum, Co Wicklow. tel. 0404-46131.

Writers' Week, Listowel (May/June)

Ireland's longest-running writers' festival. Five days of workshops in short fiction, poetry, writing for radio, theatre, etc. A number of writing competitions are run in conjunction with the festival. Also readings, lectures and theatre. PO Box 147, Listowel, Co Kerry. tel. 068-21074 (Mondays and Thursdays, 10 a.m.-1 p.m.).

Yeats International Summer School, Sligo (August)

Study of Yeats' poetry, prose and plays, life and work, together with history, politics, culture, folklore and literature of Irish renaissance and its aftermath. Also poetry workshop. Secretary, Yeats Society, Douglas Hyde Bridge, Sligo. tel. 071-42693.

A list of awards, prizes and competitions open to Irish writers or writers resident in Ireland. Where the prize or award is for a published book, the onus is generally on the book's publisher, in consultation with the author, to submit a book for consideration. Where the prize or award is non-competitive, unsolicited submissions are usually not welcome: books are nominated by a panel of judges and copies called in from the publisher. In the case of competitions for previously unpublished work, it is often necessary to submit an official entry form, which can be obtained from the address given. Either way, it is unwise to submit entries without first checking with the organisers that conditions of entry have not changed since the competition was last held. Competitions with a high entry fee should be treated with caution.

Aldeburgh Poetry Festival Prize

Michael Laskey, Goldings, Goldings Lane, Leiston, Suffolk IP16 4EB. tel. 00-44-728-830631.

Established by the Aldeburgh Poetry Trust and sponsored jointly by Waterstones and the Aldeburgh Poetry Trust. Awarded for the best first collection of poetry published in Ireland or the UK in the preceding twelve months. Open to any first collection of at least 40 pages. First prize £500 and an invitation to read at the following year's festival. Deadline October.

Aosdána

The Arts Council, 70 Merrion Square, Dublin 2. tel. 01-661-1840. Literature Officer: Laurence Cassidy.

Aosdána is an affiliation of creative artists engaged in literature, music and the visual arts, and consists of not more than 200 artists who have gained a reputation for achievement and distinction. Membership is by competitive sponsored selection and is open to Irish citizens or residents only. Members are eligible to apply for a Cnuas, an annuity of £8,000 for a five-year term, if their incomes are not sufficient to enable them to devote their energies to the full-time pursuit of their art.

Aristeion European Literary and Translation Prizes

The Arts Council, 70 Merrion Square, Dublin 2. tel. 01-661-1840.

European Literary Prize is awarded annually for the finest work of creative literature to have been published in the previous three years by an EC national. European Translation Prize is awarded for the finest literary translation published in previous three years. The Arts Council appoints a jury which selects Ireland's nominations for the prizes. The deadline for publishers' submissions is normally 1 February of each year, with the winners announced usually in November in the European City of Culture for that particular year. Prize money is ECU20,000 in each category (approx IR£16,000).

Artflight: Arts Council/Aer Lingus Travel Awards

The Arts Council, 70 Merrion Square, Dublin 2. tel. 01-661-1840. Literature Officer: Laurence Cassidy.

Scheme jointly funded by Arts Council and Aer Lingus to enable people working in the arts to travel outside Ireland. Creative artists and performers, managers and production staff may apply for a travel award, which will provide a return air journey on the Aer Lingus network.

Arts Council Bursaries in Creative Literature

The Arts Council, 70 Merrion Square, Dublin 2. tel. 01-661-1840. Literature Officer: Laurence Cassidy.

Bursaries in literature are awarded to creative writers of fiction, poetry and drama, in Irish or English, to enable them to concentrate on, or complete, specific projects. A limited number of bursaries may also be offered for non-fiction projects. Bursaries range from £3,000 to £10,000, but the Council also makes available one or two larger two-year bursaries of be-

tween £14,000 and £20,000. The deadline for submissions is normally in mid-April, with the decision made known in mid-Summer.

Arts Council Travel Grants

The Arts Council, 70 Merrion Square, Dublin 2. tel. 01-661-1840. Literature Officer: Laurence Cassidy.

To enable writers of purely creative literature (poetry, fiction and drama) to go abroad to engage in research or to take part in events which will further their work as creative writers. Travel grants are available four times per annum—applications should be submitted by 18 February, 18 May, 18 September and 18 November.

Arts Council of Northern Ireland Annual Awards

The Arts Council of Northern Ireland, Stranmillis Road, Belfast BT9 5DU. tel. 08-01232-381591. Literature Officer: Ciaran Carson.

Awards are offered for specific projects or for the acquisition of equipment or materials to enable an artist to achieve specific objectives. Awards may also be made for travel or to attend masterclasses or short-term advanced training courses. Applicants may be creative or interpretative artists working in any field of the arts. Applications for awards are invited during April of each year by public advertisement. Applications received during the year will generally be held over until April.

Arvon Foundation International Poetry Competition

Kilnhurst, Kilnhurst Road, Todmorden, Lancashire 0L14 6AX. tel. 0044-1706-816582. Administrator: David Pease.

Biennial competition for poems written in English and not previously published or broadcast. There are no restrictions on the number of entries, number of lines, themes, age or nationality of entrants. Entry fee £3.50 per poem. First prize £5,000. Deadline for next competition November 1995.

Athlone Festival Writer of the Year Competition

Festival Writer Competition, Festival Office, Jolly Marnier Licency, Coosan, Athlone, Co Westmeath.

Short stories up to 4,000 words, poetry up to

50 lines. Entry fee of £2 per short story or poem, £5 for three entries. First prize £200 and a trophy plus publication in the local press. Deadline May.

Bass Ireland Arts Awards

Arts Council of Northern Ireland, Stranmillis Road, Belfast 5DU. tel. 08-01232-381591.

Two awards made annually by Bass Ireland and administered with assistance from the Arts Council of Northern Ireland. The major award of £3,000 is open to artists working in any field of the arts; the second award of £1,500 is for an artist working in a nominated discipline. The deadline for submissions is 31 August.

Beck's Bursary

Arts Council of Northern Ireland, Stranmillis Road, Belfast 5DU. tel. 08-01232-381591.

An annual award made by Beck's Beer and administered with assistance from the Arts Council of Northern Ireland. The bursary is made to a creative person or company who, in the judgement of four assessors, has made a significant and lasting contribution to the cultural life of Northern Ireland. Open to young as well as established artists.

Ballyshannon Allingham Arts Society Competition

Catherine Breslin, Bridge End, Ballyshannon, Co Donegal. tel. 072-51760.

Poetry and short stories (up to 5,000 words), in two categories, adult and post primary. Entry fee of £3 per entry. First prize (poetry) £100 and trophy, first prize short story £100. Deadline November.

Birmingham (George A.) /Westport Arts Festival Short Story Competition

Secretary, Short Story Competition, 6 Horbans Hill, Westport, Co Mayo.

Open to all writers resident in Ireland. Previously unpublished stories of 1,500-3,000 words. Entry fee £5 waged, £3 unwaged. First prize £250. Deadline September.

Bisto Book of the Year Award

Mary Murphy, Irish Children's Book Trust, 19 Parnell Square, Dublin 1.

Awarded for published children's book, by

author or illustrator born or resident in Ireland. First prize £1,500. Publishers submit seven copies of children's titles published in previous year, before end December.

Booker Prize for Fiction

Book Trust, Book House, 45 East Hill, London SW18 2QZ. tel. 00-44-181-870-9055.

The leading British literary prize, open to citizens of Britain, the Commonwealth, the Republic of Ireland and South Africa. Awarded for novels published in the UK between 1 October and 30 September of the year of the prize. Prize: £20,000.

Bookstop Short Story Competition

John Davey, Bookstop, Dun Laoghaire, Co Dublin. tel. 01-280-9917.

Short stories (up to 2,000 words) and poetry . First prize in each category, trophy and £100 book token. Deadline May.

Bookwise Annual Short Story Competition

Kells Heritage Festival, Bookwise, Kennedy Road, Navan, Co Meath.

Short stories up to 2,000 words. Entrants must be over 18 and resident in Co Meath. One entry per person. First prize £100. Deadline May.

Boyle Arts Festival Poetry Competition

Fergus Ahern, Poetry Competition, Boyle Arts Festival Office, Boyle, Roscommon.

Poems in English or Irish from writers of any nationality. Entry fee £4 per poem. First prize £200. Deadline July.

Breathnach (Micheál) Literary Memorial Award

Cló Iar-Chonnachta Teo, Indreabhán, Conamara, Co na Gaillimhe. tel. 091-93307.

To be presented annually from 1996 for an Irish language work in any literary form (i.e. novel, drama, poetry collection or short story collection) by a writer under 30 years of age. First prize £1,000. Deadline 1 December.

Carlingford Lough Writers' Circle Young Writers' Competition

John Haugh, 3 St Oliver's Park, Carlingford, Co Louth. tel. 042-73329 (after 6pm).

Poetry and short story competition open to national school classes (fifth and sixth) in the Cooley Peninsula between Omeath and Dundalk. First prize books, tokens and a trophy. Deadline May.

Cló Iar-Chonnachta Literary Award

Cló Iar-Chonnachta Teo, Indreabhán, Conamara, Co na Gaillimhe. tel. 091-93307.

Launched 1995 to mark CIC's tenth anniversary. For a newly written and unpublished work in Irish—best novel 1995, best poetry collection 1996, best short story collection or drama 1997. First prize £5,000. Deadline 1 December.

Clonmel Writers' Weekend Library Competition

Marie Boland, Secretary, Clonmel Writers' Weekend Committee, c/o Clonmel Library, Emmet Street, Clonmel, Co Tipperary.

Poetry, short stories (300 words), plays (15-45 minutes). Entry fee £2 per entry, £10 for six entries. First prize £100. Deadline July.

College Journalist of the Year Competition

ICL, Harcourt Street, Dublin 2.

For the best published material—print or broadcast—relating to science and technology. Administered by Science Journalists' Association, sponsored by ICL, open to all third level students. First prize personal computer. Deadline May.

Cootehill Literary Award

Marion Mulligan, Station Road, Cootehill. tel. 049-52554.

Poetry and short story competition. Entry fee £5 per short story, £2 per poem. First prize £100. Deadline August.

Craven Poetry Competition

Geraldine Lavery, Dundalk, Co Louth. tel. 042-36776.

Open to junior/secondary schools. Poems not less than eight lines in English or Irish. Deadline March/April.

Denis Devlin Memorial Award for Poetry

Arts Council, 70 Merrion Square, Dublin 2. tel. 01-661-1840.

Triennial award of £1,500 for book of poetry in English by an Irish poet.

Duais don bhFilíocht i nGaeilge

The Arts Council, 70 Merrion Square, Dublin 2. tel. 01-661-1840. Literature Officer: Laurence Cassidy.

Triennial award of £1,500 for the best book of Irish poetry published in the Irish language in the preceding three years.

Ewart-Biggs (Christopher) Memorial Prize

Liz Travis, 3/149 Hamilton Terrace, London NW8 9QS. tel. 00-44-171-624-1863.

Instituted in memory of the British Ambassador to Ireland murdered by the IRA in 1976. Biennial award for work of fiction or non-fiction which increases understanding between the peoples of Britain and Ireland, promotes peace and reconciliation in Ireland or closer co-operation between partners of the European Community. First prize £4,000.

European Prize for the Translation of Poetry

European Poetry Library, P Coutereelstraat 76, Leuven, Belgium B-3000. tel. 00-32-16-235351.

Triennial prize offered by the European Commission in Brussels for translations of poetry, written by living poets from other Community countries. Both poems and translations must be in one of the nine official Community languages and the translations must have been published in book form in the previous four years. Next prize, of £6,000, to be awarded in 1996. Deadline for submissions late 1995.

Fish Short Story Prize

Fish Publishing, Durrus, West Cork. tel. 027-61355.

Short stories up to 5,000 words. Entry fee £5 per story. First prize £1,000. First eleven stories to be published in an anthology. Deadline September.

Forward Prizes for Poetry

Colman Getty PR, Carrington House, 126-130 Regent Street, London W1R 5FE. tel. 00-44-171-439-1783.

Sponsored by Forward Publishing, Waterstones Booksellers and Tolman Cunard, under the direction of the Forward Poetry Trust.

Annual awards in three categories: best collection of poetry (£10,000); best first collection of poetry (£5,000); and best poem published but not as part of a collection (£1,000). Open to UK or Irish citizens. Deadline June.

Hennessy/*Sunday Tribune* New Irish Writing Award

Ciaran Carty, *Sunday Tribune*, 15 Lower Baggot Street, Dublin 2. tel. 01-661-5555.

Short stories (up to 3,000 words) and poetry selected for publication in the Sunday Tribune *on the first Sunday of every month are considered for the annual Hennessy/*Sunday Tribune *Irish Writer Awards. Four awards of £1,000 each are presented in December: First Fiction (for previously unpublished writers); Emerging Author (published but not yet established); Poetry; and the overall New Irish Writer Award, which may be selected from any of the foregoing categories.*

Higham (David) Prize for Fiction

Book Trust, Book House, 45 East Hill, London SW18 2QZ. tel. 00-44-181-870-9055.

Annual award for a first novel or book of short stories published in the UK by an author who is a citizen of Britain, the Commonwealth, the Republic of Ireland or South Africa. First prize £1,000.

Hopkins (Gerard Manley) International Summer School Poetry Competition

Breda Reid, Co-Ordinator, Poetry Competition, 71 Allen View Heights, Newbridge, Co Kildare. tel. 045-32444.

Poems of any length. Entry fee £3 per poem. First Prize £300. Deadline June.

Ian St James Awards

The New Writers' Club, PO Box 101, Tunbridge Wells, Kent TN4 8YD. tel. 00-44-1892-511322.

Previously unpublished short stories in two categories, under 3,000 words (Category A) and over 3,000 words (Category B). Entry fee £6 per story (Category A) or £9 per story (Category B). First prize £5,000, plus 12 stories published by HarperCollins in anthology. Deadline February.

Image Short Story Competition

Image Publications Ltd, 22 Crofton Road, Dun Laoghaire, Co Dublin. tel. 01-280-8415.

Short story 1,500-3,000 words. First prize £1,000 plus publication. Deadline December.

International IMPAC Dublin Literary Award

Dublin City Public Libraries, Cumberland House, Fenian Street, Dublin 2. tel. 01-661-9000.

Sponsored to the tune of £100,000 by Florida-based productivity enhancement company IMPAC (whose chairman James B. Irwin is amongst the top 100 Irish Americans), this is the largest literary award in the world. Launched in 1995, the first award will be presented in 1996. A non-competitive award for a work of fiction written and published in English or published in English translation. Titles are nominated by selected libraries in capital cities throughout the world and a winner chosen by an international panel of judges. Nominated entries to be submitted before 31 October.

Irish American Cultural Institute Awards

University of St Thomas, 2115 Summit Avenue, St Paul, Minnesota 55105, USA. tel. 612-962-6040.

Annual arts awards, including O'Shaughnessy Poetry Award ($5,000) and Butler Literary Award ($5,000), which alternates between English- and Irish-language literature each year. Open to Irish residents only. Awards presented in September following selection by IACI members.

Irish Times International Fiction Prize

Gerard Cavanagh, Irish Times Ltd, 11-15 D'Olier Street, Dublin 2. tel. 01-679-2022.

Biennial award for a work of fiction written in English and published in Ireland, the UK or the US. Prizes will be awarded in November 1995 for books published in previous two years. Books are nominated by literary critics and editors only. First prize £7,500.

Irish Times Irish Literature Prizes

Gerard Cavanagh, Irish Times Ltd, 11-15 D'Olier Street, Dublin 2. tel. 01-679-2022.

Biennial prizes for published books, awarded in three categories—fiction, non-fiction and poetry. Open to authors who are Irish citizens or born in Ireland. Prizes will be awarded in November 1995 for books published in previous two years. Books are nominated by literary editors and critics and then called in from publishers. First prize: £5,000 in each category.

Kavanagh (Patrick) Poetry Award

The Patrick Kavanagh Society, c/o Mrs M. Quinn, Lisaolagh, Inisheen, Dundalk, Co Louth.

Collection of 20-30 unpublished poems in English, not more than 60 lines each. First prize £1,000. Deadline August.

Kilkenny Prize, The

The Kilkenny Prize, Heron Cottage, Tobernabrone, Piltown, Co Kilkenny.

Poetry (any length) and short stories (up to 3,000 words). Entry fee £2 for first entry, £1 for each subsequent entry. First prize £150. Deadline October.

Listowel Writers' Week

Literary Competitions, Writers' Week, PO Box 147, Listowel, Co Kerry.

One act play, short story (up to 3,000 words), poetry. Entry fee £4 in each category. First prize £500 in each category. Deadline March. Prizes presented during Listowel Writers' Week (May/June).

Macaulay Fellowship

Arts Council, 70 Merrion Square, Dublin 2. tel. 01-661-1840.

Annual award of £3,500 presented on a rotating basis in visual arts, music and literature, to further the liberal education of young creative artists. Applicants must be under 30 years of age on 30 June in the year of application (or under 35 in exceptional circumstances) and must have been born in Ireland. Next literature award 1997.

Macdonald's Young Writer Competition

The O'Brien Press, 20 Victoria Road, Rathgar, Dublin 6. tel. 01-492-3333.

Poetry, plays, short stories, rhymes, riddles and prose, up to 1,500 words. Entrants must be under 16 and resident in Ireland. Winning entries published in an anthology; authors receive £25 copyright fee. Deadline January.

MacManus (Francis) Short Story Competition

RTÉ, Radio Centre, Donnybrook, Dublin 4. tel. 01-208-3111.

Short stories up to 1,850 words in English or Irish. First prize £1,000 plus winning stories broadcast on Radio One. Deadline Sept. (See also 'Writing for Radio' listings).

Mobil Playwriting Competition

Mobil Oil Ireland Ltd, 24 Merchants Court, Merchants Quay, Dublin 8. tel. 01-679-6600.

Full-length plays in English which have not been previously produced. Open to writers in Ireland and the UK. London's Royal Theatre Company buy an option to produce winning plays. First prize £15,000. Deadline August.

National Poetry Competition

The Poetry Society, 22 Betterton Street, London WC2H 9BU. tel. 00-44-171-240-4810.

The major annual open poetry competition in the UK, open to any poet over the age of 16. Poems written in English (maximum of 15 per entrant) up to 40 lines. First prize £3,000. Deadline October/November.

National Women's Poetry Competition

The Works, St Brendan's, Waterloo Road, Wexford. tel. 053-41193.

Poetry (up to six poems). Open to women only. Entry fee £2 per poem, £10 for six poems. First prize £2,000 and publication in anthology. Deadline December.

Oireachtas Literary Awards

Conradh na Gaeilge, 6 Sraid Fhearchair, Baile Átha Cliath 2. tel. 01-478-3814.

Prizes awarded to Irish language writers in various disciplines, including broadcast journalism, scriptwriting, fiction (long and short), poetry and playwriting. Prizes range from £150 to £1,000. Deadline July.

Peterloo Poets Open Poetry Competition

2 Kelly Gardens, Calstock, Cornwall PL18 9SA. tel. 00-44-1822-833473.

Annual competition sponsored by Marks &

Spencer for unpublished English language poems of up to 40 lines. First prize £2,000. Deadline January.

Pushkin Prizes

Jayne Hartley, Barons Court, Omagh, Co Tyrone.

P. J. O'Connor Awards

RTE, Radio Centre, Donnybrook, Dublin 4. tel. 01-208-3111.

Radio play of 30 minutes duration, in English or Irish. First prize £500 and broadcast on Radio One. Six plays selected for Amateur Drama Radio Festival and awarded £250 each. Deadline November. (See also 'Writing for Radio' listings).

Reading Association of Ireland Awards

Blackrock Teachers' Centre, Carysfort Avenue, Blackrock, Co Dublin. tel. 01-289-4102.

Two bi-annual, non-monetary awards, the RAI Children's Book Award and the RAI Special Merit Award, to encourage the writing, publication and appreciation of children's literature in Ireland. Open to works of fiction and non-fiction (but not school text books) published during previous year. Deadline February.

Rooney Prize for Irish Literature

Rooney Prize, Strathin, Templecarrig, Delgany, Co Wicklow. tel. 01-287-4769.

Annual award to encourage young Irish writing to develop and continue. Authors must be Irish, under 40 and published. Non-competitive award—no application procedure. First prize £5,000.

Royal Liver Assurance/*Live at Three* Creative Writing Awards

PO Box 4022, Dublin 2. tel. 01-676-2728.

Poems up to 40 lines and short stories up to 1,500 words. First prize £2,000 in each category. Deadline November.

Stand Magazine Short Story Competition

Stand Magazine, 179 Wingrove Road, Newcastle upon Tyne NE4 9DA. tel. 00-44-191-273-3280.

Biennial award for a short story written in English and not yet published, broadcast or

8,000 words, by authors anywhere in the world. Next award 1995. Deadline 31 March. Total prize money £2,250.

Tia Maria/U *Magazine* Short Story Competition

U Magazine, 126 Lower Baggot Street, Dublin 2. tel. 01-660-8264.

Short stories up to 2,500 words. First prize personal computer. Entry forms published in U Magazine October, deadline January.

Toonder (Marten) Award

The Arts Council, 70 Merrion Square, Dublin 2. tel.01-661-1840. Literature Officer: Laurence Cassidy.

Sponsored by the Dutch author Marten Toonder and presented on a rotating basis in literature, music and visual arts to honour an artist of established reputation. Literature award of £3,500 presented 1995.

Walsh (Maurice) Memorial Short Story Competition

The Friends of Maurice Walsh, Ballydonoghue, Lisselton, Co Kerry. tel. 068-21799/27275 (after 6pm).

Launched 1995 to commemorate author of The Quiet Man. Stories up to 2,500 words. Entry fee £3 per story. First prize £500. Deadline May.

Waterford Review Competition

Margaret Power, Garter Lane Arts Centre, 22a O'Connell Street, Waterford. tel. 051-55038.

Poetry (any length), short stories and non-fiction (up to 2,000 words). Entry fee £4 for three pieces of poetry or two pieces of prose, £1 for each additional entry. First prize £100 in each

category, plus publication in The Waterford Review *anthology. Deadline October.*

Whitbread Book of the Year and Literary Awards

Booksellers Association, Minster House, 272 Vauxhall Bridge Road, London SW1V 1BA. tel. 00-44-171-834-5477.

Annual awards for published books made in two stages. Five category winners (novel, first novel, biography, children's novel, poetry) are awarded prizes of £2,000 each, and an overall winner is then named Book of the Year (£20,500).

Whitehead (O. Z.) Play Competition

Society of Irish Playwrights, Irish Writers' Centre, 19 Parnell Square, Dublin 1. tel. 01-872-1302.

One act stage play. Open to Irish playwrights and foreigners resident in Ireland. Entry fee £10. First prize £500. Deadline May.

Windows Poetry Competition for Students

Windows Poetry Competition, Nature Haven, Ligaginney, Ballinagh, Co Cork.

Poetry in English or Irish. Open to students 12-18 years. Entry fee £1 per poem. First prize £30.

Very Special Arts Young Playwright Programme

Very Special Arts, City Arts Centre, 23-25 Moss Street, Dublin 2. tel. 01-677-0643.

Plays on theme of disability, any length, written for maximum of four actors. Open to anyone 12-18 years or still in full-time second level education. First prize professional production and tour of play. Deadline June.

Organisations

The Arts Council

70 Merrion Square, Dublin 2. tel. 01-661-1840. fax 01-676-1302. Literature Officer: Laurence Cassidy.

Founded in 1951 to stimulate public interest in and promote the knowledge and appreciation of the arts, the Arts Council operates under the Arts Acts 1951 and 1973, which define the arts as: painting, sculpture, architecture, cinema, print-making, design, theatre, dance, music, opera, literature and "the fine and applied arts generally". The Council operates three main strategies to achieve its goals: the giving of advice on the arts; the giving of grant-aid to artists and arts organisations; and policy-making in the different art forms and arts practices.

The work of the Arts Council's Literature Department is focussed on the following five strategic areas.

Writers

The Council's support for the writer includes the Aosdána scheme, an annual programme of bursaries in creative literature, and a number of other monetary awards such as the Denis Devlin Memorial Award for Poetry, An Duais don bhFilíocht i nGaeilge, the Macaulay Fellowship and the Marten Toonder Award, as well as travel grants and the Artflight scheme (see Bursaries and awards). The Council is also prepared to co-fund writers in residence with various institutions such as county libraries, universities, hospitals, prisons, etc. subject to available budget. In addition, the Council offers assistance to literary festivals.

Literary organisations

The Council supports a number of literary organisations, usually of international, national or regional significance, which in turn promote different sectors of literature and the book world—e. g. the Irish Writers' Centre, Ireland Literature Exchange (ILE), the Irish Book Publishers' Association (CLÉ), and Poetry Ireland.

Publishers

The Council offers grants and loans to Irish publishers to enable them to publish books of contemporary literature and other works of contemporary culture. It offers three types of assistance: (1) Company Profile Assistance, for companies which create "mixed lists", i. e. lists which are part literary and part other categories; (2) Administration Grant Assistance, for literary houses, i. e. where the majority of titles are literary or artistic; (3) Title-by-title Assistance, whereby the publisher requests that the Council examines individual titles for grant aid.

Grant aid is also available for the publication of bilingual titles and translations from the Irish. The Council is anxious to assist the publication of translations in English of contemporary literature in Irish, thereby making it available to a wider readership. The bilingual format, especially for poetry, is one which the Council considers. In addition, Irish publishers may apply for translation fees for the translation into English of contemporary literary works in foreign languages. Projects involving translations of foreign-language works into Irish should be addressed to Bord na Leabhar Gaeilge. Detailed advice on all matters relating to literary translation is available from ILE (Ireland Literary Exchange, see below). Further assistance for the publication of translations is available under the Authors' Royalty Scheme, a fund of grants and loans to assist publishers to commission new work, to commission translations, to repatriate the rights of titles, etc. Of special interest to the Council here is the translation of significant works from contemporary Irish into English.

Applications for assistance by publishers are accepted twice yearly by the Council, on 1 February and 1 September. Details of the procedures for applying for such assistance are available from the Council.

Literary magazines

The Council supports a range of literary magazines, mostly in the English language, though it encourages the magazines it supports to also carry work in Irish. Irish-language literary magazines are assisted by Bord na Leabhar Gaeilge. The literary magazines supported by the Arts Council are usually magazines of national significance and national distribution, such as *Books Ireland*, the magazine of the Irish book world. Community writing magazines are not supported financially by the Council—their editors should apply for assistance to their local authorities.

European programmes

The Arts Council is the national Liaison Office for two action programmes of the European Commission, the Aristeion Prizes (see Bursaries and awards) and the European Pilot Literary Translation Scheme (see ILE below). At press date, the European Commission is developing an expanded programme principally to assist with literary translations. This is expected to replace the European Pilot Literary Translation Scheme in 1996 though no details are available yet.

Publications

Aspects of the Arts Council's literature policy are described in the following publications: *Services in Literature/ Seirbhísí don Litríocht* (1985—on bilingual policy); Developing Publishing in Ireland by Charles Pick (1988); *Translating the Success of Irish Literature* by Laurence Cassidy (1992—on translation policy); *Report on the Strategic Future of the Irish Book Publishing Industry* (1995); *The Arts Plan 1995-1997* (1995).

Arts Council of Northern Ireland

181 Stranmillis Road, Belfast BT9 5DU. tel.08-0232-381591. Literature Officer: Ciaran Carson.

The Council provides grants, awards, bursaries and commissions to artists to encourage and facilitate creative work, as well as supporting professional arts organisations on specific conditions designed to secure arts programmes of high quality. Applications for awards are invited during April of each year by public advertisement. The Arts Council of Northern Ireland and the Arts Council jointly fund a number of awards and initiatives. See also Bursaries and Awards.

Booksellers' Association of Great Britain & Ireland (Irish branch)

54 Middle Abbey Street, Dublin 1. tel. 01-873-0108. Chairman: David O'Mahony.

Represents interests of over 100 Irish booksellers, wholesalers, school and library suppliers and provides potential members with information on opening a bookshop. Also administers Book Tokens scheme in Ireland and compiles a weekly bestseller list for the media.

Booksellers Association of Great Britain & Ireland (Northern Ireland branch)

Secretary: Elizabeth McWatters, 89 Galwally Park, Belfast BT8.

Chartered Institute of Journalists

EETPU Section, 5 Whitefriars, Aungier Street, Dublin 2. tel. 01-478-4141. Chairman: James Wims, tel. 044-74615.

Inaugurated in Ireland in 1890, the Chartered Institute is the world's oldest professional body for journalists and others working in the print and broadcast media. It awards the letters MCIJ to suitably qualified members as well as its Fellowship (FCIJ), and its multilingual press card is recognised internationally. The Irish region of the Institute represents members north and south. Its aims are the protection of its members, the advancement of journalism as a profession and the upholding of ethics and a code of professional conduct in journalism.

CLAI (Children's Literature Association of Ireland)

The Church of Ireland College of Education, 96 Upper Rathmines Road, Dublin 6. tel.01-4970033. Secretary: Liz Morris.

CLAI's primary aim is the promotion, through lectures, seminars and publications, of quality reading for the young. Issues lists of recommended children's books and publishes a magazine, Children's Books in Ireland, *twice a year. Membership is open to anyone interested in any aspect of children's reading.*

CLÉ (Cumann Leabharfhoilsitheoirí Eireann: Irish Book Publishers' Association)

Irish Writers' Centre, 19 Parnell Square, Dublin 1. tel. 01-872-9090. President: John Spillane. Administrator: Hilary Kennedy.

Clé was founded in 1970 to promote Irish published books both at home and abroad. The association presently has 49 members for whom it organises training and educational activities. Also lobbies and liaises with government agencies and the EU to protect and enhance the interests of its members.

Film Base

(Centre for Film and Video) Ltd, The Irish Film Centre, 6 Eustace Street, Dublin 2. tel. 01-679-6716. Information Officer: Tom Maguire.

A non-profit organisation whose remit is to provide information, assistance and support to its 450 members on all aspects of the film business. Offers advice on ground level training in the different aspects of the film industry and opportunities for employment. Administers a low budget short film fun in conjunction with RTÉ and assists with hiring of production equipment and film distribution. Also provides information to production companies both here and abroad on financial and logistical possibilities of making films in this country. Publishes bi-monthly magazine, Film Ireland.

Film Makers Ireland

6 Eustace Street, Dublin 2. tel. 01-671-3525. Chairman: Kevin Moriarty.

Sole representative organisation of independent film and television directors and producers. Its main aim is to represent the interests of independent film makers in the economic and cultural development of an indigenous Irish film and television industry.

ILE (Ireland Literature Exchange)

Irish Writers' Centre, 19 Parnell Square, Dublin 1. tel. 01-872-7900. fax 01-872 7875. Administrator: Mark Caball.

Supported by the Arts Councils in the Republic and Northern Ireland, by the Cultural Relations Committee of the Department of Foreign Affairs and by Bord na Leabhar Gaeilge, ILE aims to increase the readership of the literature of Ireland, primarily through translation, in international markets. Working in cooperation with the publishing industry, ILE's primary role is the provision of financial support for the translation of Irish literature, in both English and Irish, into other languages. Under the provisions of the European Pilot Literary Translation Scheme, ILE also offers assistance to Irish publishers wishing to commission translations of foreign-language works into English or Irish. Publishers in the target language are eligible for grants of up to 100% of the translator's fees. ILE also acts as an information centre for Irish and foreign publishers and is establishing a database on the Irish book world which includes information on writers, translators and publishers.

Irish Children's Book Trust

The Irish Writers' Centre, 19 Parnell Square, Dublin 1. tel. 01-872 1302. Chairman: Robert Dunbar. Secretary: Mary Murphy.

Founded in 1989, the ICBT is a voluntary organisation whose aims are to make books more accessible to children of all ages, and to encourage and facilitate Irish authors of children's books. Administers the annual Bisto Book of the Year Award and runs a Summer School for Children's Literature in association with CLAI (see above). The Trust is also building a collection of Irish children's books which is housed at its room in the Irish Writers' Centre and will be made available for students and researchers.

Irish Copyright Licensing Agency

Irish Writers' Centre, 19 Parnell Square, Dublin 1. tel. 01-872 9090. Administrator:

Orla O'Sullivan.

The Irish Copyright Licensing Agency encourages respect for copyright, licences users for copying of extracts from published works, collects fees for such copying, pays authors and publishers their share of the collected fees, and institutes legal proceedings for the enforcement of the rights entrusted to it.

Irish Educational Publishers' Association

c/o Gill & Macmillan Ltd, Goldenbridge Industrial Estate, Inchicore, Dublin 8. tel. 01-453-1005. Chairman: Maurice O'Driscoll. Secretary: Hubert Mahony.

Represents the principal publishers of educational books and materials in Ireland: Folens, Veritas Publications, School and College Publishing, Educational Company of Ireland, CJ Fallon, Gill & Macmillan, Celtic Press, An Gúm, Authentik, Exemplar Publications and Mentor Publications.

Irish Film Board

The Halls, Quay Street, Galway. tel. 091-61398. Administrator: Tracy Geraghty.

Promotes the creative and commercial elements of Irish film-making and film culture for a home and international audience. Each year the Board supports a number of film projects in development and production by way of debt/equity. Normally three submission deadlines annually - dates and application procedures are available from the above address.

Irish Film Institute

The Irish Film Centre, 6 Eustace Street, Dublin 2. tel. 01-679-6716.

Administers the Irish Film Archive, which is responsible for acquiring relevant film material, restoring, preserving and cataloguing it and making it accessible to interested parties, professional or otherwise. Also runs a reference library for use by film students, researchers, scriptwriters, etc. Both services are available by appointment only.

Irish Translators' Association

Irish Writers' Centre, 19 Parnell Square, Dublin 2. tel. 01-872-1302. Secretary: Miriam Lee.

Represents the interests of translators at both national and international level. Members benefit from inclusion in the ITA Register, which provides up-to-date information on each member to publishers and other users. Members also receive information on recommended rates for translation, on professional indemnity insurance and on new developments in the profession. The ITA publishes a quarterly newsletter containing information on job opportunities and news and articles on subjects of specific interest to translators. There are two categories of membership, ordinary and professional: the first is open to all translators, full- or part-time, staff or freelance, and anyone with a professional interest in translation; the second is open to translators who meet certain criteria laid down by the membership committee—this is aimed at raising the status of the translation profession in the European market. Application forms are available from the above address.

Irish Writers' Centre

19 Parnell Square, Dublin 1. tel. 01-872-1302. Director: Peter Sirr. Administrator: Jacinta Douglas.

As well as providing accommodation and an administrative structure for the Irish Children's Book Trust, the Irish Translators' Association, the Irish Writers' Union and the Society of Irish Playwrights, the Irish Writers' Centre aims to: assist writers pursue their work; promote cultural exchange of a literary nature between Ireland and other countries; organise and promote a programme of literary activities, including seminars, readings, lectures and workshops; cultivate an interest both at home and abroad in the work of contemporary Irish writers.

The events programme runs throughout the year and covers all kinds of writing, providing a platform for emerging as well as established writers. You don't have to be a member of any of the Centre's constituent organisations to attend these events or to avail of its information services. The office is open for inquiries 10am-6pm, Monday to Friday.

The Centre also runs a programme of workshops and courses in all forms of writing, including writing for radio and television, poetry and journalism. All of the instructors are writers with experience of teaching crea-

tive writing. Workshops are generally limited to 15 participants, and the emphasis is practical rather than theoretical, focussing on basic writing skills.

In addition, the Irish Writers' Centre is the national centre for community writing and provides a number of services in this regard, including the Writers in the Community scheme.

Irish Writers' Union

19 Parnell Square, Dublin 1. tel. 01-872-1302. Secretary: Clairr O'Connor.

Aims to advance the cause of writing as a profession, to achieve better remuneration and conditions for writers and to provide advice and support to individual writers in their relations with publishers and other users of their work. The Union has been particularly active in the area of copyright and is currently engaged in setting up a mechanism for licensing and collecting in relation to the reproduction of copyright material. Part-time or full-time writers may apply for membership. Full membership is open to writers who have published at least one book. They may be creative or non-fiction writers and may write in English, Irish or any other language. A category of associate membership is open to writers whose work is as yet unpublished in book form. The membership fee for all categories is £20. Application forms are available from the above address.

Library Association of Ireland

53 Upper Mount Street, Dublin 2. tel. 01-661-9000. Secretary: Brendan Teeling.

Established in 1928 to represent the profession of librarianship in Ireland, to promote the professional and educational interests of members, and to promote and develop high standards of librarianship and of library and information services in Ireland. Publishes a quarterly journal, An Leabharlann, The Irish Library *and* Directory of Libraries in Ireland, *both jointly with the Library Association, Northern Ireland Branch.*

Library Association (Northern Ireland branch)

Tollycarnet Library, Kinrosse Avenue, Belfast BT5 7GH. tel. 08-012318-5079. Secretary: Adrienne Adair.

The Northern Ireland branch of the UK Library Association, works closely with the Library Association of Ireland to promote the interests of libraries and librarians throughout Ireland.

National Newspapers of Ireland

Clyde Lodge, 15 Clyde Road, Dublin 4. tel. 01-668 9099. Chairman: Louis O'Neill. Representative body of Ireland's daily and weekly newspapers.

National Union of Journalists

9th Floor, Liberty Hall, Dublin 1. tel. 01-874-8694. Secretary: Eoin Ronane.

The NUJ's primary aim is to seek and secure employment of staff journalists in all areas of the media, including newspapers, magazines, broadcasting and PR, and most of its resources are channelled in this direction. But it does have a freelance sector (there are 400 members of the Dublin freelance branch alone) and will intervene wherever possible to protect the rights of freelancers. To qualify for membership, a journalist must be able to show that the bulk of his earnings come from journalism (though there is a reduced earnings facility which ensures that members never pay more than 1% of their earnings), must be proposed and seconded by two other members, and must be voted in by his local branch. Application forms are available from the above address.

Poetry Ireland

44 Upper Mount Street, Dublin 2. tel. 01-6610320. Director: Theo Dorgan. Administrator: Niamh Morris.

Ireland's national poetry organisation. Publishes a quarterly magazine, Poetry Ireland Review, *and a bi-monthly newsletter of upcoming events and competitions. Also organises tours and readings by Irish and foreign poets and administers the Austin Clarke Library, a collection of 6,000 volumes. Members qualify for discounts on selected poetry books. Poetry Ireland is the national centre for literature-in-education and administers the Writers in Schools scheme.*

Provincial Newspapers Association of Ireland

33 Parkgate Street, Dublin 2. tel. 01-679 3679.

An association of weekly regional newspapers which negotiates on behalf of its members with the National Union of Journalists.

Reading Association of Ireland

Blackrock Teachers' Centre, Carysfort Avenue, Blackrock, County Dublin. Secretary: Muireann Máirtín, tel. 01-289-4102.

Aims to stimulate and promote interest in reading, to assist the professional development of teachers in reading and to disseminate knowledge helpful to the solution of reading problems. To encourage the writing, publication and appreciation of children's literature in Ireland, the RAI presents two awards biannually, the RAI Children's Book Award and the RAI Special Merit Award. Also publishes the magazine Reading News.

Society of Irish Playwrights

19 Parnell Square, Dublin 1. tel. 01-872-1302. Chairman: John Lynch. Secretary: Vera O'Donovan.

Represents the interests of playwrights in Ireland. Membership is confined to playwrights "who have written substantial texts requiring the services of actors for performance", and who have had at least one such text publicly and professionally performed by a recognised professional management. Membership is determined by majority vote of the Council of Officers and costs £30. Members of the Irish Writers' Union who fulfil the requirements of the Society do not need to pay a subscription.

Trade and Professional Publishers Association

31 Deansgrange Road, Blackrock, Co Dublin. tel. 01-289-3305. Chairman: David Markey.

Voluntary body set up in 1976 to represent the interests of trade magazine publishers.

Tyrone Guthrie Centre

Annaghmakerrig House, Newbliss, Co Monaghan. Administrator: Bernard Loughlin. tel. 047-54003.

Former home of Sir Tyrone Guthrie, the legendary theatre director, who bequeathed it as a residential centre for artists from both north and south. The centre is supported jointly by the two Arts Councils and residents make a contribution towards costs. Mainly intended for serious creative artists in any discipline, but may be available for small group projects according to circumstances. Enquiries and applications should be made to the Resident Director at the above address.

Subsidise or do it yourself?

It's a common enough scenario. You've sent your manuscript off to every publisher in the country, and beyond, and all you've got to show for your efforts is a huge collection of rejection slips. You're seriously thinking about giving up the writing game and channelling your creative energy into train-spotting instead. Then one day you're flicking through the newspaper and a small advert catches your eye: "Authors Wanted: Does Your Book Deserve to be Published? We Offer a Professional Publishing Service." Well, you're an author, and yes, your book deserves to be published, so you apply forthwith and spend the next few days in euphoric anticipation of a positive reply.

Into the honey-trap

Your publisher replies all right, and he's mad keen to publish your book. But times are hard, and he's wondering if you could see your way to contributing to the cost of production. About £3,000 should do it . . .

What you're dealing with here, of course, is a vanity publisher, one of the sharks of the publishing business. They prey, literally, on the vanity of the unpublished writer, exploiting his or her burning desire for publication. It's a sound enough principle on which to run a successful business—it's probably fair to say that no vanity publisher ever lost money—but it's a business underpinned by a fundamental deception.

The vanity publisher promises publication, but he is really not likely or even able to deliver on that promise. He'll take your money and he'll *print* your book, sending you a few finished copies as proof, but that's as far as it goes. He won't bother to sell it to the bookshops and libraries (they know his kind and wouldn't buy it anyway), and he won't send review copies to the press (most wouldn't touch a vanity book with a bargepole), or undertake any of the other activities normally associated with publication. Why bother? Where's the incentive? He's already covered his costs and made a tidy profit: time to move on to the next mug.   But how can you tell whether or not somebody is a bona fide commercial publisher or a vanity publisher? Well, the very fact that the company is advertising for authors is a giveaway. Commercial publishers don't need to advertise: they get more than enough unsolicited submissions already, from authors and literary agents. But then you already know that—they keep telling you in their rejection letters, and the only reason you've even considered the vanity route is that no other publisher will give you the time of day. So where do you go from here?

Subsidy publishing

There are some sorts of book that real (or 'ethical') publishers would be happy to have on their lists but which they cannot see as profitable, or which would represent too great a risk for them. These are likely to be academic works of limited potential sale or those for some other specialist and restricted readership, written or compiled by an acknowledged expert or a symposium. Other such books might include the histories of major companies or institutions or those aimed mainly at the members of some association.

Honest-to-goodness real publishers might well be open to the suggestion that the risks in such publishing should be carried by the academic body, institution or firm in question, or conceivably by a commercial sponsor. They are less likely to be interested in coming to an agreement with an individual who wants to bet on the likelihood of commercial success for a book which they or other publishers have rejected. If the publisher genuinely admires the book—even a novel—to the extent that he would be proud to see it under his imprint, a rare exception may be made.

Only approach publishers with a good track record. Vanity publishers like to call themselves subsidy publishers, and real publishers are therefore shy of the expression—and certainly never advertise for books or like to show they are in the market for 'shared-risk' publishing, which is perhaps the better term for it. Occasionally they may drop a hint in their rejection letter with some such remark as "We would have liked to see this book on our list, but unfortunately cannot see how we could sell enough copies to justify taking it on."

At all events, if you can come to such a subsidy-publishing agreement, the publisher will insist on applying his own editorial, design and production standards, and the author or institution will be in the position of any other author in this respect. The piper, essentially, must call the tune.

Such agreements should provide for payment to the 'client' on a fixed or sliding scale when and if sales exceed some agreed quantity, so that he can preserve some hope, however faint, of recouping some of his investment. The publisher may agree to fix the price at something lower than the economically reasonable level if the client wants the book to be accessible for instance to students or to members of his association, and this is reasonable from the publisher's point of view too, since he does not want clearly overpriced books on his list.

There must be strong mutual respect between client and publisher in such an arrangement, and no hidden agenda on either side but, however much the two parties trust each other, it is wise to define everything in a clear written agreement, with provision for what happens if there is disagreement, or if the book sells better or not so well as expected. Are the books the client's property in the final analysis, or is he only subsidising production by and for the publisher? Such details should be clearly defined from the start.

Do-it-yourself

The other alternative to vanity publishing is doing it yourself, whether as author, as private entrepreneur or as a firm, institution or association.

Self-publishing was a popular option at the beginning of this century, especially amongst maverick authors like D. H. Lawrence and James Joyce, and it's currently enjoying something of a revival. Booker Prize-winner Roddy Doyle published his first novel, *The Commitments*, himself, having been rejected by several commercial publishers. And one of the books on the 1994 Booker short list, Jill Paton Walsh's *Knowledge of Angels*, was also self-published. So, why isn't everybody doing it?

Well, first of all, it's a high-risk venture—you just might lose every penny you put into it (with vanity publishers, at least, there's the perversely reassuring certainty that you *will* lose everything!). Secondly, it's a lot of hard work: you're responsible for everything, from typesetting your manuscript to selling and distributing the finished book. And finally, it's not a cheap option: producing a relatively modest 3,000 copies of a 240-page paperback will set you back over £3,000. Almost as much as a vanity publishing deal—but at least you can be sure that any profits on this venture go straight into *your* pocket.

Local history societies, writers' groups and such bodies are regular self-publishers, usually on the basis of furthering their aims and—hopefully—breaking even.

But what are the chances of covering your costs? There are any number of variables. The received wisdom with regard to self-publishing, and indeed publishing in general, is that non-fiction is a safer bet than fiction. The institution, firm or specialist writer who puts out his own book will have a clear idea of the kind of person who will buy it, and how to sell it to them. Fiction, on the other hand, is a more instinctive affair, and poetry even more so: either you've got a well-written, engaging story, which will appeal to a substantial readership or you haven't, and that's very much a matter of opinion. But even in the field of fiction there have been some self-publishing success stories in this country in recent years. Nobody—not even Roddy Doyle—has been known to make a mint out of publishing their own fiction (much less poetry), but then it's not money that motivates most self-publishers. Rather, it's the satisfaction of seeing their books in print and in the bookshops by virtue of their own unstinting efforts.

Of course, regardless of the market for a book, unless it is produced to a professional standard, nobody is going to take it seriously. But that doesn't mean it's going to cost you a small fortune. Basically, the more you can do yourself, the less the book is going to cost, and the greater your chances of making a profit, though it's

important to recognise from the outset that there are certain tasks which are beyond your expertise. The following sections on producing and marketing books are to help you decide what you can do yourself and what you need help with.

Further Reading

Vanity & Press: the Proper Poetry Publishers by Johnathon Clifford (available from the author at 27 Mill Road, Fareham, Hampshire at Stg£6 + £1.50 p&p) is as much a guide for unpublished poets as an exposé of vanity publishing, but still the most thorough insight into the sinister workings of the vanity press you're likely to find.

How to Publish Yourself by Peter Finch (Allison & Busby, £6.99) is the definitive guide to self-publishing, from somebody who's been through it all before.

Producing a book

Editing

Particularly if you are publishing your own book, you would be very well advised to use the services of a professional editor or, at least, a literate and scrupulous person who will not mind questioning you and suggesting cuts or improvements. There are two quite different editing operations, substantive and textual. Substantive editing is done early, perhaps even when the manuscript is still incomplete, and is concerned with what the author perhaps (because it is his or her baby!) is blind to.

The substantive editor reads critically, on the look-out for padding and repetition, over-complexity or inconsistency of style, and generally reads for 'sense'. In fiction he or she might suggest re-ordering of material, more or less explanation or description, tightening passages, adding or deleting dialogue, even some variation of the plot. In non-fiction there can be even more sweeping suggestions. A writer who does not welcome and consider such ideas (however painful!) may be foolish, for the editor represents the reader, and the reader is who the book is for. Professional writers polish and re-write—sometimes several times—as a matter of course, but still welcome the suggestions of their editors.

Text editing is more laborious and mechanical, dealing with spelling, punctuation and grammar, consistency in the use of names, dates and numbers and such dull minutiae. Again it is hard to edit ones own work because one tends to see what one expects to see, and it is best if possible to find a professional or someone familiar with print who will check points with you.

Considerable costs can be saved by preparing a manuscript before it is set in type, rather than making heavy proof corrections which have to be paid for.

Indexes

Not every book needs one but, in those that may be used for reference or study as well as reading, an index may add greatly to the value. Professional indexers (see page 127) should be consulted early and, if possible, commissioned to work with you on this difficult job, which will involve decisions about subject-headings and which names or placenames are to appear. There is no fixed rule as to what is indexed or how, and you should think in terms of who will use the book and what for, rather than provide endless references that will never be used. A book on the Little People does not need an index showing that the Little People are mentioned on pages 2, 4, 10-12, 47 etc. A well-organised reference or text book may not need an index at all if everything is where you would expect to find it. Your typesetter's machine may be able to produce an index automatically from reference codes placed in the text on your word-processor, so that when the book is paged and in its final stages, the correct page numbers will be automatically generated with the list of references, but final editing will surely be necessary to ensure that the conventions of alphabetical order are followed, and that cross-references ('see' or 'see also') are properly placed.

Footnotes

There is much to be said for the argument that if information is worth giving in a footnote it would be better given in the text. The habit of footnoting springs from the academic thesis in which the writer has to show he has done his research thoroughly. Certainly critical readers of academic works often want to know the source of information, and then be able to extend their own research into it by using a bibliography, but even for them there is much to be said for mentioning the source in the narrative. Properly, footnotes are at the foot of the page where they are referred to, but more and more often nowadays writers are cleaning up their pages by putting their notes either at the end of the chapter or at the end of the book. The second strategy is the better, since it is often difficult to find the end of the chapter. At the end of the book the notes can still be grouped under chapter numbers, so that the reference numbering can start again with each new chapter, and instead of seeking note 325, you look for note 10 of chapter 16. However when this expedient is used, remember that the reader may not remember which chapter he is in, and you should provide the information in the running head, instead of making him turn back to seek the chapter heading.

Printers

For books or magazines, go to a printer who specialises in books or magazines. Have a very clear idea of what you want, specify it in writing (it may help to talk to a printer first), and then submit the specification to two or three printers for quotation, naming a quantity and also getting a price for 'per hundred run-on' (or thousand). Ask to see other books they have produced, and don't go by the price alone, but consider quality and the printer's attitude to scheduling.

Typesetters

It is more and more common nowadays to have the typesetting done by a specialist typesetter and for the printer to work from 'camera-ready copy', so shop around among typesetters as well as printers, asking to see what they have set before. Be clear exactly what you want, and ask for sample pages. Desk-top publishing (which simply means typesetting on a small computer) is available even from amateurs and semi-amateurs, who output the finished pages either on their own laser printer or via a professional typesetter from their discs. Such DTP op-

erators are not all experienced in book design and production, and you should be extra careful that they can do what you want to reasonable standards and deadlines. Professional firms accustomed to book or magazine work may well be cheaper and better in the long run, and there is a lot to be said for using the printer's own typesetting, since his commitment to quality and to deadlines will then be stronger.

Bookbinders

Most book printers are associated with bookbinding firms—if they don't have their own plant—and it is usually best for the part-time publisher to ask the printer to be responsible for the binding (to subcontract it), so that there is no confusion between the two and the printer is responsible for deadlines and final delivery.

How many to print?

It is quite normal not to bind all the books you print, but to ask the printer to hold some of the sheets and bind up more if and when the book is selling well, since some binding processes (particularly sewn case binding) are less quantity-sensitive than printing. That way you commit less capital and could bind the remainder as paperbacks at a reduced price. Another strategy is to have a commitment from the printer on the price and likely time-schedule for a reprint, and to 'go back for more' if the book sells unexpectedly well. Some publishers, with this in mind, will print extra quantities of covers, jackets and even colour illustrations in the first instance, since the set-up costs for these might make a short-run reprint too complicated and costly, while a 'run-on' is relatively cheap. The most common mistake is to print too many books, and the quantity decision is perhaps the hardest the publisher has to make, balancing quantity against unit cost and price and all these against the probable or possible demand. The best figure to start with is the *certain* sale, and to treat the potential additional sales with great caution.

Casting off

It is important to know as early as possible how many pages your book will make in the type and layout you have chosen. This is called casting off and, although the printer's estimator sees it as part of his job, it is something you should consider doing first, since it may make you change your mind about the format, type or layout. At its simplest it is a matter of counting how many words the specimen page contains, and dividing that into the total words of the book. For greater accuracy, count the letters (printers talk in terms of so many thousand ens, meaning characters and spaces), which is not as laborious as it sounds if your typescript is fairly consistent—multiply average characters per line by lines per page and then by pages. Allow for a half-page blank at the end of each chapter and for the space taken by chapter headings, illustrations, index and prelims. You are then in a position to plan and design more accurately, and to make such decisions as whether chapters should always start on a right-hand ('recto') page, which will in turn demand an allowance of *more* than a half-page white at the end of chapters. There's a lot of arithmetic in good publishing!

Pricing

Because of the nature of printing—high prime costs and relatively low running costs—there is a temptation to over-estimate the sale using the backwards-logic that the books will then be cheaper. But paper is very expensive, and you do have to pay for running-on, so it is wise to price a book on the basis that you will only sell a *certain* quantity, and will move into greater unit profits if sales exceed that number. Different publishers use different formulas for the delicate calculations involving quality, quantity and price.

In general it is false economy to reduce the typesize or margins to make fewer pages. It is better to decide on the page design and pagination appropriate to the book and keep that as a fixed datum, trying variations of quantity, paper qual-

ity, binding style and perhaps number of illustrations to achieve the right price. Books (except perhaps for children's ones) are not very price-sensitive; people buy them by subject, author, reputation or simply on impulse and do not seem to be much influenced by the difference between £5.95 and £6.95, or between £14.95 and £16.95. It is quality rather than pence that will make them hesitate.

Book design

As with editing, there is much more to designing a book than most first-time publishers realise. The decision on page size ('format'), the choice of paper and of the binding method and materials and the basic typography can all make the difference between an attractive book, appropriate to subject and readership, and one that looks amateurish—and all these things affect the cost of production.

'Appropriate' is the key word because people judge books by reference to other books. They expect a novel to look like a novel and to be priced like a novel and the same goes for cookery books, guidebooks, biographies, poetry and the rest.

You will probably not sell any more copies by producing your book very much more cheaply or more elaborately than comparable books. Good taste and care for details of editing and design cost little and are what will make the difference.

Design-it-yourself?

An amateur with a good eye, an interest in how books look and a lot of care—ideally with the collaboration of typesetter and printer accustomed to book production—can design a satisfactory book, but you should consider seeking the services of a professional, particularly for a complex book. For illustrations (including maps or diagrams), covers and jackets there is no substitute for professionalism and experience, and it is by accepting poor work (perhaps not wanting to hurt the feelings of a friend or relation with artistic ambitions) that first-book publishers very often spoil the ship for a ha'porth of tar. There are many more competent designers and illustrators than we list below who are not members of the Society of Designers in Ireland or of Illustrators Ireland. Judge them on the work they have done, and on their enthusiasm and ideas.

Dummies

Even experienced book designers usually ask for a 'dummy' to be made up and bound to see how the book feels, and what the thickness ('bulk') and weight will be. A dummy is also useful for designing the cover (for a paperback) or jacket (for a cased book) so that it fits exactly.

Typography

Readers and book-buyers are generally conservative about book typography, and publishers unfamiliar with the basic traditional rules of thumb should look at books in a bookshop or library and study the conventions carefully. Books for continuous reading (as distinct from reference works) are generally set in a 'roman' or serif typeface in a size between 10pt and 14pt, and justified (i. e. with right margins squared off). Sanserifs (like this) or **less familiar designs (like this)** are seldom used for straight text, but there is scope for experiment with poetry or other books that are to be enjoyed for their own qualities. The size of type and the space between lines ('leading') must relate to the length of line so that ideally on average there are no more than twelve words to the line, so the reader's eye doesn't tend to skip or repeat lines. Breaking and hyphenating words at the end of lines is generally preferred to the expedient of letterspacing to fill out a line, or to overwide word-spacing. With a wide book or a small typesize it is often wise to consider setting the type in two columns for optimum legibility, as we have done here.

Margins and running heads

Margins should be carefully planned.

There is a convention that the outer and bottom margins should be slightly wider than the inner and top ones, but care should be taken that the inner margins are not so narrow as to prevent easy reading of a book with a tight binding—the dummy will help here too. Page numbers (often called folios) can be centred at top or bottom or ranged ('flush') to the outer margin. Unless there is good reason to number the prelims separately (often i, ii, etc.), it is sensible to count from the first page of the book, though the convention is not to show a number on the title-page or other display pages. Where a running head is necessary (book title on the left pages, chapter title on the right is a good idea), it can be centred or flush to the back margin, ideally in the same size as the text or smaller, and distinguished by being in italics or small capitals. Often the page number can be conveniently included on the same line as the running head. The intelligent 'analytic' use of running heads can be very helpful in text or reference books so that the browser can find a section or subject. In histories and biographies one should consider running the year as a changing running head, in guide-books a place or county name and so forth. Novels and such need no running heads.

Text setting

Generally for continuous reading there should be no extra space between paragraphs, and the first line of a paragraph should be indented by about the same width as the type size. Usually the first paragraph of a chapter or after a heading is 'full out' and not indented. Get two specimen pages set (or two copies of one) and paste them into the dummy. Continuous reading demands simplicity and 'plainness', so don't use fancy typefaces or elaborate decorations. Inviting pages are those in a type big enough to be easy on the eye, with good spacing between the lines. Long quotations or excerpts are often indented and set in a smaller type. The indentation can be helpful (it need be only from the left margin, not both), and avoids the need for quotation marks, but the change in typesize is a poor tradition better abandoned: if a passage is worth quoting, it is no less important than the main text—and indeed is often more important.

Set it yourself

Most typesetters can now produce setting from the author's word-processor discs at considerable savings (since no second keyboarding is necessary) and it is well worth checking beforehand exactly what can be reproduced and how. For instance the codes for italics or for accented characters on your word-processor may or may not be translated properly by the typesetter and you may have to insert codes like <I> for italics or <B> for bold, followed by <D> to revert to roman. The normal typist's habit of making two spaces after a full stop should be abandoned, and the typewritten convention for a dash (space, hyphen, space) will not look well in print - as this shows; many typesetters can convert two hyphens together without spaces into a proper dash or 'em-rule'—thus—or a spaced 'en-rule' – thus – is acceptable. Opening and closing quotation marks are often not differentiated on word-processors, but most typesetters can programme their machines to alternate them. The search-and-replace facility of word-processors can be used to insert or change codes, either automatically or on a replace-or-skip command. Spelling programmes are dangerous, and should be used with care and intelligence.

Prelims

Design of the 'prelim' pages and chapter headings should be simple and clear. Where possible stick to the same typeface as for the text, and use only one or two bigger sizes of type. Amateur typographers tend to use bold, italic, capitals and many different sizes and achieve only ugly confusion. Decide whether titles should be centred or ranged from the

left, and be consistent in this. Contents lists and indexes are for looking up a page quickly and easily, so don't follow the annoying old convention of separating the title from the page number with a long row of dots, particularly if the lines are spaced close together.

Proof reading

Guidebooks for writers traditionally show elaborate examples of the professional way to correct proofs, but in fact such marks can be misunderstood, particularly now that typesetting is often done by non-professional compositors. The only important thing is to make absolutely clear what you want. Correct boldly in a coloured ink or your marks may be missed altogether. Mark the word or passage for correction with a neat circle and put the correct form (not in capitals but *as you want it set*) in the nearest margin. Show where an insertion should go with an inverted V, and put what is to be inserted in the margin followed by a diagonal stroke /. What is to be put in italics is usually underlined once, with 'ital' in the margin, double-underline for SMALL CAPITALS, triple-underline for FULL CAPITALS, wavy-underline for **bold type**, with the appropriate 'sm. caps' or 'bold' in the margin. Delete by striking through the letter or words with 'del' or d/ in the margin; change a letter or word by striking through it, adding the inverted V and putting the correct form in the margin followed by the diagonal stroke /. Distinguish clearly between I and 1, O and 0, Z and 2 etc. (put 'fig.' in brackets to indicate a number). Don't leave anything to the intelligence or imagination of the typesetter; if there can be doubt write out clearly what you want done. Don't query anything unless some more decisive proof-reader will follow you. 'Line out, see copy' is not very helpful: it is better to write out the line (or word) that has been missed and show where it is to be inserted.

Above all, be scrupulous: it pays.

Illustrations

Nowadays illustrations including photographs can often be well printed on the ordinary text pages, and so next to any references to them. Those that must go sideways on the page should *all* run up the page (i. e. with the caption on the right) whether on a right-hand page or left. Illustration sections on art (shiny) paper may be necessary if the desired quality cannot be achieved on the text paper, and that is better and cheaper than choosing a shiny paper for the whole book, which can make it tiring to read.

It is common to bind-in 'sections' of eight, twelve or sixteen illustration pages, but instead consider breaking them down into four-page sheets and inserting them or wrapping them round the text sections. That way illustrations can be scattered through the book and placed nearer the references to them. Particularly with colour illustrations, the small added expense of this bindery hand-work is repaid because the book may look—and be—better value for it. In choosing photographs, be very firm about quality and reject grey or fuzzy shots unless they have some unique intrinsic value. A good picture well reproduced in a decent size is much better than six small or poor ones. In commissioning illustrators, get them interested and involved in the book and its design, and see how their work can be integrated into the page design.

Covers of cased books

It is the convention for lettering (usually 'blocked' with gold or other foil rather than printed) to run *down* the spine, not up, if it cannot be fitted legibly across the thickness of the book. That way, when the book is lying face up, the spine of case or cover is legible.

Jackets and paperback covers

Paperback covers and the jackets for cased books are all-important in selling books, and amateurism here and in illustrations can spoil an otherwise good book. Few amateur artists or designers can compete successfully with professionals in illustration or jacket design, and most publishers who design their books in-house commission such artwork from experienced artists. Rather than specify exactly what you visualise, it is usually better to let the artist see the typescript or proofs, explain what needs explaining, and ask for his or her own ideas. A good designer or illustrator is likely to have better ideas than yours, and will certainly carry them out better than if he or she has to 'work to rule'.

Simplicity is the hallmark of good cover design, and amateurs often make the mistake of trying to include too many graphic ideas or images. Striking lettering alone may make a better cover than an illustration, and a strong two-colour combination is likely to be better than a rainbow effect.

Specify the very minimum of wording and expect the artwork to do the selling. Ask the designer to design the whole cover or jacket, including the blurb and whatever other material is necessary on the back or the flaps.

Magazines

Much that is said of books above is true of magazines too, with obvious differences. Regularity and punctuality are vital, not least because otherwise contributors, advertisers, typesetters and printers will learn not to respect your deadlines—and readers will get confused or tire of it.

Often a magazine will be started as a quarterly or half-yearly with the aim of becoming more frequent later—but the change is seldom made. It is probably a mistake because magazines are very much a matter of *habit* for both their producers and readers, and it is best to start as you mean to go on. It takes two or three issues before a magazine finds its real character, and frequency helps you reach that stage before you have lost your readership. A slim monthly or two-monthly is likely to be much more viable than a thicker quarterly or half-yearly (and much more topical and useful in terms of news and coming events), and you are likely to get higher advertising sales—usually the main revenue—that way.

You should foster a very good working relationship with your printer, and if possible have a written contract covering two or three issues in advance, specifying deadlines for copy and delivery. If you do not pay the printer and typesetter regularly, they cannot be expected to produce your magazine on time.

Producing a magazine is hard work but good fun, and it can do a lot for a company, association, trade or any group of people with shared special interests.

Book production stages

To sum up, producing a book should be done more or less in this order:

Writing, rewriting, polishing.

Substantive editing.

Text editing.

Choice of illustrations or commissioning an illustrator.

Decision on index or no index.

Planning the prelims.

Designing the basic page.

Rough cast-off.

Specification for quotation including format, paper, type, margins and binding—and schedule dates.

Specimen pages from typesetters.

Quotations from printers and typesetters.

Revised cast-off.

Dummy from printer/bindery.

Commission cover or jacket design.

Price and quantity decisions and reconsideration of earlier decisions.

Last polishing, text editing and (if setting from discs) editing of codes.

Typesetting.

Proof-reading and correction, placing illustrations and captions.

Page adjustments, prelims editing.

Final proofs.

Indexing.

Camera-ready copy to printer.

Printing and binding.

But you're not a publisher yet—you have to market the book, for it won't sell itself, and that's another day's work.

Editors and indexers

The following are members of the Association of Freelance Editors, Proofreaders and Indexers, all people of skill and experience in one or more of those capacities.

The association recommends standard hourly rates from £11.75 for proof-reading and simple indexing to £13.85 for rewriting, sub-editing and research, with £1 added for on-screen work. For project management the rate is £16 per hour. The AFEPI's liaison officer is Éilis Brennan (address below). In addition two experienced indexers are listed below.

Ashe, Eleanor
58 Woodford Lawn, Monastery Road, Clondalkin, Dublin 22. tel. 01-459-1302.
Editing; experience in publishing, literary and educational; BA.

Brennan, Éilis
27 St Mary's Road, Ballsbridge, Dublin 4. tel. 01-668-8491.
Experience in research in humanities, editing and proof-reading in English and Irish, indexing own editing work, layout and keyboarding. BA, HDipE.

Caslin, Pauline
11 Eglinton Court, Donnybrook, Dublin 4. tel. 01-269-6684 fax 01-269-6684.
Editing, proof-reading, rewriting, translating from French; experience in design, photography and printing.

Clancy, Julitta
Parsonstown, Batterstown, Co Meath. tel. 01-825-9438 fax 01-925-9438.
Indexing (inc. IBM computer), archives; experience in law, industrial relations, humanities. Registered Society of Indexers, highly commended in Wheatley indexing awards. BA, Diploma in Archival Studies.

Croker, Colm
Cronaguiggy, Crolly, Letterkenny, Co Donegal.
Copy editing, proof-feading, rewriting; experience in history (esp. Irish), humanities, theses, reference apparatus.

Cuffe, Nuala
Ashley, Quinn's Road, Shankill, Co Dublin. tel. 01-282-3630.
Editing, proof-reading; experience in science, medicine, education, business, technical. BSc, HDipE.

Farren, Gráinne
74 George's Avenue, Blackrock, Co Dublin. tel. 01-283-2848.
Editing in English and French, proof-reading, indexing; experience in humanities, feminism, music, photography, periodicals.

Greenwood, Gloria
Skeagh, Skibbereen, Co Cork. tel. 028-38259 E-mail BrendanLyons@top-psi.gn.apc.org
Editing (Apple Mac), rewriting, proof-reading, indexing, typesetting; experience in humanities; BA Hons.

Hamilton, Olivia
Moyne, Durrow, Co Laois. tel. 0502-36135
Editing, research, proof-reading, word-processing. Experience in humanities. MA.

Hassell, Aisling
1 Ulverton Court, Ulverton Road, Dalkey, Co Dublin. tel. 01-280-7027 fax 01-280-6753.
Editing, abstracting, rewriting, proof-reading; experience in engineering, sciences, mathematics, computing; WordPerfect, Lotus 123, MacWrite. BA, MSc, BAI.

Litton, Helen
45 Eglinton Road, Donnybrook, Dublin 4. tel. 01-269-2214 fax 01-269-2214.
Indexing (IBM, both disc sizes, WordPerfect 5.1 or ASCII), proof-reading, copy editing; experience in history and archaeology. Member of the Society of Indexers. MA.

Lunn, Bridget
2 James Street North, Dublin 3. tel. 01-836-4062.
Editing and copy editing, rewriting, indexing, proof-reading; experience in religion (esp. Catholic theology), literary criticism.

O'Brien, Brendan

62 Broadford Lawn, Ballinteer, Dublin 16. tel. 01-494-2442 fax 01-494-2442.

Copy editing, proof-reading, book design and production, DTP; experience in scientific, technical and other non-fiction.

Ó Brógáin, Séamas

Lexis Editorial Service, 2 Upper Galloping Green, Stillorgan, Co Dublin. tel. 01-283-6511 fax 01-288-4068.

Editing in English and Irish, consultancy, manuscript evaluation; experience in non-fiction, reference and educational.

Power, Winifred

7 Donnybrook Terrace, Douglas, Cork. tel. 021-894030.

Editing, copy editing, rewriting, proof-reading; experience with academic and educational texts; IBM, 3.5" discs, WordPerfect 5.1 and Word 2.0; MA.

Reeners, Roberta

Cronroe, Ashford, Co Wicklow. tel. 0404-40517.

Full editorial and production service to disc or bromides; associated with designers, artists, photographers etc. Apple Mac with MS Word, Quark XPress and Adobe Illustrator.

Roberts, Helen

15 Glen Park, Comber, Newtownards, Co Down. tel. 08-01247-878983.

Editing, proof-reading; experience in scientific and educational, primary through college. BSc.

Williams, Jonathan

2 Mews, 10 Sandycove Avenue West, Sandycove, Co Dublin. tel. 01-280-3482.

Literary agency; evaluating, editing, rewriting, proof-reading, consultancy; experience in Canada as well as Ireland; represents 32 writers as agent.

Winder, Stephen

38 Hamilton Street, Dublin 8. tel. 01-454-2516.

Editing, proof-reading; experience of reports, theses, law, periodicals; BA Hons.

Indexers

In addition to the above, some of whom are also members of the Society of Indexers, there are two members of the latter available for indexing work in Ireland.

McGoldrick, Fiona

16 Ballycannon Heights, Meelick, Co Clare. tel. 061-454458.

Accredited by the Society of Indexers.

Smith, Gráinne

4 Victoria Terrace, Bangor, Co Down BT20 5JB.

Indexing; experience of law work.

Designers and illustrators

The following members and licentiates of the Society of Designers in Ireland are those who provide either specialised book design services or general graphic or typographic design or illustration—we have not excluded those who say they specialise only in commercial, packaging and other such design work. SDI members are bound by a code of professional conduct. Full membership (MSDI, the first list) is for qualified and experienced designers; licentiates (LSDI) are those not yet elected to full membership, but who are likely to be very competent. For clients who are not familiar with designers' work, SDI recommends two alternative forms of commission. **'Limited competition'** is where the client invites written quotations from two or more designers for a specified job and also invites rough design proposals, for which a rejection fee should be stated and paid to the unsuccessful invitees. A **'Commission'** may similarly be an invitation to more than one designer, the successful one to be selected only on the basis of a written quotation, which should include fees for clearly defined stages of design development, including a rough design proposal; thus the client is free at each stage to continue to the next or, if unhappy with the rough proposal or a later stage of development, is committed only to the fee quoted to that stage. The SDI suggests a scale of fees which, with other details of their code, is available to interested parties. In either form of commission, copyright in final design work belongs to the the client unless otherwise agreed, but copyright in rough design proposals remains the property of the designer. A list of illustrators follows.

MEMBERS OF SDI

Adams, Aislinn
24 Abercorn Square, Inchicore, Dublin 8. tel. 01-453-0714.
Graphic design and illustration.

Banahan McManus
30 Morehampton Road, Dublin 4. tel. 01-668-9322 fax 01-668-9367.
Graphic design.

Michael Begley & Associates
60 Percy Lane, Haddington Road, Ballsbridge, Dublin 4. tel. 01-668-9988 fax 01-660-8808.

Beirne, Brendan
149 Gaybrook Lawns, Malahide, Co Dublin. tel. 01-845-2291 fax 01-845-2920.

BFK Design Group
29 Westland Square, Pearse Street, Dublin 2. tel. 01-671-8844 fax 01-671-8045.
Graphic design, cartoons.

Bolger, Bill
31 Morehampton Terrace, Donnybrook, Dublin 4. tel. 01-668-4405.
Book design and typography.

Cooke, David
21 Shanard Road, Santry, Dublin 9. tel. 01-842-9083 fax 01-842-9083.

Book and magazine design and illustration.

Corporate Image
64 Northumberland Road, Ballsbridge, Dublin 4. tel. 01-660-8944 fax 01-660-9817.
Graphic design.

Creative Inputs
121-123 Ranelagh, Dublin 6. tel. 01-497-2711 fax 01-497-2779.
Graphics and DTP.

Creavin, Ann
83A Grosvenor Lane, Rathmines, Dublin 6. tel. 01-496-0863.
Typography.

Custodian
48 Fitzwilliam Square, Dublin 2. tel 01-676-9299 fax 01-676-9299.
Graphic design, print management consultancy.

Design Desk, The
4 Lower Mount Street, Dublin 2. tel. 01-676-5518 fax 01-661-9879.
Design administration.

Design ID (Dublin)
9 Morehampton Road, Donnybrook, Dublin 4. tel 01-667-0044 fax 01-667-0127.
Design administration.

Design Image
Kingram Mews, 6 Kingram Place, Dublin 2. tel. 01-676-2465 fax 01-676-4508.
Book design.

Design Point
12 Princes Street, Derry BT48 7EY. tel 08-01504-263504 fax 08-01504-263504.
Graphic design, design management.

Design Works
42 Eastmoreland Lane, Upper Baggot, Street, Dublin 4. tel 01-668-8235 fax 01-660-0586.
Graphic design and consultancy.

Dowling & Dowling Design
8 Barrymore Court, Sallybrook, Glanmire, Co Cork. tel 021-821971 fax 021-866352.
Graphic and comprehensive design service.

Dry, Simon
188 South Circular Road, Dublin 8. tel. 01-453-9973.
Graphic design consultant.

Em Space
Cullellen, Lower Glenageary Road, Dun Laoghaire, Co Dublin. tel. 01-284-2152 fax 01-284-2152.
Graphic design and illustration.

Dynamo Design Consultants
58 Tritonville Road, Sandymount, Dublin 4. tel. 01-668-6300 fax 01-660-8261.
Graphic design.

Flanagan, Paul Creative Photography
Tramway House, 17a Gilford Road, Sandymount, Dublin 4. tel. 01-269-7533 fax 01-269-7645.
Photography.

Graphiconies, The
22 South Great George's Street, Dublin 2. tel. 01-679-4173 fax 01-679-5409.
Graphic and book design.

Hooper, Síobhra
97 Upper Georges Street, Dun Laoghaire, Co Dublin. tel. 01-280-3770 or 01-280-6972 fax 01-280-1558.
Graphic design and photography.

Hope, Steven
21 Shenick Grove, Skerries, Co Dublin. tel. 01-849-1697 fax 01-849-1697.

Book jackets and illustration.

Identity Business, The
Distillery Building, Fumbally Court, Dublin 8. tel. 01-454-6377 fax 01-454-6383
Graphic design.

Information Design
11 Mountpleasant Parade, Ranelagh, Dublin 6. tel. 01-497-4288 fax 01-497-4826.
'Design systems for publishing'.

Joseph & Co
Shankill, Co Dublin. tel. 01-282-2311.
Graphic and DTP design.

Kell Marketing Design
14 Grattan Court East, Lower Mount Street, Dublin 2. tel 01-676-4320 fax 01-676-1785.
Graphic design.

Kilkenny Design Consultancy
Castle Yard, Kilkenny. tel. 056-22441 fax 056-22104.
Graphic design.

Kingram Studios
Shaw's Lane, Bath Avenue, Dublin 4. tel. 01-660-1369 fax 01-668-7850.
Graphic design.

Kummer, Ditte
5 Woodcliff Heights, Howth, Dublin 13. tel. 01-839-1572.
Graphic design and illustration.

Kyne, Raymond Design Associates
27 South Frederick Street, Dublin 2. tel. 01-678-9514 fax 01-678-9670.
Graphic design.

McGuinne, Dermot
31 Ballymace Green, Rathfarnham, Dublin 14. tel. 01-494-4247 fax 01-494-4247.
Graphics consultant.

Mason, Barry, Photographer
3 Wilton Place, Dublin 2. tel. 01-676-1449 or 088-566832 fax 01-676-1449.
Photography.

Matthews, Brendan
9 Upper Leeson Street, Dublin 4. tel. 01-668-7803 fax 01-660-2792.
Graphic design and consultancy.

Desmond Meade Design
1 Cedarwood Avenue, Carrigaline, Co Cork. tel. 021-371166 fax 021-373096.

Graphic design.

Meagher, Darina
63 Dartmouth Square, Dublin 6. tel. 01-660-5483 fax 01-660-3710.
Graphic design consultant.

Murphy, Bill
27 Mespil Road, Dublin 4. tel. 01-668-1346 fax 01-660-9660.
Graphic design consultant.

Daniel O'Brien Creative Design
Millmount House, Mary Street, Drogheda, Co Louth. tel. 041-32658 fax 041-32868.
Graphic design.

O'Connor O'Sullivan
52 Northumberland Road, Dublin 4. tel 01-668-2833 fax 01-668-2297.
Graphic design.

PDI (Photo Display Images)
11 Enterprise Centre, Pearse Street, Dublin 2. tel 01-671-7210 fax 01-671-7674.
Photography.

Pinnacle Design Practitioners
5 Herbert Street, Dublin 2. tel. 01-661-0443 fax 01-676-8781.
Graphic design consultancy.

Propellor
Letteragh House, Letteragh, Galway. tel. 091-22786 fax 091-22786.
Graphic and book design.

Rainey Associates
Derryloran Industrial Estate, Cookstown, Co Tyrone BT80 9LU. tel. 08-016487-65335 fax 08-016487-65000.
Graphic design consultancy.

Swan Design Group
13 Clyde Road, Ballsbridge, Dublin 4. tel 01-668-2071 fax 01-668-2729.
Design administration.

Tobin Associates
25 Sibthorpe Lane, Leeson Park, Dublin 2. tel. 01-660-9282 or 088-542060 fax 01-660-9295.
Graphic design.

Nicola Troy
Ardkenna, Bandon, Co Cork. tel 023-41412.
Graphic design.

20-20 Vision
16 Morehampton Road, Donnybrook, Dublin 4. tel 01-660-8044 fax 01-660-8346.
Graphic design.

Visual Image
20 Orchard Green, Blanchardstown, Dublin 15. tel. 01-821-3545 fax 01-821-3545.
Graphic design.

XMI Marketing Services
60a Percy Lane, Haddington Road, Dublin 4. tel. 01-660-3411 fax 01-668-5595.
Graphic design.

Zeus
38 Leeson Place, Dublin 2. tel 01-661-6360 fax 01-661-9298.
Graphic design.

LICENTIATES OF SDI

Breslin, Patrick
Kinacasslagh, Letterkenny, Co Donegal. tel. 075-43165.
Graphic design.

Centraline Creative
1 Fitzwilliam Square, Dublin 2. tel. 01-661-1653 fax 01-661-9899.
Graphic design consultants.

Collins, Jane
Manderley, Woodlawn Road, Killarney, Co Kerry. tel. 064-32322.
Graphic design.

Coughlan, Gillian
26 Dargle Valley, Grange Road, Rathfarnham, Dublin 16. tel. 01-494-3622.
Graphic design.

Cowper, John
123 Lakelands, Naas, Co Kildare. tel. 045-66754.
Graphic design.

Foley, Eamonn
17 Upper Leeson Street, Dublin 4.
Graphic design.

Glynn, Ann

Monmore, Kilrush, Co Clare. tel. 065-51830.

Graphic design.

Healy, John Martin

7 Burgh House, Ardilaun Court, Patrick Street, Dublin 8. tel. 01-660-5590.

Graphic design.

Johnson, Wendy

Kildallon Rectory, Ardlougher, Ballyconnell, Co Cavan. tel. 049-26259.

Graphic design.

Kenna, Hilary

Multimedia Technologies Ireland, Schuman Building, University of Limerick, Castletroy, Co Limerick. tel. 061-333644 ext 5044 fax 061-338173.

Graphic design.

Kilkenny, Geraldine

Newtown, Ballinagh, Co Cavan. tel. 049-37137.

Graphic design.

McIvor, Neil

Design Factory, 3 & 4 Merrion Place, Dublin 2. tel. 01-661-2600 fax 01-661-0572.

Graphic design.

Miller, Brian

c/o 4 Brickhillwest, Cratloe, Co Clare.

Graphic design.

Mustard, Elaine

102 Cabra Park, Phibsboro, Dublin 7. tel. 01-868-2462.

Graphic design.

Sharkey, Niamh

Stonehaven, Dublin Road, Malahide, Co Dublin. tel. 01-845-2365.

Illustration.

Spögler, Lisa

Sycamore Lodge, Deerpark, Killarney. tel. 064-32202.

Graphic design.

Swan, Daniel C.

746 Howth Road, Raheny, Dublin 3. tel. 01-831-0843.

Graphic design.

Thompson, Stephen

9 Pinley Meadow, Ballygowan Road, Banbridge, Co Down BT32 3XT. tel. 08-018206-24978.

Graphic design.

Walsh, William T.

5 Holborn Villas, Bangor, County Down, BT20 5DX. tel. 08-01846-663377.

Graphic design and illustration.

Wilson, Fiona

Apartment 4, Hazelbrook, 65/69 Terenure Road West, Dublin 6W. tel. 01-660-4700 fax 01-660-4918.

Graphic design.

ILLUSTRATORS IRELAND

This is a recently formed association and, while a certain professionalism may be expected from members—many of whom are very experienced, and some also appear also in the SDI list of designers above—no code of conduct has yet been adopted. Organiser is Ed Miliano.

Adams, Aislinn

24 Abercorn Square, Inchicore, Dublin 8. tel. 01-453-0714.

Berkeley, Jon

42 Park Vale, Baldoyle, Dublin 13. tel. 01-668-7945.

Byrne, Tom

10 Stephen's Place, Dublin 2. tel. 01-676-9943.

Cooney, Aidan

35 Maywood Avenue, Raheny, Dublin 5.

tel. 01-831-4533.

Dineen, Cathy

15 Anville Drive, Kilmacud, Co Dublin. tel. 01-288-9910.

Emoe, Nicola

12 Bancroft Park, Tallaght, Dublin 24.

Fitzgerald, Brian

PO Box 4389, Dublin 4. tel. 01-284-6373 or 088-538606.

Graphiconies, The

22 South Great Georges Street, Dublin 2.

tel. 01-679-4173.

Hutchinson, Conor
43 Stillorgan Park, Blackrock, Co Dublin.

Johnson, Shane
9 Kenilworth Lane, Dublin 6. tel. 01-492-4751 or 01-496-5315.

Lynch, P. J.
86 Upper Leeson Street, Dublin 4. tel. 01-668-0317.

MacNamara, Moira
20 Eyre Square, Galway.

Miliano, Ed
Cullellen, Lower Glenageary Road, Dun Laoghaire, Co Dublin. tel. and fax 01-284-2152.

Murphy, Mary
53 Parnell Road, Dublin 12. tel. 01-454-2161.

Pomphrey, Helen
7 Lower Albert Road, Sandycove, Co Dublin. tel. 01-284-1252.

Reid, Chris
52 Stapleton House, 33 Mountjoy Square, Dublin 1. tel. 01-855-1056.

Rohu, Owen
1 Sandymount Road, Dublin 4. tel. 01-668-8273.

Rooney, David
The Loft House, Woodbrook, Bray, Co Wicklow. tel. 01-282-5635.

Short, John
7 Lower Albert Road, Sandycove, Co Dublin. tel. 01-284-1252.

Marketing a book

Assessing the market

Optimism is your worst enemy. Beware of your own enthusiasm, and avoid telling yourself "Everyone will want a copy." Convey realistic enthusiasm to other people and tell them *why* your book may sell, but don't be too credulous about your own sales pitch. Many good books—even potential bestsellers—have been put out by professional publishers never to sell in any appreciable numbers, and this can be due to bad luck as much as to bad planning or marketing. You must be ruthlessly realistic, and if you think your local bookseller will sell a hundred or a thousand copies, go and talk to him and listen carefully to what the real potential is. Booksellers have many thousands of new books to choose their stock from—far more than they could ever stock at one copy each—and they know what really sells and how and why. But don't expect firm orders from bookshops until you can show a jacket or cover, a firm date and a firm price.

Direct-mail selling

If you can identify who are most likely to want your book and can get their names and addresses—perhaps members of an association or of a profession etc.—you may be able to sell copies by mailing a leaflet direct to them with an order form on which publication date, price, postage and order address are clearly stated. You may ask for payment with the order (in which case you are committed to publish or to return the money), or offer to invoice at the offer price on publication. You may get your leaflet enclosed with a magazine or an association's newsletter, which will be cheaper and maybe more effective than an individual mailing. Sometimes you might do a deal with an association or club to offer the book to their members

or subscribers, whereby the organisation makes a small profit on sales.

Pre-publication price

Specialist books, in particular, are often advertised at a 'pre-publication' price with a deadline order date, so that you know the minimum sure sale even before the printing begins—invaluable information! Such a discount offer can be made to and through booksellers (who *may* pass the extra discount on to their customers) as well as direct to potential buyers. But people are lazy and forgetful, and if you mail a thousand leaflets it would be quite normal to receive no more than fifty orders. Thus you must calculate the cost of the leaflet and of addressing and mailing it and be prepared for the value of a few orders to swallow up your expenses.

Pricing

Pricing is dealt with under 'Producing a book', but marketing factors should be strong in your decision. Underpricing is the amateur's most frequent mistake, leaving him with insufficient margins to cover marketing expenses and discounts, but there are other factors: the bookseller earns a smaller margin on a cheap book, and his customer may be suspicious of a book at £3.95 when comparable ones are priced at two or three pounds more.

Advance information

Booksellers and wholesalers are accustomed to being informed of forthcoming books six months or more before publication, with reliable details of pagination, size and price, a good short 'blurb' and a reproduction (at least) of the jacket or cover. Keep the information very short and to the point, as they are busy people. The information comes in the form of advance trade information sheets (often accompanied by the jacket or cover itself) or in catalogues, and is often directed at libraries as well as the book trade. It should also go to book-trade magazines. In Ireland, *Books Ireland* magazine publishes seasonal lists of forthcoming titles without charge to the publisher in September, February and April. In Britain and other countries trade magazines are more selective, but free listing is available in Whitaker's weekly microfiche *New and Forthcoming Books* and in their CD-ROM *Bookbank* which in turn gets a listing in *The Bookseller* magazine in the week for which publication was announced. For this you should fill in and return one of Whitaker's yellow forms at least three months before publication. *BookFind* CD-ROM is similar to *Bookbank* but includes quite elaborate descriptions of content and reader level. It is published by Book Data Ltd, who make a small charge to publishers for inclusion of forthcoming and in-print titles. Addresses on p. 01420.

Cataloguing in Publication

Another form well worth getting and completing three months or more before publication is an application for Cataloguing-in-Publication (CIP) data from the British Library. The catalogue data as supplied by them (don't prepare or change it yourself) may be printed on the book's title verso (copyright page) as an aid to librarians and bibliographers. It will also automatically appear in the *British National Bibliography* (see p. 142) and get you some orders from other libraries.

ISBNs

There is an worldwide scheme whereby each book is assigned an International Standard Book Number, which can be (and is quite often) used by shops and libraries to order copies. Publishers usually apply for a group or block of numbers, and then assign one to each book themselves; a one-off publisher can apply for a single number for a book. The number consists of ten digits in four groups, thus: 1-98765-456-2. The single first digit 1 or 0 indicates a British, US or Irish pub-

lication, the next group is special to the publisher, and the same for all his books (unless he runs out of numbers and has to be assigned a new 'publisher prefix'). Big publishers have a 2-digit prefix, the smallest have 7 digits. The next group identifies the book, and strictly a new number should be got for a new (revised) edition; different ones are assigned for instance to the hardback and paperback. The last digit is arrived at by an arithmetical formula, and computers are programmed to recognise it as correct or incorrect and so reject or query ISBNs which are misquoted.

You should apply for an ISBN (or choose one from a block assigned to you) as soon as the book's title is settled from the ISBN agency (see page 142). The ISBN should be given on the title verso; it should also appear on the cover or jacket, often (but not necesarily) as part of a bar code.

Bar codes

If your book is likely to be sold in major bookshops or by other retailers, they will appreciate the provision of a machine-readable bar code, preferably on the back cover for their Electronic Point of Sale (EPOS) system. Bar codes for books incorporate the ISBN, but prefixed with the European Article Number for books, 978, and with a different final check digit. The artwork is available from suppliers of bar codes listed in the Golden Pages directory.

Statutory deposit copies

The publisher is required by the Copyright Act to deliver (in effect post) a free copy of a newly-published book or magazine to each of fifteen named libraries. This requirement has little or nothing to do with copyright, which belongs to the author or publisher whether or not the free copies are sent. The only advantage accruing to the publisher is the consequent free listing of the book by the libraries, which ought to engender orders from other libraries and institutions. The two

134

most significant listings are those by the British Library in the *British National Bibliography* (which also includes Irish-published titles) and by the National Library of Ireland in an annual book, the *Irish Publishing Record*, which appears up to eighteen months after the year in question. The copies required by Irish law for British libraries are generally sent together to a Copyright Agent in Dublin. This and the addresses of other 'statutory libraries' are listed on page 142.

Dates

Fix a publication date well in advance (six months or more) allowing time and to spare for all the production and publicity work, which should be carefully scheduled so that everything—particularly bookshop stock—comes together on publication date, with allowance for delays and accidents. In advance publicity you may just name a month, but as soon as possible fix a firm date that you can stick to. Apart from the confidence it gives to the trade and media, this helps you organise deadlines and insist on them. Your realistic scheduling and confidence in it will be conveyed to the people who matter. Too many books are announced for September and then appear two weeks before Christmas, when booksellers are too busy selling the stock they've got to be bothered with a new book. Few printers or binders can be counted on to adhere precisely to promised delivery dates (often justifiably blaming the publisher), and it takes time to invoice and deliver to the trade, so fix publication for at least two weeks after you are sure copies will be available. Some booksellers may be tempted to start selling before publication date, but that shouldn't bother you much; it is better than failing to get copies to them on time.

Leaflets

Mailshots, advance information sheets and other such leaflets can themselves be expensive. Consider whether one all-purpose leaflet would serve, but remember that if it incorporates an order form it should encourage the user to address it to a bookshop, with a space for the shop's rubber stamp, perhaps. When used as a direct-mail shot, your own rubber stamp could be used instead.

Subscribing

Most publishers have salesmen ('reps') who visit bookshops regularly, either bringing advance information sheets or backing up the mail-shots and showing the covers, or even proof copies of the books. They will look for advance orders for ('subscribe') their books between six and two months before publication. Often the bookseller will simply take a note of what he might require and, only when he has seen all the new books announced for that month or season, will make his final decisions and send out his orders.

Freelance reps

Most publishers' representatives 'carry' more than one publisher's list. Those who aren't employed exclusively by one firm or group may be open to taking on a small publisher's product(s) on commission, since this may help to defray their travelling expenses. You might find one in the list below (page 143), or a bookseller might recommend someone who is known to take small commissions. Like most other people in the book trade, reps are often well-read and interested in the products they deal in. Get them personally interested, give them a proof copy to read, and seek their advice about your publicity strategies, and the design and pricing of your book; they know better than most what works and what doesn't.

Trade discount

Booksellers expect full trade terms, which means 35% discount off the selling price. A shorter discount may be expected on single-copy orders, or at least the cost of delivery or postage may reduce the effective discount on such orders to 25%. Staff are paid salaries, shops cost money to rent and run, and a publisher would be foolish to begrudge such discounts. Bookselling is not a very profitable business.

Wholesalers

Booksellers generally do not like having to order a book from a 'once-off' or new publisher (except perhaps for a book of local interest), and prefer such books to be available from a wholesaler, to minimise their paper-work and accounting. Your first priority marketing should therefore be to book wholesalers who, in order to give full trade terms, will need a discount of 50% or more on the selling price. This may be negotiable according to the quantity they order—but see 'Returns' below: it may be in your best interests to supply wholesalers with smaller quantities and top up the stock after a regular check on actual sales. A good wholesaler with an interest in your book will encourage his reps to sell the book to shops, so make a point of seeking wholesalers' advice, keeping them informed and generally trying to make them feel partners in your enterprise.

There are very few important wholesalers in Ireland, and you might get a better deal by appointing one of them as the sole distributor, named in all your publicity. But make sure first that he covers *all* the bookshops.

Returns

Most books nowadays (but not where a single copy is ordered for a customer) are supplied on sale or return, and it is impossible for a bookseller to display a book and let customers handle it and at the same time to keep it in mint condition. Sunlight through a shop window may make the cover inks fade; dust and handling and time will take their toll, but still the book may be returnable for credit if the bookseller has used his best efforts and it remains unsold. If not, he will be very wary about his next order for that publisher's books. Some publishers keep a spare stock of jackets (which reps may carry with them on their visits) to refresh

booksellers' or returned stock of casebound books. Returned paperbacks very often have to be written off. Even the 'remainder' merchants who wholesale bargain books—your last resort for old stock—want their books to look fresh and new.

Settlement terms

The book trade is not known for rapid payment. Three months' credit is quite normal, but be prepared for it to be stretched to six.

Distributing yourself

Fulfilling orders means invoicing, packing books and delivering or mailing them, all of which is laborious and expensive. You will begin to see how useful and important wholesalers and distributors are when orders begin to come in in quantity, and you may well decide to pass your own orders on to the the wholesaler as being simpler and cheaper than despatching and invoicing yourself. If mailing yourself, choose simple but protective packing materials for different quantities well in advance and note weights and the different postal rates. Booksellers are accustomed to getting a delivery note with books, and an invoice separately. If you enclose the invoice with the books, draw attention to it on the packing with a large 'invoice enclosed'. The invoice should clearly show the selling price (which ideally should be printed on cover or jacket as well), and the discount, and should quote the order number or the name of the person you received the order from.

Trade advertising

It is very seldom indeed that press or magazine advertising will pay for itself. There are only two sorts of press advertising most publishers find worth while, and one only in very special circumstances. The first is in trade magazines to back up their advance information sheets and their reps' visits—which can indicate the strength of their commitment to a title, and suggest that there will be commensurate publicity to the public when the book appears to back up the booksellers' efforts.

Such specialised trade advertising is cheap, and the size of the advertisement is probably relatively unimportant, since those concerned will scan all the advertising as a matter of course. Part-time and small publishers may use this as a substitute for reps' visits or even instead of mailing advance-information sheets, but nothing can replace the human touch in the book trade, and the telephone is another possible substitute for personal bookshop calls. We have to declare an interest, because we publish the only Irish trade magazine, *Books Ireland*. Look at a copy and assess the likely selling-value of a small space, bearing in mind all the reservations about advance information mentioned above.

Consumer advertising

The other sort of book advertising to be considered—very cautiously—is in consumer papers and magazines, on radio and on television, especially where the audiences are of the sort you want to target. Mostly such advertising is only used to 'keep the top spinning' for books that are already stocked and selling widely, because the costs and the risks are so high. Where a book is being talked about and written about, the sales may be reaching the point at which prime costs are well covered, and the profit margin on each sale is therefore high, but it takes a careful calculation to decide whether the margin is high enough to benefit from advertising; you may simply be throwing the margin away, just when it is turning profitable. Publishers who resort to such expenditure often think equally in terms of encouraging booksellers to re-order, and to display the book in question prominently—if possible in a window. Particularly with books there is a lot in the motto that "success breeds success". Some mass-market publishers may risk money to make a book look like a success before it has begun to sell, but such invest-

ment is seldom for the small publisher. Another characteristic of the trade is that a book can 'take off' and head the bestseller lists, and next week promptly stop selling for no reason.

Point-of-sale publicity

For a book that promises well in the shops, booksellers may welcome display material like 'crowners', posters, dumpbins and window-dressing material. But if they don't see the book as promising sales in real quantities, such material will be an embarrassment to them and a waste of the publisher's money, since space in the shop is valuable, and they will dump unnecessary display material. Booksellers may also like publisher's catalogues and leaflets to give out to their customers, but again such things take valuable space, and they know that customers' first priority is to browse among books. Some shops maintain a mailing list and send out catalogues or other sales material regularly to customers. Find out what they want and will use, and provide it.

Reviews

Most magazines and newspapers, and many radio and TV chat-shows, give space to book reviews or news, but very selectively. The more important ones receive many hundreds of books in a year and publish reviews of at most ten per cent of them—often much less. Literary editors tend to have a leaning to certain sorts of book (or feel their readers do). The problem for publishers is that most of their books won't be reviewed, but if they don't send copies they *certainly* won't; like so much else in publishing, sending out review copies is an incalculable risk. Unfortunately at the heel of the hunt reviews are not believed to be very influential in terms of sales.

The best strategy is to pick your review media carefully in the light of the sort of books they do review, and the sort of readers you hope to influence. Send copies well before publication date, even scheduling different lead times for different media, with the object of getting maximum exposure on or just after publication date. Our own *Books Ireland* magazine is unique in guaranteeing at least a mini-review (a listing and comments on potential, market, design, value and so on) in the first issue after a book is received—as long as it is from an Irish publisher, or an Irish author, or of particular Irish interest—but we need the copy two or three weeks before our publication date. The chance of a longer review thereafter is higher than in most other magazines.

Don't ask or expect media to *request* a review copy; they see such a request as a commitment which they might not be able to fulfil. Don't enclose a long letter—or any letter—with a review copy, but just a slip stating the title, author, price, publisher and publication date "for the favour of a review"—with any useful information (distributor's address) which is not given on the book itself. An enclosed press release may help to underline newsworthiness.

News

The best free publicity is to make news with your book. In local media that is relatively easy, but with a little thought some controversial or topical point might attract national news editors' interest. Press releases about books being published are seldom used unless there is a genuinely newsworthy angle and the copy can be seen as really interesting rather than simply a disguised effort to obtain free advertising. A big launching party with important people present might get you a photograph or a gossip-column mention. Select periodicals and radio and TV programmes that might be tempted to interview the author or even set up a discussion about the book, and lay siege to their producers and researchers. Chat shows are a happy hunting ground, and Gay Byrne's radio show is said to sell more books than any other medium—but every other publisher is trying to get his books mentioned on it! There are a few

professional book publicists practising in Ireland, and their addresses are given at the end of the list of publishers' representatives on page 144.

Word of mouth

Personal recommendation sells most books, other than those by famous names or about a subject in the news. In all your publicity seek to emphasise interesting talking points. Prepare the ground for press releases or approaches to features editors, columnists or chat-shows by telephoning first, and/or follow up a mailing with a phone call. Don't waste journalists' time with sales talk, but get them personally interested and leave them with the impression that they are getting something 'exclusive', or would be privileged to run an author interview or whatever.

Serialisation

An extract in a newspaper or magazine is a very desirable form of publicity—and even an unexpected windfall in terms of revenue. You should try to sell serial rights to any periodical that might regard the book as likely to make a good 'feature', and some features editors have been known to fall for the carrot of exclusivity, and pay handsomely for the privilege of publicising your book. A national Irish paper is reputed to have paid £8,000 for a recent single piece featuring extracts from an Irish author's new book, which must have gone a long way to paying its production costs—and of course engendered a lot of bookshop sales.

The 'serialisation' might consist of only one extract (or several edited to make a single article). Careful editing may be required to single out and knit together the most newsworthy excerpts to the right length for the publication in question. This may be best done by author or publisher, especially if they have journalistic experience, since they know the bits to go for. Such pre-editing of feature-length pieces could make the difference between acceptance and rejection. Magazines, especially those for women, often carry serialised novels, and again these usually have to be specially edited so that instalments are the right length. Payment for these may not be very high, but the resultant book sales make them worth pursuing.

Readings

Public readings in bookshops or libraries, particularly of poetry or short stories, are occasionally organised and can spark off word-of-mouth sales, but the public do not as a rule find them very attractive events unless the author is famous. Prepare them well and exert good showmanship and stagecraft so that the audience is really entertained and not bored. Writers are sometimes shy or not good at public performance; don't force such people into readings that might do them more harm than good. Radio stations—even local ones—might be interested in putting out a short story or the serial reading of a novel. As with magazine serials, special editing may be needed to make an extract or instalments fit the time-slot, and this is well worth while, since book sales will certainly follow.

Launches

A party to launch the book for local booksellers, journalists and the author's friends need not be expensive, and you might get a commercial firm to host or sponsor it. Such parties seldom get reported at all, but if you can get a VIP to do the launching that might attract the media, and even TV cameras if they've nothing better to do. Invitations to press people should enclose a 'teaser' press briefing to make the most of anything topical or controversial about the book, so that they feel they'll miss a good story if they don't come. Mainly such parties are a little thank-you or ego-boost for the author and those who helped with the book. If the party is reasonably big, invite a local bookseller to attend (with credit-card machines) to look after sales on the spot. The publisher can sell his own books, but for goodwill and diplomacy it is no harm to give this help to (and get this help from) a bookseller, who will then tend to push your book all the harder on his shop floor. Plan the order of events at such parties, with the bare minimum of speeches, which should all be short, entertaining and to the point. If people are to be thanked by name, make very sure that nobody is left out.

Signings

Bookshops like to host an autographing session, as it brings people into their shop and guarantees some sales. Advance media and shop-window publicity is important for such events, and the thoughtful publisher will make sure there's a crowd (his staff and the author's friends and relations perhaps), which itself will attract passers-by and ensure the author doesn't feel lonely sitting at a table with nobody asking him to autograph his books.

Bestseller lists

These are widely published and read, and influence the reading public, the trade and literary editors. The Irish ones are compiled and supplied to the media by the Booksellers Association, who telephone different shops and wholesalers every week to determine (not very scientifically!) what is selling best. Such is human nature and the book trade that sometimes the books that are most heavily stocked (rather than most heavily sold) get into the listings on the 'success breeds success' principle, especially in quiet times.

Tell the trade

If you have advance warning about media exposure—an interview, news item or feature—tell bookshops and wholesalers about it, telephoning or faxing if necessary with essential details. Often with beginner's luck or through some original idea or a contact a new publisher will achieve a publicity coup, only to find that there are no books in the shops—or not enough—to satisfy the sudden demand.

After the event booksellers will be reluctant to order more because they know the public have short memories. Make sure there is stock *before* the appearance of a press piece or the broadcasting of an interview, even if it means special delivery and the promise of collection of returns afterwards. But don't cry wolf until you are certain what will appear and when.

Getting everything together

All the above should keep you very busy. Books do not sell themselves, and every phone call or visit you make, every publicity strategy, pays off if you have a good product at the right price, and can orchestrate production and marketing properly. The book trade and the media are hungry for good books and interesting authors, but titles tend to come and go quickly and briefly.

Most books will sell from fifty to a hundred per cent of their total sales in the first few weeks—sometimes days—after publication, so everything you plan and do should be aimed to accomplish the maximum exposure and sale then. The greater the initial sale, the more likely the book will be kept on the shelves in the weeks and months afterwards as a 'sleeper' with a continuing demand. Even books whose main sale will be steady rather than immediate (like a tourist guide) need a launch with initial publicity. Once booksellers get into the habit of stocking such steady sellers, they will continue, but the process has to start somewhere.

Magazines

Marketing a magazine is more difficult than marketing a book, and there are no media that review periodicals. Of the strategies discussed above, only direct-mail selling, wholesaling, 'making news' and word of mouth can be used effectively. The subscriptions resulting from even a well-targeted mailshot will be no better than those for a book, though there is one advantage here: you can mail free sample copies, since the aim is subscriptions rather than single-copy sales.

Formalities for periodicals

While, as with books, the Copyright Act 'statutory deposit' copies of each issue have to go to the fifteen libraries, they usually only list the first issue, so the expenditure will bring you nothing. Magazines should obtain an eight-digit International Standard Serial Number (ISSN) from the agency listed on page 142, and print it on the cover or title page. The consequent listing may bring you subscriptions. In Ireland VAT (currently 21%) is charged on magazines, and your cover price should include it ("£2 inc. VAT"), even if you are not registered as a VAT trader; in that case include an equivalent amount in your invoices to recover enough to pay the VAT that your printer will charge.

News wholesalers

With a new magazine, news wholesalers may 'box copies out' (i. e. on spec) to newsagents, and if sales are good the newsagents will then order regular copies, but if they're not and they don't, there is not much you can do the second or thirtieth time around. Wholesalers expect a 40 per cent discount—on the copies they sell. Those they don't sell will be nominally returned, which means in effect destroyed unless you are quick on your feet.

Subscription agencies

In Britain, America and Europe there are a few big subscription agencies whom you should inform about your magazine (even if the demand is likely to be restricted to Ireland, because they get subscriptions from libraries and institutions here), offering them at least 15 percent discount on your postal subscription rates. Blackwells, Dawson, Swets & Zeitlinger, Ebsco and Faxon are the big international agencies to pursue, and when they list your magazine, many smaller national ones will pursue *you*, but strangely there is no good agency based in Ireland.

Publicity for periodicals

If you break a good news story, the news media may mention where it first appeared, but probably won't, and there's no copyright in news. A strong controversy in your columns may get you better mentions and word-of-mouth sales. The best strategies are to provide *benefits* to the reader like discounts on other purchases or—and this is really the same thing in another guise—to be really *useful* to them in providing information they might otherwise miss. For entertainment and distraction, people buy mass-circulation magazines; for useful information on their profession, trade, hobby or other special interest—anything from local history to technology, slimming or the shoe trade—they will subscribe to the sort of magazine that one man or a spare-time group can produce. Literary magazines enjoy (or rather suffer from) a very restricted readership, though booksellers, as distinct from newsagents, may agree to stock them.

Advertisements in periodicals

The advertisements in specialised magazines may be as valuable to the reader as the editorial, but beware of letting the advertising tail wag the editorial dog. If you woo advertisers by promising articles on their products or services, your game will soon become obvious to readers, and you won't be seen as balanced or impartial. If your magazine is authoritative and independent, people will buy the advertising for what it is worth to them—which may be just prestige and goodwill.

Subscription renewals

It is worth repeating what we said about magazines in the notes on producing a book: frequency and regularity are all-important, because magazines are a matter of habit, even addiction. It is easy to forget to renew a subscription, and once you have lost a reader you may not regain him, so insert clear and forceful reminders when the subscription is due to expire, and continue sending a few more issues with increasingly urgent reminders; it will pay you handsomely, and the renewal will of course date from the previous expiry. That way your circulation will increase instead of taking two steps back for every step forward.

Copyright Act libraries

Publishers in the Republic must by law deliver thirteen copies of every publication (including periodicals, maps, etc.) to the following within a month of publication. The best edition should go to those marked *, the most numerous edition to the others. Although this requirement is part of the Copyright Act, compliance with it—or otherwise—does not affect copyright, which belongs in any case to the author or the commissioner of the publication. The requirement is thus not only misleading, but is also a baneful imposition particularly upon publishers of small or special editions, and is of little or no benefit to them or to the public. While it is desirable that the National Library should have a copy of each publication for the public record, there is no reason why they should not be endowed by the state to purchase copies, rather than require publishers to supply them free as a tax. It is notable that the law in both the United Kingdom and Ireland ignores Northern Ireland, while recognising Scotland and Wales as 'nations'.

Dublin City University
Glasnevin, Dublin 9
1 copy

Irish Copyright Agency
Trinity College, Dublin 2
6 copies for
Bodleian Library, Oxford
British Library *
Cambridge University Library
National Library of Scotland
National Library of Wales
Trinity College Library, Dublin

National Library of Ireland *
Kildare Street, Dublin 2
1 copy

National University of Ireland
Merrion Square, Dublin 2
4 copies for
University College Cork
University College Dublin
University College Galway
St Patrick's College, Maynooth

University of Limerick Library
1 copy

NORTHERN IRELAND

Publishers in Northern Ireland have to deliver six copies of each of their publications to the Copyright Agent, 100 Euston Street, London NW1 2HQ for the following. Note that the British Act recognises Trinity College Dublin, not our National Library—but it does not add new universities from time to time as does the Irish Act did recently.

Bodleian Library, Oxford
British Library *
Cambridge University Library

National Library of Scotland
National Library of Wales
Trinity College Library, Dublin

Bibliographical services

Book Data Ltd (BookFind CD)
2 King Street, Twickenham, TW13RZ.

Books Ireland (Listings)
11 Newgrove Avenue, Dublin 4.
tel. + fax 01-269-2185.

Cataloguing in Publication
CIP Office, British Library, Store Street, London WC1. tel. 00-44-171-636-1544.

International Standard Book Number
ISBN Agency, 12 Dyott Street, London WC1A 1DF. tel. 00-44-171-836-8911.

International Standard Serial Number
ISDS Centre, National Library of Ireland, Kildare Street, Dublin 2.

Whitaker (Books in Print, Bookbank)
address as for ISBN agency above.

Publishers' representatives

Members of the Book Representatives Association of Ireland which is mainly a social organisation of reps and publishers' agents. The secretary is Genny Kelliher (address below).

Adamson, David
41 Shandon Park, Knock Down, Belfast BT5 6NW.
Macmillan representative.

Brookside Publishing Services
2 Brookside Road, Dundrum, Dublin 14. tel. 01-298-9937.
Agents for various imprints, represented by Edwin Higel, Billy Doran, Steven Anderson and Suzanne Barnes.

Binchy, Jim
7 Heathervue, Greystones, Co Wicklow.
Little, Brown representative.

Butler Sims
78 Ranelagh Village, Dublin 6. tel. 01-497-2836.
Brian Blennerhasset is a publisher's agent.

Boyne, Brenda
39 Seafort Avenue, Sandymount, Dublin 4.
Wolfhound and O'Brien Press representative.

Clooney, Liam
Manor Lodge, Baptist Grange, Lisronagh, Clonmel, Co Tipperary.
Mercier Press representative.

Carr, Gregory
83 Tudor Grove, Ashbourne, Co Meath.
Gregory Carr and Joan O'Connell are publishers' agents.

Corcoran, Fergus
The Gorse Bush, Killegar, Enniskerry, Co Wicklow.
Agent for different imprints.

Dollard, Paddy
8 Lorcan Crescent, Santry, Dublin 9.
Brown Watson representative.

Grace, Chris
47 Moorefield Drive, Newbridge, Co Kildare.
Tiger Books representative.

Greer, Lawrence
Blackstaff Press, 3 Galway Park, Dundonald, Belfast BT16 0AN.
Blackstaff Press representative.

Hamilton, Peter
1155 Osberstown, Naas, Co Kildare.
Publishers' agent.

Hess, Gill
15 Church Street, Skerries, Co Dublin. tel. 01-849-1901.
Publishers' agency; Gill Hess, Simon Hess and Geoff Bryan representatives.

Kelliher, Genny
36 Rialto Cottages, Dublin 8.
Publishers' agent.

Killeen, Fiona
109 Upper Kilmacud Road, Stillorgan, Co Dublin.
Macmillan representative.

Montague, Terry
303 Swords Road, Santry, Dublin 9.
Publishers' agent.

Harper Collins
Temple Court, Temple Road, Blackrock, Co Dublin.
Represented by Charlie Byrne, Ann Murphy and Barbara Flood.

McMahon, John
42 Woodland Grange, Finaghy, Belfast BT11 9NJ.
Represents Little, Brown.

Munroe, Gerardine
184 Sutton Park, Dublin 13.
Publishers' agent.

Neilan, Paul
Gill & Macmillan, Goldenbridge, Inchicore, Dublin 8.
Represents Gill & Macmillan.

Ó Flatharta, Pádraig
ÁIS, 31 Fenian Street, Dublin 2.

Represents ÁIS, the wholesaler of Irish-language books.

O'Neill, David
10 Ardagh Crescent, Blackrock, Co Dublin.
Publishers' agent.

O'Mahony, Donal
22 Castleknock Pines, Castleknock, Dublin 15.
Publishers' agent.

Penguin Group
Represented by Phil Twomey and Dave Devaney.

Poolbeg Group Services
123 Baldoyle Industrial Estate, Dublin 13.
Represented by Breda Purdue and Ivan Kerr.

Pritchard, David
123 Wheatfield, Bray, Co Wicklow.
Publishers' representative.

Redmond, Dave
Hibernian Book Services, 18 Lorcan O'Toole Park, Dublin 12.
Publishers' agent.

RepForce Ireland
12 Longford Terrace, Monkstown, Co Dublin.
Agents, represented by Vivienne Lavery and Louise Dobbin.

Roberts Books
Unit 12 Benson Street, Enterprise Centre, Hanover Quay, Dublin 2.
Don Roberts sells bargain books.

SL Agencies
Kilbrew, Ashbourne, Co Meath.
Sheila Lavery is a publishers' agent.

Smith, Dudley
The Gables, Watterstown, Dunboyne, Co Meath.
Publishers' agent.

Tallon, Richard
114 Rowanbryn, Blackrock, Co Dublin.
Represents Hodder & Stoughton.

Towers, Robert
2 The Crescent, Monkstown, Co Dublin.
Publishers' agent.

Walker, Brian
3 Seaview, Kilcade, Co Wicklow.
Represents Dorling Kindersley.

Book publicists

Eveleen Coyle
46 Heytesbury Street, Dublin 8. tel. 01-497-1700.

Margaret Daly
15 Lullymore Teerrace, Dublin 8. tel. 01-453-9989 fax 01-453-9490 mobile 088-568833.

Booksellers

Members of the Booksellers Association
* indicates wholesalers

bookshops are indexed by county and town on pp 153-155

Academy Library Services
(Phyllis O'Keeffe) 12 Kilbracken Lawn, Blackrock, Cork.

Anchor Bookshop
(Donald Stauffer) 2 Fair Street, Drogheda, Co Louth.

APCK Book Centre
St Anne's Cathedral, Donegall Street, Belfast BT1 2HD.

Apsleys
(J. Elliot) 11-13 Main Street, Larne, Co Antrim BT40 1JQ.

Ards Evangelical Bookshop
(Richard McCoubrey) 7 High Street, Newtownards, Co Down BT23 4JN.

Argosy Libraries
*(Fergal Stanley) 96 Haddington Road, Dublin 4. tel. 01-668-4670 fax 01-668-5226.

ÁIS
*Áisinteacht Dáiliúchán Leabhar, 31 Sráid na bhFíníní, BÁC 2. tel. 01-661-6522. Irish-language wholesale.

Assisi Bookshop & Repository
(Denise McMahon) 4 Merchant's Quay, Dublin 8.

Automobile Association
(J. J. Cassidy) 108-110 Great Victoria Street, Belfast BT2 7AT.
(Mr Whealan) 23 Suffolk St., Dublin 2.

Belfast Book & Bible House
(Karen Tolcher) 64 Ann Street, Belfast BT1 4EG.

Bell's Corner
(Samantha Dale) 2 High Street, Carrickfergus, Co Antrim BT38 7AF.

Bennett Brothers
(O. N. Gill) 52 Ogle Street, Armagh, BT61 7EW.

Bethel Bookshop
(Timothy Anderson) 4 Broad Street, The Diamond, Magherafelt, Co Londonderry BT45 6EA.

Boland
(Colette Boland) Barry's Place, Kinsale, Co Cork.

Book Centre, Ballybofey
(Emer Reilly) College Court, Ballybofey, Co Donegal.

Book Centre, Clonmel
(Yvonne Browne) 2 O'Connell Street, Clonmel, Co Tipperary.

Book Centre, Kilkenny
(John Cantwell) 10 High Street, Kilkenny.

Book Centre, Waterford
(Michael McNena) 25 Barronstrand Road, Waterford.

Book Centre, Wexford
(Caroline Thomas) 5 South Main Street, Wexford.

Book Choice
(Mark Pearson) The Rock, Midleton, Co Cork.

Book Nook, The
(T. Liddle) 98 Main Street, Larne, Co Antrim BT40 1RE.

Book Stop
(John Davey) Dun Laoghaire Shopping Centre, Dun Laoghaire, Co Dublin.
Blackrock Shopping Centre, Blackrock, Co Dublin.

Book World
(Ireneus Shortt) Village Centre, Orchard Road, Clondalkin, Co Dublin.

Bookends

(F. W. T. Hunter) 10 Society Street, Coleraine, Co Londonderry BT52 1LA.

Books Etcetera

(Richard Doig) 7 Riverdale, Larne, Co Antrim BT40 1LB.

Books Unlimited

Northside Shopping Centre, Coolock, Dublin 17.

(Lesley Doyle) 70 Talbot St., Dublin 1.

(R. White) Unit 46 Donaghmede Shopping Centre, Dublin 13.

(Mary White) 307 The Square, Tallaght, Dublin 24.

Books Upstairs

(Maurice Earls) 36 College Green, Dublin 2.

Unit 25 Omni Park, Santry, Dublin 9.

Bookshop at Queen's, The

(Tim Smyth) 91 University Road, Belfast BT7 1NL.

Bookshop, Enniscorthy

(James Byrne) 2 Court Street, Enniscorthy, Co Wexford.

Bookshop, Navan

(Anne Dunne) Trimgate Centre, 38 Trimgate Street, Navan, Co Meath.

Bookshop, Nenagh

(Ms J. Cadell) 63 Kenyon Street, Nenagh, Co Tipperary.

Bookshop, Rathfarnham

(Rosemarie Mitchell) Rathfarnham Shopping Centre, Dublin 14.

Bookshop, Westport

(Michael McLoughlin) Shop Street, Westport, Co Mayo.

Bookwise

(Geraldine O'Dea) 4 Kennedy Road, Navan, Co Meath.

Bookworm, Ballymoney

(P. McIlveen) 19 Church Street, Ballymoney, Co Antrim BT53 6HS.

Bookworm Community Bookshop

(Angela Carlin) 16 Bishop Street, Londonderry BT48 6PW.

Bookworm, Thurles

(John Butler) Westgate, Thurles, Co Tipperary.

Boots the Chemist

314 Richmond Centre, Londonderry.

Bevans, Henry P.

(Maureen Denn) 114 The Quay, Waterford.

Bray Bookshop

(Gemma M. Barry) 10 Main Street, Bray, Co Wicklow. tel. 01-286-9370 fax 01-286-9886.

Brodericks

21 O'Connell Street, Sligo.

Buckland & Co

(Ms I. T. A. Buckland) 50 South Main Street, Wexford.

Byrne, P. & Sons

(Patrick O'Dwyer) The Square, Tuam, Co Galway.

Camerons

(Jim Hughes) 23-29 Broughshane Street, Ballymena, Co Antrim BT43 6EB.

Carlisle Bookshop

(Ms K. Wilson) 25 High Street, Omagh, Co Tyrone BT78 1BA.

Carlow Books & Card Shop

(Ms Evelyn McHugh) 143 Tullow Street, Carlow.

Carlow Newagency

(Paul O'Neill) Paul's New Bookshop, 1 Tullow Street, Carlow.

Castlebar Book Centre

(Ms M. O'Loughlin) Castle Street, Castlebar, Co Mayo.

Cathedral Books

(Alex Tarbett) 4 Sackville Place, Dublin 1.

Celtic Bookshop

(Máire Ní Laoi) 6 Harcourt Street, Dublin 2.

Cenacle Christian Bookshop

(Ms C. Fitzgerald) 25 Henrietta Street, Wexford.

Christian Book Centre, Ballyclare

(Mrs Campbell) 18 Rashee Road, Ballyclare, Co Antrim BT39 9HJ.

Christian Book Centre, Randalstown
(A. T. Poots) 14 New Street, Randalstown, Co Antrim BT41 3AF.

Christian Literature Distributors
(Roy Semple) 2-4 Mill Street, Ballymena, Co Antrim BT43 5AE.

Christian Publications Centre
(Ms E. Mawhinney) 110 Middle Abbey Street, Dublin 1.

Cill Dara Education
Limerick Lane, Newbridge, Co Kildare.

Clements Newsagent
(E. Clements) 7a-9 Eglinton Street, Portrush, Co Antrim BT56 8XD.

Coleraine Books & News
(Ms F. Donnelly) 12 Bridge Street, Coleraine, Co Londonderry.

Collins Bookshop
(Con Collins) Carey's Lane, off Patrick Street, Cork.

Columba Bookservice
(Cecilia West) 93 The Rise, Mount Merrion, Blackrock, Co Dublin.

Covenanter Book Shop
98 Lisburn Road, Belfast BT9 6AG.

Day's Bazaar
(James J. O'Donnell) The Mullingar Bookshop, 30-32 Oliver Plunkett Street, Mullingar, Co Westmeath. tel. 044-48251 fax 044-43178.

Dillons the Bookstore
(Angela Brown) 44-46 Fountain Street, Belfast BT1 5EE.

Douglas Books
(Mark O'Hagan) Unit 18 Douglas Shopping Centre, Cork.

DRC Bookshop
(Revd P. Gallinagh) 13-15 Donegall Lane, Belfast BT1 2LZ.
105 Anderstonstown Road, Belfast BT11 9BS.

Dublin Bookshop
(Gemma Barry) 24 Grafton Street, Dublin 2.

Duffy's Booksellers
(Edward Greevey) 4 South Leinster Street, Dublin 4.

Dundrum Books
(Liz Meldon) Unit 15 Dundrum Shopping Centre, Dundrum, Dublin 14.

Eason & Son
✱(Wholesale) Brickfield Dr., Dublin 12
40-42 Lower O'Connell Street, Dublin 1.
(Gordon Bolton) 80 Middle Abbey Street, Dublin 1. tel. 01-453-6211 fax 01-453-8632.
113-115 Patrick Street, Cork.
33 Shop Street, Galway.
9 O'Connell Street, Limerick.
5 Upper Georges Street, Dun Laoghaire, Co Dublin.
The Square, Town Centre, Tallaght, Dublin 24.

Eason & Son (NI)
✱*Wholesale only* (D. J. Martin) 25 Boucher Road, Belfast BT12 6QU
Unit 33-35 Castle Centre, Market Square, Antrim BT41 4DN.
Tower Centre, Wellington Street, Ballymena, Co Antrim BT43 6AH.
29-33 Main Street, Bangor, Co Down BT20 5AF.
Castle Court Shopping Centre, Royal Avenue, Belfast BT1 1DD.
16-22 Ann Street, Belfast BT1 4EF.
35 Church Street, Coleraine, Co Londonderry BT52 1AW.
Unit 28 Craigavon Shopping Centre, Craigavon, Co Armagh BT64 1AA.
34 Bow Street, Lisburn, Co Antrim BT28 1BN.
(Ms K. Enright) Ards Shopping Centre, Circular Road, Newtownards, Co Down BT23 4EU.
Unit 2/3 Buttercrane Quay, Newry, Co Down BT35 8HJ.

Eblana Bookshop
4 Scaney Court, Dublin Industrial Estate. Glasnevin, Dublin 11.

Educational Company
(Ms C. Moffitt) 47-49 Queen Street, Belfast BT1 6HP.
(R. A. McBride) 1 Mallusk Park, Newtownabbey, Co Antrim BT36 8GW.

Ennis Bookshop
(Mary Evans) 13 Abbey Street, Ennis, Co Clare. tel. 065-29000 fax 065-29000.

Evangelical Book Shop
(John Grier) 15 College Square East, Belfast BT1 6DD.
(Letitia Moffitt) 8 Dublin Road, Enniskillen, Co Fermanagh BT74 6HH.

Exchange Bookshop
(M. Simonds) 34 Castle Street, Dalkey, Co Dublin.

Faith Mission Bookshop
(Edward Douglas) 5-7 Queen Street, Belfast BT1 6EA.

Familia
(Shane McAteer) 64 Wellington Place, Belfast BT1 6GE.

Familybooks
(Betty Bell) Church House, Fisherwick Place, Belfast BT1 6DW.

Fax & Fiction
(Gerry Daly) Ashbourne Town Centre, Ashbourne, Co Meath.

Fitzmaurice Bookshop
9/10 Barronstrand Street, Waterford.

Four Masters Bookshop
(Louise O'Rourke) The Diamond, Donegal town.

Gallery Bookshop
(Lisa Irvine) 56-60 Dublin Road, Belfast BT2 7HP.

Galway Cathedral Bookshop
(Margaret Dooley) The Cathedral, Galway.

Galway University Bookshop
(A. Bundschu) University College, Galway.

Gardner, J. P. & Son
(Joe Beattie) 70-72 Botanic Avenue, Belfast.

Gibson, D.
(Jean Wylie) 5 Northland Place, Dungannon, Co Tyrone BT71 6AN.

Gray's
(Dorothy Smith) 49 Main Street, Strabane, Co Tyrone BT82 8AU.

Greene's Bookshop
(E. J. Pembrey) 16 Clare St., Dublin 2.

Hall, L.
34-36 Darling Street, Enniskillen, Co Fermanagh BT74 7EW.

Hanna, Fred
(Fred Hanna) 27-29 Nassau Street, Dublin 2. tel. 01-677-1255.
University College, Belfield, Dublin 4.

Hannigan's Bookshop
(Tom Hannigan) Unit 23 Queens Old Castle, Cork.

Hawkins House
(Bridget Hawkins) 14 Churchyard Street, Galway.

HMSO Books
(Dan Lavery) 16 Arthur Street, Belfast BT1 4GD.

Hodges Figgis & Co
(Walter Pohli) 57/58 Dawson Street, Dublin 2.

Hughes & Hughes
(Frank Moore) Departure floor, PO Box 2394, Dublin Airport, Co Dublin.
(Liam Hughes) 12 Cruises Street, Limerick.
Stephen's Green Centre, Dublin 2. tel. 01-478-3060 fax 01-475-0014.
(L. Morrissey) Nutgrove Shopping Centre, Rathfarnham, Dublin 14.

Hughes Book Services
✱**Wholesale only** (Derek Hughes) 21 Lee Road, Dublin Industrial Estate, Glasnevin, Dublin 11.

Hughes Book Services NI
✱Wholesale only (R. Anderson) Lisburn, Co Antrim

Hurley
(Tony McGuire) Castle Street, Tralee, Co Kerry.

Hyland's Educational Bookshop
(Jim Hyland) 22 Lower Cork Street, Mitchelstown, Co Cork.

International Books
(Brendan Storey) South Frederick Street, Dublin 2.

International Educational Services
(John P. Treacy) Weston Industrial Estate, Salmon Leap, Leixlip, Co Kildare.

Irish Film Centre Bookshop
(Mary Sherlock) 6 Eustace Street, Temple Bar, Dublin 2.

Irish Georgian Society
(Jane Fenlon) 74 Merrion Square, Dublin 2.

Irish Library Suppliers
(Allen Hanna) Rathmines Road Lower, Dublin 6.

Jeffers, D. & Co
(D. Jeffers) 1 West Street, Portadown, Co Armagh BT62 3JY.

Keohane, J. M.
(Mr Keohane) Castle Street, Sligo.

Keohane's Bookshop
Aran Street, Ballina, Co Mayo.

Kerr's Bookshop
(Patricia Kerr) Ashe Street, Clonakilty, Co Cork.

Killarney Bookshop
(David O'Mahoney) 32 Main Street, Killarney, Co Kerry.

Kinsale Books
(Geoff Dyson) Unit 3 Market Street, Kinsale, Co Cork.

Laois Education Supplies
(John McNamee) Portlaoise, Co Laois. tel. .0502-20466 fax 0502-20466.

Lennox, A. & Sons
(D. Lennox) 17-21 Market Street, Armagh BYT61 7BT.

Library Shop
(J. G. Duffy) Trinity College, College Street, Dublin 2.

Limerick Christian Bookshop
(Tim O'Connell) Upper Gerald Griffin Street, Limerick.

Lisburn Bookshop
(Karen McFarlane) 58 Bow Street, Lisburn, Co Antrim BT28 1BN.

Live'n'Learn Bookshop
(G. Quigley) Stockwell Court, Drogheda, Co Louth.

McAuley, Albert, Bible Bookshop
9 Linenhall Street, Ballymoney, Co Antrim BT53 6DP.

McCarthys' Newsagent & Bookseller
(Dolly McCarthy) 22 Main Street, Kenmare, Co Kerry.

McGuire & Co
(P. McGuire) Church Street, Listowel, Co Kerry.

McIntyre
60-61 The Promenade, Portstewart, Co Londonderry BT55 7AF.
(Colin McDowell) 5 High Street, Ballymoney, Co Antrim.

McMurray & Son
(Ms Tracy Duke) 32 Market Street, Lurgan, Co Armagh BT66 6AH.

Mainly Murder Bookstore
(Patricia Barry) Paul Street, Cork.

Maynooth University Bookshop
(John Byrne) St Patrick's College, Maynooth, Co Kildare.

Mercier Bookshop
(Loretto McNamara) PO Box 5, French Church Street, Cork.

Methodist Bookroom
(Richard J. Mairs) Aldersgate House, 13 University Road, Belfast BT7 1NA.

Midland Books
(Patricia Ryan) High Street, Tullamore, Co Offaly.

Miller, Stewart, & Sons
(Michael Miller) 112 Main Street, Bangor, Co Down BT20 4AG.
(Stephen E. Miller) 97 High Street, Holywood, Co Down BT18 9AQ.

Mizen Books
(Jeanne Schuster) Main Street, Schull, Co Cork.

Mizpah Bible & Book Shop
(Ms A. Harrison) 41 Kingsgate Street, Coleraine, Co Londonderry BT52 1LD.

MJ's Newsagency & School Centre
(John Howard) 33 Trimgate Street, Navan, Co Meath.

Moonstone
(Rita Wild) 39 Church Road, Holywood, Co Down BT18 9BY.

Mullan, William, & Son
(Mr Irvine) 56 Windmill Road, Hillsborough, Co Down BT26 6LX.

Murray Richardson
(Ms A. B. Rafferty) 15 Church Street, Dungannon, Co Tyrone BT71 6AB.

Music and Book Centre
(L. McGuigan) 45 High Street, Ballynahinch, Co Down BT24 8AB.
(Mary Wilson) 27b Market Street, Downpatrick, Co Down BT30 6LP.

Nás na Ríogh Bookshop
(Joan Kehoe) 14 Main Street, Naas, Co Kildare.

National Bible Society of Ireland
(Fergus O'Ferrall) 41 Dawson Street, Dublin 2.

National Gallery Shop
Merrion Square West, Dublin 2.

Newry Bookshop
(Geraldine Lynn) Unit 5, Kingsway, Monaghan Street, Newry, Co Down BT35 6BB.

Northern Ireland Book Service
✱*Wholesale only* (B. H. Gray) 53 High Street, Ballymena BT43 6DT

Northern Publishing Office
(Morag Andrew) 4 Marshalls Road, Castlereagh, Beflast BT5 6QU.
(Steward Hamilton) Springhill Shopping Centre, Bangor, Co Down BT19 1ND.
(Ben Jones) Connswater Shopping Centre, Bloomfield Avenue, Belfast.
(Edith McManus) Northcott Shopping Centre, Glengormley, Co Antrim.
(Ann Kerrigan) Abbeycentre, Longwood Road, Newtownabbey, Co Antrim BT37 9UH.

O'Connor, A. B. & Co
(Ann O'Connor) Shelbourne Street, Kenmare, Co Kerry.

O'Mahony & Co
120 O'Connell Street, Limerick. tel. 061-418155 fax 061-414558.

(Bridget Leen) 9 Castle Street, Tralee, Co Kerry.

Open Book Co
(Robert Redmond) Sutton Cross Shopping Centre, Dublin 13.

O'Sullivan, D. F.
(William V. O'Sullivan) 72 High Street, Killarney, Co Kerry.

Paddy's
Church St., Greystones, Co Wicklow.

Page One (First Edition)
(Rosemary McNena) 14 Tullow Street, Carlow.

Page One Bookshop
The Reader Ltd, 7 Regent Street, Newtownards, Co Down BT23 4AB.

Paper Shop, The
(R. Johnston) 4 The Square, Ballyclare, Co Antrim BT39 9BB.

Paperback Centre
(J. R. Montgomery) 14 Stillorgan Shopping Centre, Blackrock, Co Dublin.

Paperchase
(Anne Cole) 34 Shipquay Street, Londonderry BT48 6DW.

Pembrey's Bookshop
(Vivian Pembrey) 78 Lower Georges Street, Dun Laoghaire, Co Dublin.

Philip's Bookshop
(Catherine O'Flynn) 34 Bank Place, Mallow, Co Cork.

Porter, J. R.
Wilton Shopping Centre, Cork.

Powers Book Shop
(Michael Power) 11 Mary Street, Dungarvan, Co Waterford.

Rathmines Bookshop
(James P. Kinsella) 211 Lower Rathmines Road, Dublin 6.

Reader's Choice
(Catherine O'Donnell) Lower Main Street, Dungarvan, Co Waterford.

Reader's Digest Shop
18 Lower Liffey Street, Dublin 1.

Reid's

(Ms J. Reid) 4 Barrack Street, Armagh BT60 1AD.

Reigate Press

(Betty Dugdale) 10 Hawthorns, Castletroy, Co Limerick.

Roselawn Bookshop

(Anne Dunne) Roselawn Shopping Centre, Blanchardstown, Dublin 15.

Roughans Newsagent

(Vincent Roughan) 16 The Promenade, Portstewart, Co Londonderry BT55 7AD.

Royal Bookshop

(Carol Cobbe) Main Street, Dunshaughlin, Co Meath.

Royal Kilmainham Bookshop

(Lindsay Grant) Royal Hospital, Kilmainham, Dublin 8.

Russell, Liam

(Liam Russell) 49-50 Oliver Plunkett Street, Cork.

St Ann's Book Centre

(Fergus McCullough) St Ann's Church, Dawson Street, Dublin 2.

St Paul Book Centre

(Revd J. Pius) Castle Street, Athlone, Co Westmeath.

St Paul's

(George Thanickal) Clarendon Street, Dublin 2.

Scholars Bookstore & Stationery

(Monica Cahillane) 8 John Street, Waterford.

Scripture Union Book Centre

(Rosalie McCabe) 87 Lower Georges Street, Dun Laoghaire, Co Dublin.

Scripture Union Resource Centre

(Ms G. Fortheringham) 157-159 Albertbridge Road, Belfast BT5 4PS.

See 'ere

51-53 Spencer Road, Londonderry BT47 1AA.

Selskar Bookshop

(Joe Seery) Selskar Street, Wexford.

Serridge, Ambrose

Units 15/16 Workwest Industrial Park, 301 Glen Road, Belfast BT11 8BU.

Setanta Books

(Denis Courtney) 29 Hawthorn Lodge, Castleknock, Dublin 15.

Sheehy, T. & Sons

(Tom Sheehy) 44-46 William Street, Cookstown, Co Tyrone BT80 8NB.

Shipquay Books

10 Shipquay Street, Londonderry BT48 6DN.

Sibley & Co

(D. Sibley) Dundrum Shopping Centre, Dublin 14.

Simpson, James

28 Main Street, Ballymoney, Co Antrim BT53 6AL.

Smyth, Gavin

(Roger Wort) Unit 4 Windsor Business Park, Boucher Place, Belfast BT12 6HT.

Smyth's Bookshop

(Hugh Smyth) 12 Railway Street, Newcastle, Co Down BT33 0AL.

Stationery Centre, The

7 Rainey Street, Magherafeld, Co Londonderry BT45 5DA.

Stewart-McElheran Company

(R. B. Stewart) 66-70 Mill Street, Ballymena, Co Antrim BT43 5AF.

SU Book & Music Centre

(Howard Hall) 40 Talbot Street, Dublin 1.

Sunday School Society for Ireland

(Norah Bedlow) Holy Trinity Church, Church Avenue, Dublin 6.

Tower Books

(Patricia Daly) 13 Hawthorn Avenue, Inniscarra View Estate, Ballincollig, Co Cork.

Tuam Bookshop

(Sean Tierney) Vicar Street, Tuam, Co Galway.

Unibooks (Ulster)

(Ms A. Teskey) Central Buildings, University of Ulster, Cromore Road, Coleraine, Co Londonderry BT52 1SA.

University of Limerick Bookshop
(David O'Mahony) National Technological Park, Limerick.

Veritas Company
(Chris Cunningham) 7-8 Lower Abbey Street, Dublin 1.
(Tom Egan) 14-15 Bridge Street, Cork.

Veritas Family Bookshop
(Chris Cunningham) 4 Dublin Road, Stillorgan, Co Dublin.

Walsh, Patrick Bernard
(Timothy Walsh) 10 Scarva Street, Banbridge, Co Down BT32 3DA.

Waterstone's Booksellers
(Lois Brown) Queen's Building, 8 Royal Avenue, Belfast BT1 1DA.

(Phil Davies) 7 Dawson Street, Dublin 2.
(P. Ó Flaitheartaigh) 69 Patrick Street, Cork.
Boole Basement, University College, Cork.

Wicklow Street Bookshop
(Ms N. Shields) 21 Wicklow Street, Dublin 2.

Wise Owl, The
(Eoin Murphy) West Street Arcade, Drogheda, Co Louth.

Wordsworth Bookshop
(Tony Hayes) Unit 21 Merrion Centre, Merrion Road, Dublin 4.

Booksellers by place

Index by county and town

to the alphabetical list on pp. 145-152

Book Centre
Donegal
Four Masters

Down
Ballynahinch
Music & Book Centre
Banbridge
Walsh, Patrick Bernard
Bangor
Eason & Son
Miller, Stewart, & Sons
Northern Publishing
Downpatrick
Music & Book Centre
Hillsborough
Mullan, William, & Son
Holywood
Miller, Stewart, & Sons
Moonstone
Newcastle
Smyth's Bookshop
Newry
Newry Bookshop
Newtownards
Ards Evangelical
Page One Bookshop

Dublin
Blackrock
Book Stop
Clondalkin
Book World
Dalkey
Exchange Bookshop
Dublin 1
Books Unlimited
Cathedral Books
Christian Publications
Reader's Digest Shop
Eason & Son
SU Book & Music
Veritas Company
Dublin 2
Automobile Assoc.
Books Upstairs
Celtic Bookshop
Dublin Bookshop
Greene's Bookshop
Hanna, Fred
Hodges Figgis & Co
Hughes & Hughes
International Books

Irish Film Centre
Irish Georgian Society
Library Shop, TCD
National Bible Society
National Gallery Shop
St Ann's Book Centre
St Paul's
Watersone's
Wicklow St. Bookshop
Dublin 4
Argosy Libraries
Duffy's Booksellers
Wordsworth Bookshop
Dublin 6
Irish Library Suppliers
Rathmines Bookshop
Sunday School Society
Dublin 8
Assisi Bookshop
Royal Kilmainham
Dublin 9
Books Upstairs
Dublin 11
Eblana Bookshop
Hughes Book Service
Dublin 13
Books Unlimited
Open Book Co
Dublin 14
Bookshop, Rathfarnhm
Dundrum Books
Hughes & Hughes
Sibley & Co
Roselawn Bookshop
Setanta Books
Dublin 17
Books Unlimited
Dublin 24
Eason & Son, Tallaght
Books Unlimited
Dublin Airport
Hughes & Hughes
Dun Laoghaire
Book Stop
Eason & Son
Pembrey's Bookshop
Scripture Union
Mount Merrion
Columba Bookservice
Stillorgan
Paperback Centre

Veritas Family Bkshop
Fermanagh
Enniskillen
Evangelical Bookshop
Hall, L.
Galway
Galway
Eason & Son
Galway Cathedral
Galway University
Hawkins House
Tuam
Byrne & Sons
Tuam Bookshop
Kerry
Kenmare
McCarthy's
O'Connor, A. B.
Killarney
Killarney Bookshop
O'Sullivan, D. F.
Listowel
McGuire & Co
Tralee
Hurley
O'Mahony & Co
Kildare
Leixlip
International Educ. S.
Maynooth
Maynooth University
Naas
Nás na Ríogh Bookshop
Newbridge
Cill Dara Education
Kilkenny city
Book Centre
Laois
Portlaoise
Laois Educ. Supplies
Limerick
Castletroy
Reigate Press
Limerick
Eason & Son
Hughes & Hughes
Limerick Christian
O'Mahony & Co
Univ. of Limerick

Londonderry see Derry

Louth
Drogheda
Anchor Bookshop
Live'n'Learn Bookshop
Wise Owl, The

Mayo
Ballina
Keohane's Bookshop
Castlebar
Castlebar Book Centre
Westport
Bookshop

Meath
Ashbourne
Fax & Fiction
Dunshaughlin
Royal Bookshop
Navan
MJ's Newsagency
Bookshop
Bookwise

Offaly
Tullamore
Midland Books

Sligo
Sligo
Brodericks
Keohane, J. M.

Tipperary
Clonmel
Book Centre
Nenagh
Bookshop
Thurles
Bookworm

Tyrone
Cookstown
Sheehy, T. & Sons
Dungannon
Gibson, D.
Murray Richardson
Omagh
Carlisle Bookshop
Strabane
Gray's

Waterford
Dungarvan
Powers Book Shop
Reader's Choice

Waterford
Book Centre
Fitzmaurice Bookshop
Bevans
Scholars Bookshop

Westmeath
Athlone
St Paul Book Centre
Mullingar
Day's Bazaar

Wexford
Enniscorthy
Bookshop
Wexford
Book Centre
Buckland
Cenacle Christian
Selskar Bookshop

Wicklow
Bray
Bray Bookshop
Greystones
Paddy's

Libraries

Here are listed the headquarters of public, college, specialist and such private libraries as may be accessible to researchers. For public libraries we state the number of branches and the main other services provided; opening hours vary from branch to branch. For other libraries generally accessible to researchers we give opening times. Where times are not given, we provide telephone and fax numbers since access is only by special arrangement. Libraries with special collections are indexed by subject on pp. 165-168. We are indebted to the North-South Liaison Committee of the two Library Associations in Ireland for this information which is abridged from their superb *Directory of Libraries and Information Services in Ireland* (4th edn, 1993).

Accountancy & Business College Library, Little Longford Street, Dublin 2. tel. 01-475-1024 fax 01-475-1043. *Reference by arrangement.*

Age Concern Northern Ireland, 6 Lower Crescent, Belfast BT7 1NR. tel. 08-01232-245729. *Monday-Friday 9-17.00.*

Agency for Personal Service Overseas (APSO), 30 Fitzwilliam Square, Dublin 2. *Monday-Friday 9.30-13.00, 14.00-17.30.*

Agriculture see Department of Agriculture

Agriculture Library, QUB, Newforge Lane, Belfast 9. tel. 08-01232-661166. *By arrangement.*

AIB Group, Bankcentre, Ballbridge, Dublin 4. tel. 01-660-0311 ext. 3412 fax 01-660-1696. *By arrangement.*

All Hallows Missionary College, Gracepark Road, Drumcondra, Dublin 9. tel. 01-837-3745 ext. 265 fax 01-837-7642.

AONTAS (National Association of Adult Education), 22 Earlsfort Terrace, Dublin 2. tel. 01-475-4121/4122 fax 01-478-0084. *By appointment.*

APSO see Agency for Personal Service Overseas

Archbishop Marsh's Library, St Patrick's Close, Dublin 8. Restoration service for old books and manuscripts. *Monday and Wednesday-Friday 10.00-12.45, 14.00-17.00, Saturday 10.30-12.45; closed Tuesday.*

Armagh Observatory, College Hill, Armagh BT61 9DG. tel. 08-01861-522928 fax 08-01861-527174. *Monday-Friday 9.00-17.00.*

Armagh (Robinson) Public Library, Abbey Street, Armagh BT61 7DZ. tel. 08-01861-523142 fax 08-01861-524177. *Monday-Friday 10.00-12.30, 14.00-16.00 or by arrangement.*

Athlone Regional Technical College, Dublin Road, Athlone, Co Westmeath. tel. 0902-72647 fax 0902-74529.

Austin Clarke Library, Poetry Ireland, Dublin Castle, Dublin 2. *Monday-Friday 14.00-17.00 or by arrangement.*

BBC Northern Ireland, rooms 106/109 Broadcasting House, Ormeau Avenue, Belfast BT2 8HQ. tel. 08-01232-338648 fax 08-01232-338800. *Research by arrangement; commercial customers charged fees.*

Belfast Education and Library Board, Belfast Public Libraries, Central Library, Royal Avenue, Belfast BT1 1EA. tel. 08-1232-243233 fax 08-1232-332819. 27 branches including colleges, plus special services to hospitals, housebound, visually impaired and prisons and by 2 mobile libraries.

Belfast Institute of Further and Higher Education, Park House, 87 Great Victoria Street, Belfast BT2 7AG. tel. 08-01232-325312. 6 libraries.

Boole Library, University College, Cork. tel. 021-276871 fax 021-273428.

Bord Altranais, An, 31-32 Fitzwilliam Square, Dublin 2. tel. 01-676-0226 fax 01-676-3348. *By arrangement.*

Bord Iascaigh Mhara, PO Box 12 Crofton Road, Dun Laoghaire, Co Dublin. tel. 01-284-1544 fax 01-284-1123. *Fax and letter service, open by appointment, Monday to Friday.*

Bord na Móna, Droichead Nua, Co Kildare. tel. 045-31201 fax 045-33240. *By appointment.*

Bord Tráchtála/Irish Trade Board, Merrion Hall, Strand Road, Sandymount, Dublin 4. *Monday-Friday 9.00-13.00, 14.00-17.00.*

Bryson House, 28 Bedford Street, Belfast BT2 7FE. tel. 08-01232-325835. *By arrangement for members of voluntary and community groups.*

Carlow County Library, Dublin Street, Carlow. tel. 0503-31126. 3 branches, mobile library and primary schools service.

Carlow Regional Technical College, Kilkenny Road, Carlow. tel. 0503-31324 fax 0503-43787.

Cavan County Library, Farnham Street, Cavan. tel. 049-31799 fax 049-31384. 14 branches, mobile library and primary schools.

Central Catholic Library, 74 Merrion Square, Dublin 2. *Monday-Saturday 11.00-19.00.*

Central Remedial Clinic, Vernon Avenue, Clontarf, Dublin 3. *Monday-Friday 9.30-17.00.*

Central Statistics Office, St Stephen's Green House, Earlsfort Terrace, Dublin 2. *Monday to Friday 9.30-12.45 and 14.30-16.45.*

CERT, Cert House, Amiens Street, Dublin 1. *Monday-Friday 10.00-12.30, 14.30-16.30.*

Chester Beatty Library, 20 Shrewsbury Road, Dublin 4. *Tuesday-Friday 9.30-17.00, Saturday 14.00-17.00; research work by appointment.*

Chomhairle Leabharlanna, An, 53-54 Upper Mount Street, Dublin 2. tel. 01-676-1167/1963 fax 01-676-6721.

Church of Ireland College of Education, 96 Upper Rathmines Road, Dublin 6. tel. 01-497-0033 fax 01-497-0878. *By appointment.*

Clare County Library, Mill Road, Ennis, Co Clare. tel. 065-21616 fax 065-28233 telex 28144. 16 branches.

Coillte, Sidmonton Place, Bray, Co Wicklow. tel. 01-286-7751 fax 01-286-8126. *Access by arrangement.*

Colleges of Catering, Commerce, Marketing, Technology: see Dublin Institute of Technology.

Combat Poverty Agency, 8 Charlemont Street, Dublin 2. Monday-Friday 9.30-13.00, 14.00-17.00.

Commission of European Communities, 39 Molesworth Street, Dublin 2. *Monday to Friday 11-13.00 and 14.00-16.30.*

Cork City Library, 57 Grand Parade, Cork. tel. 021-277110 fax 021-275684. 6 branches, 1 mobile library.

Cork County Library, Farranlea Road, Cork. tel. 021-546499 fax 021-343254. 27 branches, 5 mobile libraries.

Cork Regional Technical College, Rossa Avenue, Bishopstown, Cork. tel. 021-545222 fax 021-545343.

Curriculum Development Unit, Sundrive Road, Dublin 12. tel. 01-453-5487 fax 01-453-7659. *By appointment.*

Department of Agriculture, Food and Forestry, Agriculture House, Kildare Street, Dublin 2. *Monday-Thursday 10.15-12.45 and 14.15-17.30, Friday to 17.15.*

Department of Agriculture for Northern Ireland, Room 612 Dundonald House, Upper Newtownards Road, Belfast BT4 3SB. *Monday-Friday 9.00-17.00.*

Department of Economic Development (NI), Netherleigh, Massey Avenue, Belfast BT4 2JP. *Monday-Friday 9.00-17.00.*

Department of Education, Marlborough Street, Dublin 1. *By appointment Monday-Thursday 9.15-12.45 and 14.00-17.30, Fridays to 17.15.*

Department of the Environment for Northern Ireland, Work Service Library, room 1408, Churchill House, Victoria Square, Belfast BT1 4QW. *Monday-Friday 9-17.00.*

Department of Health, Hawkins House, Poolbeg Street, Dublin 2. *Monday-Friday 9.30-17.30.*

Department of the Marine, Leeson Lane, Dublin 2. *Monday-Friday 9.15-13.00,*

14.30-17.30.

Department of Social Welfare, Áras Mhic Dhiarmada, floor 5, Store Street, Dublin 1. tel. 01-874-8444 ext. 2850. Researchers by arrangement.

Diocesan Library of Down and Dromore and Connor, 12 Talbot Street, Belfast BT1. tel. 08-01232 322268. By appointment.

Disability Action, 2 Annadale Avenue, Belfast BT7 3UR. tel. 08-01232-491011 fax 08-01232-491627. Enquiry line for disabled, carers etc. Monday-Friday 14.00-15.30.

Donegal County Library, Rosemount, Letterkenny, Co Donegal. tel. 074-21968 fax 074-26402. 17 branches, 1 mobile and services to islands, hospital, old people's homes and primary schools. For RTC see Donogh O'Malley.

Donogh O'Malley Regional Technical College, Port Road, Letterkenny, Co Donegal. tel. 074-24888 fax 074-24879.

Dublin City Libraries, Central Department, Cumberland House, Fenian Street, Dublin 2. tel. 01-661-9000 fax 01-676-1628. 27 local and specialised branches inc. prison and schools lib. HQ, 4 mobiles.

Dublin City University Library, Dublin 9. tel. 01-704-5212 fax 01-837-4733.

Dublin County: see Dublin South, Dún Laoghaire, Fingal and Rathdown.

Dublin Dental Hospital Library, Dunlop/Oriel House, Lincoln Place, Dublin 2. tel. 01-662-0766 ext. 205 fax 01-661-2072. *On applications for professionals and students.*

Dublin Diocesan Library, Clonliffe Road, Dublin 3. tel 01-874-1680 fax 01-836-8920. Serves Mater Dei Institute of Education and Holy Cross College.

Dublin Institute for Advanced Studies, School of Celtic Studies and School of Theoretical Physics, 10 Burlington Road, Dublin 4. tel. 01-668-0748 fax 01-668-0561. *By special arrangement.*

Dublin Institute for Advanced Studies, School of Cosmic Physics, 5 Merrion Square, Dublin 2. tel. 01-677-4321 fax

01-668-2003. *By appointment.*

Dublin Institute of Technology, College of Catering, Cathal Brugha Street, Dublin 1. tel. 01-874-7886 fax 01-874-3634.

Dublin Institute of Technology, College of Commerce, Rathmines Road, Dublin 6. tel. 01-497-0666 fax 01-497-0647.

Dublin Institute of Technology, College of Marketing and Design, 40-45 Mountjoy Square, Dublin 1. Monday-Thursday 10.00-21.00; Friday-Saturday 10.00-17.00; Vacation time Monday-Friday 10.00-17.00.

Dublin Institute of Technology, College of Technology, Bolton Street, Dublin 1. tel. 01-872-7177 ext. 369 fax 01-872-7870.

Dublin Institute of Technology, College of Technology, Lower Kevin Street, Dublin 8. tel. 01-475-7541 ext. 359 fax 01-478-0282.

Dublin South County Libraries, c/o Central Department, Cumberland House, Fenian Street, Dublin 2. tel. 01-661-9000 fax 01-676-1628. (May move HQ to Tallaght, Dublin 24.) Branches, mobiles.

Dún Laoghaire Public Library Service, Lower Georges Street, Dún Laoghaire, Co Dublin. tel. 01-280-1254/28-1147/284-5477. 4 branches, services to housebound and schools.

Dundalk Regional Technical College, Dublin Road, Dundalk, Co Louth. tel. 042-34785 ext. 312 fax 042-33505.

Dunsink Observatory, Castleknock, Dublin 15. tel. 01-838-7959 fax 01-838-7090. Restricted access.

Dupont (UK), Maydown Works, PO Box 15, Londonderry BT47 1TU. tel. 08-01504-860860 fax 08-01504-860244. *By arrangement.*

Economic Development, see Department of

Economic and Social Research Institute, 4 Burlington Road, Dublin 4. tel. 01-676-0115 fax 01-668-6231. *By arrangement.*

Edgehill Theological College, 9 Lennoxvale, Belfast BT9 5BY. tel. 08-01232-665870. *By arrangement.*

Education see Department of

Electricity Supply Board, Lower Fitzwilliam Street, Dublin 2. *Monday-Friday 8.30-16.45.*

ENFO see Environmental Information Service

Environment see Department of the Environmental Information Service (ENFO), 17 St Andrew Street, Dublin 2. tel. 01-679-31444 fax 01-679-5204. *Monday-Saturday 10-17.00.*

EOLAS, Irish Science and Technology Agency, Glasnevin, Dublin 9. tel. 01-837-0101 fax 01-837-8854. *Service to industry; charges for literature search and document delivery. Monday-Friday 9.15-13.00, 14.00-17.15.*

Equal Opportunities Commission for Northern Ireland, 22 Great Victoria Street, Belfast BT2 7BA. *Monday-Friday 9.00-17.00.*

European Business Information Centre, LEDU House, Upper Galwally, Belfast BT8 4TB. *Monday-Friday 9.00-17.00.*

European Foundation, Loughlinstown House, Shankill, Co Dublin. 01-282-6888 fax 01-282-6456. *By appointment.*

FÁS see Foras Áiseanna Saothair

Fingal County Libraries, 11 Parnell Square, Dublin 1.

Fisheries Research Centre, Abbotstown, Castleknock, Dublin 15. tel. 01-821-0111 fax 01-820-5078. *Researchers by appointment.*

Foras Áiseanna Saothair (FÁS), 27-33 Upper Baggot Street, Dublin 4. tel. 01-668-5777 fax 01-668-2691. *By appointment.*

Franciscan Library, Dun Mhuire, Seafield Road, Killiney, Co Dublin. tel. 01-282-6760. *By appointment.*

Galway County Libraries, Island House, Cathedral Square, Galway. tel. 091-62471/65039. 23 branches, mobile service with 65 stops, schools, postal service for visually impaired.

Galway Regional Technical College, Dublin Road, Galway. tel. 091-53161 ext. 215-216 fax 091-51107.

Gamble Library, Union Theological College, 108 Botanic Avenue, Belfast BT7 1JT. tel. 08-01232-325374 fax 08-01232-325397. *By arrangement.*

Garda College Library, Templemore, Co Tipperary. tel. 0504-31522 ext. 2109 fax 0504-31913.

General Consumer Council for Northern Ireland, 116 Holywood Road, Belfast BT4 1NY. *Monday-Friday 9.00-15.00.*

Geological Survey of Ireland, Beggar's Bush, Dublin 4. *Monday-Friday 9-13.00, 14.00-16.30.*

Glenstal Abbey, Murroe, Co Limerick. tel. 061-386103 fax 061-386328. *By appointment.*

Goethe Institute, 37 Merrion Square, Dublin 2. *Monday, Tuesday, Thursday 16.00-20.00; Wednesday, Friday 10.00-18.00; Saturday 10.00-13.00.*

GPA-Bolton Library, John Street, Cashel, Co Tipperary. *Monday-Saturday 9.30-17.30; Sunday 14.30-17.30; contributions expected.*

Guinness Ireland Technical Information Services, St James's Gate, Dublin 8. *Monday-Friday 9.00-17.00.*

Hardiman see James Hardiman

Health see Department of

Health Promotion Unit, Department of Health, Hawkins House, Poolbeg Street, Dublin 2. *Monday-Friday 9.30-13.00, 14.00-17.00.*

Heritage Library, Hegarty House, 14 Bishop Street, Derry BT48 6PW. *Monday-Friday 9.00-17.00.*

Holy Cross College see Dublin Diocesan Library

Institiúid Teangeolaíochta Éireann, 31 Fitzwilliam Place, Dublin 2. *Monday-Friday 9.30-12.30, 14.30-17.00.*

Institute of Chartered Accountants in Ireland, 87/89 Pembroke Road, Dublin 4. tel. 01-668-0400 fax 01-668-5685 telex 30567.

Insurance Institute of Ireland, 32 Nassau Street, Dublin 2. tel. 01-677-2582/2753 fax 01-677-2621. *On application.*

Irish Architectural Archive, 73 Merrion Square, Dublin 2. *Tuesday-Friday 10.00-13.00, 14.30-17.00.*

Irish Christian Study Centre, Glenburn House, Glenburn Road South, Dunmurry, Belfast BT17 9JP. *Monday, Wednesday, Friday 9.30-13.00; Tuesday,*

Thursday 13.20-16.30; Tuesday except Jan, July and August 19.00-21.30.

Irish Film Institute, 6 Eustace Street, Dublin 2. *Currently only Fridays 9.30-17.30.*

Irish Business and Employers Confederation, Confederation House, Kildare Street, Dublin 2. tel. 01-677-9801 fax 01-677-7823. *On application.*

Irish Management Institute, National Management Centre, Sandyford Road, Dublin 16. tel. 01-295-6911 fax 01-295-9479. *By arrangement.*

Irish Railway Record Society, (post: Box 9, Main Hall) Heuston Station, Dublin 8. *Apply in writing or in person.*

James Hardiman Library, University College, Galway. tel. 091-24411 fax 091-22394 telex 50191.

Jesuit Library, Milltown Park, Dublin 6. tel. 01-269-8411 fax 01-260-0371. *By arrangement.*

Judges' Library, Department of Justice, Supreme & High Court, Four Courts, Inns Quay, Dublin 7. *Monday-Friday 9.30-17.00.*

Kerry County Library, Moyderwell, Tralee, Co Kerry. tel. 066-21200 fax 066-22466. 8 branches, 2 mobiles, services to hospitals, housebound and schools.

Kildare County Libraries, Athgarvan Road, Newbridge, Co Kildare. tel. 045-31486/31109 fax 045-32490. 17 branches, 1 mobile, schools service.

Kilkenny County Library, 6 John's Quay, Kilkenny. tel. 056-22021/22606 fax 056-63384. 5 branches, 1 mobile, schools service.

Kimmage Institute of Theological and Missionary Formation, Kimmage Manor, Dublin 12. tel. 01-450-4174/450-4607.

King's Inns Library, Henrietta Street, Dublin 1. tel. 01-874-7134 fax 01-872-6048. *Enquire.*

Lambeg Industrial Research Association, Lambeg, Lisburn, Co Antrim BT27 4RJ. *Monday-Thursday 8.30-12.45, 13.30-17.30; Friday 8.30-13.00.*

Laois County Library, County Hall, James Fiontan Lalor Avenue, Portlaoise, Co Laois. tel. 0502-22044. 7 branches and 6 centres, primary school service.

Law Library, PO Box 2424, Dublin 7. *Monday-Friday 9.00-18.00; loans to members of the Bar only.*

Law Society of Northern Ireland, 90-106 Victoria Street, Belfast BT1 3JZ. tel. 08-01232-231614 ext. 46 fax 08-01232-232606. *By appointment for non-solicitors.*

Leabharlann na mBráithre see Franciscan Library

Leitrim County Library, Ballinamore, Co Leitrim. tel. 078-44012/44424 fax 078-44425. 7 branches.

Leprosy Mission, 44 Ulsterville Avenue, Belfast BT9 7AQ. tel. 08-232-381937. *Apply to the Director.*

Letterkenny RTC see Donogh O'Malley

Library Council see Chomhaire Leabharlanna

Library for Teachers & Students of German, 62 Fitzwilliam Square, Dublin 2. tel. 01-661-8506. *Monday-Thursday 15.30-17.30 or by appointment.*

Limerick City Library, The Granary, Michael Street, Limerick. tel. 061-314668 fax 061-415266. 2 branches, prison and schools service.

Limerick College see Limerick Regional Technical College.

Limerick County Library, 58 O'Connell Street, Limerick. tel. 061-318477 fax 061-318478. 22 branches, 2 mobiles, schools service.

Limerick Regional Technical College, Moylish Park, Limerick. tel. 061-451344 fax 061-451707.

Linen Hall Library, 17 Donegall Square North, Belfast BT1 5GD. *Monday-Wednesday and Friday 9.30-17.30; Thursday 9.30-20.30; Saturday 9.30-16.00.*

Longford County Library, Annaly Car Park, Longford. tel. 043-41124/41125 fax 043-41233. 5 branches, schools service.

Louth County Library, Chapel Street, Dundalk, Co Louth. tel. 042-35457 ext.138/138 fax 042-34549. 3 branches, schools service.

Marine see Department of the

Maritime Institute of Ireland, Haigh Terrace, Dun Laoghaire, Co Dublin. tel. 01-280-0969. *Non-members by appointment.*

Marsh's see Archbishop Marsh's

Mary Immaculate College, South Circular Road, Limerick. *Term time 9-22.00; non-term 9-17.00.*

Mater Dei Institute see Dublin Diocesan

Mayo County Library, Mountain View, Castlebar, Co Mayo. tel. 094-24444 fax 094-24444. 5 branches, 2 mobiles, schools service.

Meath County Library, Railway Street, Navan, Co Meath. tel. 046-21134/21451. 11 branches.

Medical Library, St Vincent's Hospital, Elm Park, Dublin 4. tel. 01-283-9444 ext. 210. *Tuesday-Thursday 9.15-21.00; Monday and Friday 9.15-17.15; closed during lunch.*

Medical Library, QUB, Institute of Clinical Science, Grosvenor Road, Belfast 12. tel. 08-01232-322043/321487. *By arrangement.*

Medical Library, TCD, St James's Hospital, Dublin 8. tel. 01-454-3922 fax 01-453-6709.

Mercer Library, Royal College of Surgeons in Ireland, Mercer Street Lower, Dublin 2. *Term time Monday-Friday 9.00-21.45, Saturday 9.00-12.45; Vacation Monday-Friday 9.00-17.00.*

Meteorological Service Library, Glasnevin Hill, Dublin 9. tel. 01-842-4411 ext. 325 fax 01-837-5557 telex 91444. By appointment.

Monaghan County Library, The Diamond, Clones, Co Monaghan. tel. 047-51143 fax 047-51863. 5 branches, 2 mobile, schools and old people's homes services.

Multi-disciplinary Education Centre, Altnagevin Area Hospital, Glenshane Road, Londonderry BT47 1JB. tel. 08-01504-45171 ext. 3725 fax 08-01504-49334.

National Botanic Gardens Library, Glasnevin, Dublin 9. tel. 01-837-4388 fax 01-837-0080. *Researchers by arrangement.*

National Children's Resource Centre, Barnardo's, Christchurch Square, Dublin 8, tel. 01-453-0355 fax 01- 453-0300. *Monday-Friday 9.30-13.00.*

National College of Art and Design, 100 Thomas Street, Dublin 8. *Monday-Thursday 9.30-21.00, Friday 9.30-17.00.*

National College of Industrial Relations, Sandford Road, Ranelagh, Dublin 6. tel. 01-497-2917 fax 01-497-2200. *By arrangement.*

National Gallery of Ireland Art Library, Merrion Square West, Dublin 2. tel. 01-661-5133 fax 01-661-5372 *Re-opening to public in 1995; no information yet.*

National Library of Ireland, Kildare Street, Dublin 2. *Monday 10.00-21.00, Tuesday-Wednesday 14.00-21.00. Thursday-Friday 10.00-17.00, Saturday 10.00-13.00; closed in November.*

National Museum of Ireland, Kildare Street, Dublin 2. tel. 01-661-8811 fax 01-676-6116.

National Rehabilitation Board, 25 Clyde Road, Dublin 4. *Monday-Friday 10.00-12.30, 14.30-16.30.*

National Safety Council, 4 Northbrook Road, Dublin 6. tel. 01-496-3422 fax 01-496-3306. *Monday-Friday 9.15-12.45, 14.00-17.30.*

National Social Service Board, 71 Lower Leeson Street, Dublin 2. tel. 01-661-6422 fax 01-676-4908. *By arrangement.*

NI see Northern Ireland

North-Eastern Education and Library Board, Demesne Avenue, Ballymena BT42 1AY. tel. 08-01266-41531 fax 08-01266-46680. 36 branches in 3 divisions, some served only by mobile, 10 mobiles, schools service.

Northern Ireland Assembly, Parliament Buildings, Stormont, Belfast BT4 3SY. tel. 08-01232-521250 fax 01-0232-521715. *Photocopying service by arrangement.*

Northern Ireland Association for Mental Health, 80 University Street, Belfast BT7 1HE. tel. 08-01232-328474 fax 08-01232-234940. *Monday-Friday 9.00-17.00.*

Northern Ireland Association of Citizens Advice Bureaux, 11 Upper Crescent, Belfast BT7 1NT. tel. 08-01232-231120 fax 08-01232-236522. *No hours given.*

Northern Ireland Council for Voluntary Action, 127 Ormeau Road, Belfast BT7 1SH. *Monday-Thursday 9.00-17.00, Friday 9.00-16.30.*

Northern Ireland Economic Research Centre, 48 University Road, Belfast BT7 1NJ. *Monday-Friday 9.00-13.00, 14.00-17.00.*

Northern Ireland Electricity, Danesfort, 120 Malone Road, Belfast BT9 5HT. tel. 08-01232-661100 ext. 2205. *Telephone enquiries.*

Northern Ireland Housing Executive, Housing Centre, 2 Adelaide Street, Belfast BT2 8PB. tel. 08-01232-240588 ext. 2632 fax ext. 3065. *By arrangement.*

Northern Ireland Preschool Playgroup Association, Unit 3 Enterprise House, Boucher Crescent, Belfast BT12 6HU. Monday-Friday 9.00-16.30.

NRB see National Rehabilitation Board

Nursing Board see Bord Altranais

Occupational Therapy Library, TCD, Rochestown Avenue, Dun Laoghaire. tel. 01-285-2677 fax 01-671-9003. *By appointment.*

Offaly County Library, O'Connor Square, Tullamore, Co Offaly. tel. 0506-21419 fax 0506-41160 telex 60819. 9 branches, primary schools and welfare homes services.

Office of Public Works, 51 St Stephen's Green, Dublin 2. tel. 01-661-3111 ext. 2159 fax 01-661-0747. *By arrangement.*

Pharmaceutical Society of Ireland, 37 Northumberland Road, Dublin 4. tel. 01-660-0699/0551 fax 01-668-1461. *By arrangement.*

Public Record Office of Northern Ireland, 66 Balmoral Avenue, Belfast BT9 6NY. *Monday-Friday 9.15-16.45.*

Queen's University of Belfast, University Road, Belfast BT7 1NN. tel. 08-01232-335020 fax 08-1232-323340. Inc. Agriculture, Veterinary Science, Medical and Science libraries.

Radiological Protection Institute of Ireland, 3 Clonskeagh Square, Clonskeagh Road, Dublin 14. *Monday-Friday 8.30-17.00.*

Radio Telefís Éireann programme library, RTÉ, Donnybrook, Dublin 4. *Monday-Friday 9.00-16.00.*

Rathdown County Libraries, c/o Central Department, Cumberland House, Fenian Street, Dublin 2. (May have moved HQ to Blackrock) tel. 01-661-9000 fax 01-676-1628. Branches, mobiles.

Redemptorist Community, Marianella, 75 Orwell Road, Dublin 6. tel. 01-496-1688. *By appointment.*

Regional Technical Colleges: see under place name

Religious Society of Friends in Ireland, Swanbrook House, Bloomfield Avenue, Morehampton Road, Dublin 4. *Thursday 11.00-13.00.*

Representative Church Body, Braemor Park, Rathgar, Dublin 14. *Monday-Friday 9.30-13.00, 13.45-17.00.*

Roscommon County Library, Abbey Street, Roscommon. tel. 0903-26100 fax 0903-25474. 7 branches, housebound and schools service.

Royal College of Physicians of Ireland, 6 Kildare Street, Dublin 2. tel. 01-661-6677. *By appointment for non-professionals.*

Royal Dublin Society, Ballsbridge, Dublin 4. tel. 01-668-0866 fax 01-660-4014. *Non-members by appointment.*

Royal Irish Academy, 19 Dawson Street, Dublin 2. tel. 01-676-2570/4222 fax 01-676-2346. *Non-members by arrangement or with letter of introduction.*

Royal Society of Antiquaries of Ireland, 63 Merrion Square, Dublin 2. *Monday-Friday 14.00-17.00.*

St Angela's College of Education, Lough Gill, Sligo. tel. 071-43580/42785 fax 071-44585. *By arrangement.*

St Catherine's College of Education, Sion Hill, Blackrock, Co Dublin. *Monday-Thursday 9.00-21.30, Friday 9.00-17.00, Saturday 13.00-17.00; Vacation Monday-Friday 9.00-17.00.*

St Columban's, Dalgan Park, Navan, Co Meath. tel. 046-21525 fax 046-22799. *By arrangement.*

St Lukes Institute of Cancer Research, St Lukes Hospital, Highfield Road, Rathgar, Dublin 6. tel. 01-496-5692 fax 01-497-4886.

St Mary's College, 191 Falls Road, Belfast BT12 6FE. tel. 08-01232-327678/61731 fax 08-01232-624166. *By arrangement.*

St Patrick's College, Drumcondra, Dublin 9. tel. 01-837-6191 fax 01-837-6197. *By arrangement.*

St Patrick's College, Maynooth, Co Kildare. Term time 9.00-21.30; Vacation 10.00-17.00.

St Patrick's College, Thurles, Co Tipperary. tel. 0504-21201 fax 0504-21822.

Save the Children (NI), 41 Wellington Park, Belfast BT9 6DN. Monday-Friday 9.00-16.30.

Science Library, QUB, 19 Chlorine Gardens, Belfast BT9 5EQ. tel. 08-01232-661111. *By arrangement.*

Services Industrial Professional Technical Union see SIPTU

SIPTU, 30 Parnell Square, Dublin 1. tel. 01-873-3977 fax 01-873-3062. *By appointment only.*

Social Welfare see Department of

Sligo County Library, The Courthouse, Sligo. tel. 071-42212. 2 branches and schools service.

Sligo Regional Technical College, Ballinode, Sligo. tel. 071-43261 ext. 246/305 fax 071-44096.

South-Eastern Education and Library Board, Windmill Hill, Ballynahinch, Co Down BT24 8DH. tel. 08-01238-562639 fax 08-01238-565072. 25 branches, 5 mobile, schools, prisons, hospitals and home services.

Southern Education and Library Board, 1 Markethill Road, Armagh BT60 1NR. tel. 08-01861-525353 fax 08-01861-526879. 23 branches in 3 divisions, 5 mobiles, housebound and schools services.

Spanish Cultural Institute, 58 Northumberland Road, Dublin 4. *Monday-Thursday in academic year 12.00-19.00,*

Friday 10.00-17.00; closed August.

Sports Council for Northern Ireland, House of Sport, Upper Malone Road, Belfast BT9 5LA. tel. 08-01232-381222 fax 08-01232-682757.

Sports Information Service, National Coaching and Training Centre, University of Limerick, Plassey Technological Park, Limerick. tel. 061-33644 fax 061-338174.

St alphabeticalised as if 'Saint'.

State Laboratory, Department of Finance, Abbotstown, Castleknock, Dublin 15. tel. 01-821-7700 ext. 149 fax 01-821-7320. *By appointment.*

Stranmillis College, Belfast BT9 5DY. *Term time Monday-Thursday 9.00-21.00, Friday 9.00-16.30; Vacation Monday-Thursday 9.00-17.00, Friday 9.00-16.30.*

Tallaght Regional Technical College, Dublin 24. tel. 01-459-8888 fax 01-459-8989.

Teagasc, Agriculture and Food Development Authority, 19 Sandymount Avenue, Dublin 4. tel. 01-668-8188 fax 01-668-8023. Libraries also at branches countrywide. *Monday-Friday 9-17.00.*

Tipperary Joint Libraries Committee, Castle Avenue, Thurles, Co Tipperary. tel. 0504-21555/21154 fax 0504-23442. 13 branches, schools service.

Tralee Regional Technical College, Clash, Tralee, Co Kerry. tel. 066-24666 fax 066-25711.

Trinity College Library, College Street, Dublin 2. *Term time Monday-Friday 9.30-22.00, Saturday 9.30-13.00; Long vac. Monday-Friday 9.30-17.00, Saturday 9.00-13.00.*

Trócaire, 169 Booterstown Avenue, Co Dublin. *Monday-Friday 9.30-13.00, 14.00-17.30.*

Ulster American Folk Park, Mellon Road, Castletown, Omagh, Co Tyrone BT78 5QY. *Monday-Friday 9.30-13.00, 13.30-16.30.*

Ulster Cancer Foundation, 40 Eglantine Avenue, Belfast BT9 6DX. *Monday-Friday 9.00-12.45, 14.00-17.00.*

Ulster Folk and Transport Museum, Cultra, Holywood, Co Down BT18 0EU.

Monday-Friday 9.00-17.00.

Ulster Museum Library, Botanic Gardens, Belfast BT9 5AB. *Monday-Friday 9.00-12.45, 14.00-16.30, closed bank holidays.*

Ulster Society of Chartered Accountants, 11 Donegall Square South, Belfast BT1 5JE tel. 08-01232-321600. *Monday-Friday 9.30-17.30, Saturday (Dublin only) 10.00-13.00; for registered users.*

University College Cork see Boole Library.

University College Dublin, Belfield, Dublin 4. tel. 01-706-7583 fax 01-283-7667. Includes Architecture Library, Earlsfort Terrace Library, Veterinary Medicine Library, Blackrock Campus Library.

University College Galway see James Hardiman

University of Limerick, Limerick. *Term time Monday-Friday 8.30-21.00, Saturday 9.00-12.45; Vacation 9.00-15.00.*

University of Ulster, Coleraine, Co Londonderry BT52 1SA. tel. 08-01265-44141 fax 08-01265-40928 telex 747597. Includes libraries at Jordanstown, York Street, Belfast, and Magee College.

University of Ulster Art & Design faculty, York Street, Belfast. tel. 08-01232-328515 fax 08-01232-321048. *By arrangement.*

Veterinary Research Laboratory, Abbotstown, Castleknock, Dublin 15. tel. 01-678-9011 ext. 1002 fax 01-821-3010. *9.30-17.30.*

Veterinary Science Library, QUB, Veterinary Research Laboratories, Stormont, Belfast BT4 3SD. tel. 08-01232 760011 ext. 222.

Virginia Henderson Library, Royal College of Nursing, 17 Windsor Avenue, Belfast BT9 6EE. tel. 08-01232-668236. *By arrangement.*

VMRA Consulting Engineers, Tramway House, Dartry Road, Dublin 6. tel. 01-497-5716 fax 01-497-5886. *By arrangement.*

Waterford County Library, Lismore, Co Waterford. tel. 058-54128 fax 058-54877. 8 branches.

Waterford Municipal Library, Lady Lane, Waterford. tel. 051-73501 fax 051-50031. 2 branches.

Waterford Regional Technical College, Cork Road, Waterford. tel. 051-75934 fax 051-78292.

Western Education and Library Board, 1 Spillars Place, Omagh, Co Tyrone BT78 1HL. 16 branches in 3 divisions, 9 mobiles, prisons, schools services.

Westmeath County Library, Dublin Road, Mullingar, Co Westmeath. tel. 044-40781. 6 branches.

Wexford County Library, Abbey Street, Wexford. tel 053-42211 ext. 355. 5 branches, 1 mobile, schools, youth and disabled voluntary groups.

Wicklow County Library, Greystones, Co Wicklow. tel. 01-287-4387/287-3548 fax 01-287-3297. 12 branches and schools service.

Wood & Associates, 38 Arran Quay, Dublin 7. tel. 01-872-6088 fax 01-872-6957. *By arrangement.*

Libraries by subject

To help researchers we index libraries with special collections by subject. The national, city, county and university libraries obviously offer such resources as to be the equivalent of specialist libraries in many subjects; they are only indexed here if their specialities are very notable. The Irish Joint Fiction Reserve (IJFR) is a nationwide stock, arranged alphabetically by author in particular city and county libraries and available (as are most public and some other library stocks) by the inter-library lending scheme. Details of all major libraries, including those indexed here, are given in the list on pages 156-164, either with public opening times or (if special arrangements are required by researchers) with telephone and fax numbers.

Accident prevention
National Safety Council

Accountancy
Accountancy & Business College
Inst. of Chartered Accountants in Ireland

Adult education
AONTAS

Aerial photographs
National Museum of Ireland

Agriculture
Dept of Agriculture, Dublin
Department of Agriculture for NI
Queen's University (Agriculture Lib.)
Teagasc
Royal Dublin Society

Archaeology
Royal Society of Antiquaries
Ulster Museum Library

Architecture
Dept of the Environment for NI
Irish Architectural Archive
Office of Public Works

Art
National Gallery of Ireland
National College of Art & Design
University of Ulster, York Street

Astronomy
Armagh Observatory
Dunsink Observatory
Dublin Inst. for Adv. Studies

Atomic energy
see Nuclear science

Banking
AIB Group, Bankcentre

Bibliography
National Library of Ireland
and see under Librarianship

Bibliophily
(Early school texts) Stranmillis College
(Rare bks) St Patrick's Coll., Maynooth
(Early books) Trinity College Dublin
(16th-18th c.) Archbishop Marsh's Lib.
(16th-18th c.) Armagh Public Library
(from 1522) Central Catholic Library
(from 1473) GPA-Bolton Library
(Old books) Royal Irish Academy
(Old bks from 1481) Franciscan Library
(Coverdale Bible, 1550) Edgehill
(Pamphlets 17th-19th c.) King's Inns

Botany
National Botanic Gardens Library

Brewing
Guinness Ireland Tech. Info. Services

Business
Dublin City Libraries, Central branch
Irish Bus. and Employers Confed.
Irish Management Institute
(Companies) University of Limerick
(Europe) European Bus. Info. Centre
(Marketing and Eur.) Bord Tráchtála
(Marketing) Dublin Inst. of Technology

Catering
Dublin Inst. of Technology

Celtic studies
Dublin Institute for Advanced Studies

Chemistry
State Laboratory
(Polymer) Dupont
see also Brewing and Pharmacy

Children
National Children's Resource Centre
NI Pre-school Playgroup Assoc.

Children's literature
Church of Ireland Coll. of Education
Dublin City Libraries
St Patrick's College, Drumcondra
St Mary's College

Cinema
Irish Film Institute

Consumer affairs
Bryson House
General Consumer Council for NI

Current affairs
BBC NI
Radio Telefís Éireann prog. lib.

Dentistry
Dublin Dental Hospital Library

Design
Dublin Institute of Technology
National College of Art & Design
University of Ulster, York Street

Disability
Central Remedial Clinic
Disability Action
see also Rehabilitation

Drama
Austin Clarke Library
Cork County Library

Economics
Dept of Econ. Development (NI)
Econ. and Social Res. Institute
Northern I. Economic Research Centre
(History) Ulster Folk & Transport Mus.

Education
see also Children,
Department of Education, Dublin
Mary Immaculate College
Curriculum Development Unit
Stranmillis College
St Patrick's College, Drumcondra
St Mary's College

Electricity
Electricity Supply Board
Northern Ireland Electricity
see also Engineering

Emigration
Ulster American Folk Park

Employment
Equal Opportunities Comm. for NI
(Conditions) European Found.
see also Social welfare

Engineering
Electricity Supply Board
Wood & Associates
(Building services) VMRA
see also Architecture

Environment
Environmental Information Serv.

European Community
Comm. of European Communities
see also Employment (Conditions)

Fire prevention
see Accident prevention

Fisheries
Bord Iascaigh Mhara
Department of the Marine
Fisheries Research Centre

Folk life
Ulster Folk & Transp. Museum
Ulster American Folk Park

Folklore
Heritage Library, Derry

Forestry
Coillte

Gaelic manuscripts
Franciscan Library
King's Inns
St Patrick's College

Genealogy
Public Record Office of NI
County and city libraries.

Geology
Geological Survey of Ireland
Dublin Inst. for Adv. Studies

German language
Goethe Institute
Lib. for Teachers & Stud. of German

Gerontology
Age Concern Northern Ireland
(Geriatrics) see Medicine

Government
(Publications) National Library
Belfast Education and Library Board.
Northern Ireland Assembly

Health
Department of Health
Health Promotion Unit
Multi-disciplinary Education Centre
(Cancer research) St Lukes Institute
(Cancer) Ulster Cancer Foundation
see also Children and Medicine

Horticulture
see Agriculture and Botany

History
see Irish Studies and Archaeology
(Local) City and county libraries.

Home economics
St Catherine's College of Educ.
St Angela's College of Educ.

Human rights
see Third world

Humour
Boole Library

Industry
(Ind. rels, labour hist.) SIPTU
(Ind. rels) Nat. Coll. of Ind. Relatns
see Economics and Vocational

Insurance
Insurance Institute of Ireland

Irish studies
National Library of Ireland
Public Record Office of NI
St Mary's College

Languages
Institiúid Teangeolaíochta Éireann
see also German language

Law
Judges' Library
King's Inns Library
Law Library
Law Society of N. Ireland

Leprosy
Leprosy Mission

Librarianship
Chomhairle Leabharlanna, An

Literacy
AONTAS
Cork City Library

Local authors, history, studies
County and City libraries
(Ulster) Linen Hall Library

Maps
Trinity College Library

Maritime
Maritime Institute of Ireland
see also Fisheries

Marketing
An Bord Tráchtála

Medicine
Central Remedial Clinic
Medical Lib., St Vincent's Hosp.
QUB (Medical library)
TCD (Medical Library)
Mercier Lib., Royal Coll. of Surgeons
Multi-disciplinary Education Centre
Regonal Medical Lib., Cork: see Boole
(Archive) Royal Coll. of Physicians
see also Health

Mental health
NI Association for Mental Health

Meteorology
Meteorological Service Library

Microbiology
St Lukes Institute
see also Chemistry

Music
(Sheet) Cork County Library
Dublin City Libraries, Central branch

Natural History
Office of Public Works

Newspapers
National Library of Ireland
BBC Northern Ireland
(NI) Belfast Public Libraries
(Old) GPA-Bolton Library

Nuclear science
Radiological Prot. Inst. of I.
Dublin Inst. for Adv. Studies

Nursing
Bord Altranais
Multi-disciplinary Education Centre
Virginia Henderson Library

Occupational therapy
Occupational Therapy Library, TCD

Orient
Chester Beatty Library

Overseas service
Agency for Personal Serv. Overseas

Patents
  Belfast Education and Library Board

Peat
  Bord na Mona

Pharmacy
  Pharmaceutical Society of Ireland

Photographs
  Ulster Museum Library
  see Current affairs & Archaeology

Physics
  Dublin Inst. for Adv. Studies

Plays
  see Drama

Poetry
  Austin Clarke Library

Politics
  (NI) Linen Hall Library

Railways
  Irish Railway Record Society

Rehabilitation
  National Rehabilitation Board
  see also Disability

Religion
  Central Catholic Library
  (CofI) Representative Church Body
  Gamble Library
  Irish Christian Study Centre
  Jesuit Library
  St Patrick's College, Maynooth
  (Hist.) Franciscan Library
  (Islam) Chester Beatty
  (Liturgy) Glenstal Abbey
  (Methodism) Edgehill Theol. Coll.
  (Moral theol.) Redemptorist Comm.
  (Missions) St Columban's
  (Quaker) Religious Society of Friends
  (Theology) Diocesan Library of Down

Science
  Royal Dublin Society
  QUB (Science lib.)
  see also Standards and Chemistry

Social welfare and services
  Department of Social Welfare
  National Social Service Board

Bryson House
Combat Poverty Agency
NI Assoc. Citizens Advice Bureaux
Multi-disciplinary Education Centre
see also Gerontology and Employment

Spain
  Spanish Cultural Institute

Sports
  Sports Council for Northern I.
  Sports Information Service

Standards
  EOLAS
  (British) NI Housing Executive

Statistics
  Central Statistics Office
  University of Limerick

Surgery
  see Medicine

Technology
  see Standards

Textiles
  (Linen) Lambeg Ind. Reseearch Assoc

Third world
  St Columban's
  Trócaire

Tourism
  CERT

Transport
  Ulster Folk & Transport Museum

United Nations publications
  Belfast Education and Library Board

Veterinary
  Veterinary Research Laboratory
  QUB (Veterinary Science lib.)
  see also Agriculture

Vocational training
  Foras Áiseanna Saothair (FÁS)

Voluntary organisations
  Combat Poverty
  NI Council for Voluntary Action

Youth and community
  Dublin City Libraries

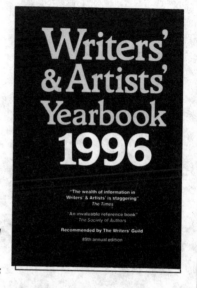

BOOKS IRELAND

Listing and reviewing over 750 Irish-interest books a year, Ireland's only national book magazine has appeared without interruption—and always punctually—since 1976. It is produced by the team that gave you the *Irish Writers' Guide* and supported by both the Arts Councils in Ireland.

Books Ireland publishes authoritative feature articles and news on the book business and lively interviews with authors, publishers and other book people.

In addition it includes seasonal lists of forthcoming books, reviews by distinguished (and entertaining) writers, and the famous 'First flush' column, which provides a brief and sometimes acerbic survey of all the month's new books.

BOOKS IRELAND

appears monthly except in January, July and August. You can buy it for £1.50 at all the best bookshops in Ireland, London and New York, and at many newsagents in Ireland.

By post anywhere in the world for £15 or $22 a year from major subscription agencies or direct from

BOOKS IRELAND

11 Newgrove Avenue, Dublin 4
tel. & fax + 353-1-269-2185
or phone or fax subscription by Visa, Access, MasterCard or EuroCard.